ON COMMON LAWS

ON COMMON LAWS

H. Patrick Glenn

OXFORD
UNIVERSITY PRESS

OXFORD
UNIVERSITY PRESS

Great Clarendon Street, Oxford OX2 6DP

Oxford University Press is a department of the University of Oxford.
It furthers the University's objective of excellence in research, scholarship,
and education by publishing worldwide in

Oxford New York

Auckland Cape Town Dar es Salaam Hong Kong Karachi
Kuala Lumpur Madrid Melbourne Mexico City Nairobi
New Delhi Shanghai Taipei Toronto

With offices in

Argentina Austria Brazil Chile Czech Republic France Greece
Guatemala Hungary Italy Japan Poland Portugal Singapore
South Korea Switzerland Thailand Turkey Ukraine Vietnam

Oxford is a registered trade mark of Oxford University Press
in the UK and in certain other countries

Published in the United States
by Oxford University Press Inc., New York

First published 2005
First published in paperback 2007

British Library Cataloguing in Publication Data
Data available

The Library of Congress has catalogued the hardback edition as follows:

Glenn, H. Patrick.
On common laws / H. Patrick Glenn.
p. cm.
Includes index.
ISBN–13: 978–0–19–928754–3
ISBN–10: 0–19–928754–6
1. Comparative law. 2. Customary law. I. Title.
K559.G547 2005
340.5′7—dc22 2005018920

Typeset by Newgen Imaging Systems (P) Ltd., Chennai, India
Printed in Great Britain
on acid-free paper by
Biddles Ltd., King's Lynn

ISBN 978–0–19–928754–3 (Hbk.)
ISBN 978–0–19–922765–5 (Pbk.)

1 3 5 7 9 10 8 6 4 2

To the memory of
John E. C. Brierley,

who knew about common laws

Preface

The concept of common law, with all its implications of universality and particularity, has been one of the great intellectual constructions of the western legal traditions. It has even been referred to as 'the essential legal tradition, allowing unity to be preserved amidst diversity.'[1] Designated as such, it is largely unknown in other legal traditions, though much can be said (see Ch. 3) on the responses of those traditions to such questions of unity and diversity. Yet under the pressures of nineteenth and twentieth century legal thought, and its insistence on the exclusivity and autonomy of national legal systems, the concept of common law, in its primary historical sense, has been largely forgotten. It does live on in the name of the common law tradition, and in the current debate on the need for a new ius commune in the European Union, but in both cases the essence of the idea has been lost. The common law is thus conceived, by common law lawyers themselves, as case law or even as a system of case law. Some may continue to maintain that it is binding case law. Within the European Union it is said that a new (single) ius commune is necessary to ensure the functioning of the common market, and the new ius commune would take the form of pan-European legislation, doctrine, or case law, depending on its particular advocate. What has been lost in all of this is the idea that law is common *in relation to* law which is not common, which is particular, and that a common law lives in constant, dialogical tension with an inescapable intellectual companion, the ius particulare. This was as much the case for the common law (the Welsh and others will tell you) as it was for the ius commune, and it was as much the case for the common laws of Europe, in Europe, as it was for their continuation beyond Europe. Common law thus understood does not presume, as does the law of a national legal system, a non-contradictory field of legal meaning, but rather its opposite, a *contradictory* field of legal meaning, in which differences are resolved in an ongoing manner without prejudice to survival of the sources of both particular and common law.

To the extent that state law is now losing its complete and exclusive nature, challenged by different forms of normativity both from within and

[1] B. Oppetit, *Droit et modernité* (Paris: Presses universitaires de France, 1998) at 74 (author's transl.).

from without, it appears appropriate to re-open the enquiry as to the nature of common law. Manlio Bellomo has thus recently declared that we must re-examine the idea of the ius commune and 'begin from the beginning,' though his important work excludes the 'interesting topic' of the Anglo-American common law.[2] The enquiry is thus necessary and, for what appears to be the first time, it must be directed to the multiple forms of common law which have existed in western law. Europe and the countries influenced by Europe have thus known the common law, the ius commune, le droit commun, el derecho común, il diritto comune and das gemeine Recht, to name only those, and each of these experiences has been different. Within the federations and confederations of the world there has also been a vigorous debate on the possibility of *federal* common law, a debate which may have relevance to the future of European law. The experience of common law has thus been plural, though almost never acknowledged as such, as the dominance of the definite article in the above expressions eloquently indicates.

Enquiry into the nature of common law entails reflection on the relations of different laws and different peoples, and necessarily involves legal history. It is here intended as normative legal history, that which the past can provide in resolving our present problems and in bridging the relations between different peoples. This will be seen, moreover, to be part of the teaching of common laws. Great reliance in this process must be placed on the work of legal historians, but in a sense there is no legal history of the common laws, in plural form.[3] It is thus perhaps more a process of interpretation of legal histories, as they have been seen by legal historians, than legal history as presently understood.[4] A distinguished practitioner of that art has recently written, however, that

[2] M. Bellomo, *The Common Legal Past of Europe, 1000–1800*, transl. Lydia G. Cochrane, (Washington, DC: The Catholic University of America Press, 1995) at 32 ('Anglo-American common law' an 'interesting topic that is beyond the scope of the present work but one whose historical relevance deserves more than passing note').

[3] Cf., however, D. Ibbetson, *Common Law and* Ius Commune (London: Selden Society, 2001)(with focus on late-16th and early-17th centuries law reports then emerging); and for work on the place of the ius commune in England, infra, Ch. 3, *The common law and the ius commune.*

[4] For such 'exploratory and interpretative' history, R. R. Davies, *The First English Empire: Power and Identity in the British Isles 1093–1343* (Oxford: Oxford Univ. Press, 2000) at iv, v, noting that it 'lays no claim to displace existing historiographical patterns.' Cf., however, for a shift in historiography towards transborder or 'world history,' L. Raphael, *Geschichtswissenschaft im Zeitalter der Extreme: Theorien, Methoden, Tendenzen von 1900 bis zur Gegenwart* (Munich: C. H. Beck, 2003) at 18, 21, 210, and for a recent view in legal history that 'National history is out,' D. Heirbaut, 'Feudal Law: the Real *Ius Commune* of Property in Europe, or: Should We Reintroduce *Duplex Dominium?*' (2003) 11 Eur. Rev. Pr. L. 301, at 303. The Journal of World History was begun in 1990.

'[l]egal history is too important to remain within the domain of specialist legal historians,'[5] so others must presume to enquire.

An earlier version of Chapters 1 and 2 of this book were presented as the Richard Youard Lectures in Legal History, Oxford University, in Hilary Term, 2003, and a more transatlantic version was presented as the Eason-Weinmann Lecture at Tulane Law School in the fall of 2004.[6] Still further versions have been presented at the Faculty of Law, University of Edinburgh; the Scuola Superiore St-Anna, Pisa; the Institute for Foreign and International Private Law, Hamburg; and the Université Laval, Quebec. I have benefited from comments received on all of those occasions. Writing of the book has been greatly facilitated by a research fellowship of the Killam Trust, Canada, a visiting fellowship of All Souls College, Oxford, and research facilities kindly provided by the Max-Planck Institute for European Legal History, Frankfurt, and the Max-Planck Institute for Foreign and International Private Law, Hamburg. I am very grateful to all.

H. Patrick Glenn
Hamburg, Germany, and
Sutton, Quebec
December 2004

[5] D. J. Ibbetson, *A Historical Introduction to the Law of Obligations* (Oxford: Oxford Univ. Press, 1999) at v.

[6] H. P. Glenn, 'The Common Laws of Europe and Louisiana' (2005) 79 Tulane L. Rev. 1041.

Contents—Summary

Preface vii
Contents—Summary xi
Contents xiii
List of Abbreviations of Periodicals and Law Reports xv

1 The Common Laws of Europe 1
2 The Common Laws of the World 44
3 On the Relations of Common Laws 95
Some Concluding Remarks 143

Index 145

Contents

Preface vii

Contents—Summary xi

Contents xiii

List of Abbreviations of Periodicals and Law Reports xv

1 THE COMMON LAWS OF EUROPE 1

Roman Law and Roman Universality 2
A Common Lex Non Scripta? 7
Mobility of People and Mobility of Laws 9
The Nature of the New Common Laws 12
The Early Expansion of the Ius Unum and the Common Law 14
The Essential Tradition of the Ius Commune 16
The Ius Commune, as Prototype 20
The Common Law, as Common Law 25
The Common Law Originating from England 32
The Common Law (droit commun) Originating from France 35
The Common Law (gemeine Recht) Originating from Germany 37
The Common Law (derecho commún) Originating from Spain 40
Other Common Laws of Europe 41

2 THE COMMON LAWS OF THE WORLD 44

National Appropriation of Common Laws in Europe? 45
A Common, Pan-European Process of Appropriation 49
Territoriality and Appropriation 53
The Identity of the Common Laws Abroad 56
The Nature of the Common Laws Abroad 62
The Common Law as Common Law, in the World 63
The Droit Commun Originating from France, in the World 70
The Derecho Commún Originating from Spain, in the World 75
Roman-Dutch Common Law, in the World 78
Pandectist Common Law, in the World 79

National Appropriation of Common Laws Abroad? The U.S.A. Experience 84
Common Law in Federations and Confederations 88
Influence within the Commons Laws of the World 91

3 ON THE RELATIONS OF COMMON LAWS 95

The Common Law and the Ius Commune 97
The Common Law and other Continental Common Laws 103
The Ius Commune and other Continental Common Laws 105
Common Laws and Canon Law 108
Common Laws and Commercial Law 114
Common Laws and Feudal Law 116
Territories at the Confluence of Common Laws 118
Common Laws and Language 124
Common Laws and Legal Education 128
Common Laws and Talmudic Law 131
Common Laws and Islamic Law 134
Common Laws and Hindu Law 140
Contemporary Relations of Common Laws 142

SOME CONCLUDING REMARKS 143

Index 145

List of Abbreviations of Periodicals and Law Reports

A.C.	Appeal Cases
AcP	Archiv für die civilistische Praxis
Alta. L. Rev.	Alberta Law Review
Am. J. Comp. L.	American Journal of Comparative Law
Am. J. L. Hist.	American Journal of Legal History
App. Cas.	Appeal Cases
Arch. phil. dr.	Archives de philosophie du droit
Aust. J. Asian L.	Australian Journal of Asian Law
Aust. J. Leg. Hist.	Australian Journal of Legal History
Aust. L. J.	Australian Law Journal
A.L.R.	Australian Law Reports
B. & Ald.	Barnewall & Alderson's Reports
Boston College Int'l. & Comp. L. Rev.	Boston College International and Comparative Law Review
Cal. L. Rev.	California Law Review
Camb. L. J.	Cambridge Law Journal
Can. Bar Rev.	Canadian Bar Review
Cardozo L. Rev.	Cardozo Law Review
C. de D.	Cahiers de Droit
Ch. D.	Chancery Division
C.J.Q.	Civil Justice Quarterly
Clevel. St. L. Rev.	Cleveland State Law Review
C.L.R.	Commonwealth Law Reports
Col. L. Rev.	Columbia Law Review
Cornell L. R.	Cornell Law Review
Cowp.	Cowper's English King's Bench Reports
Current L. & Soc. Probs.	Current Law and Social Problems
D.	Dalloz
Dal. L. J.	Dalhousie Law Journal
D.L.R.	Dominion Law Reports
Duke L. J.	Duke Law Journal
Electr. J. Comp. L.	Electronic Journal of Comparative Law
E.R.	English Reports

Eur. Rev. Pr. L.	European Review of Private Law
Georgetown L. J.	Georgetown Law Journal
Harvard Int. L. J.	Harvard International Law Journal
Harv. L. Rev.	Harvard Law Review
Hastings L. J.	Hastings Law Journal
H.C.	High Court of Australia
Hofstra L. Rev.	Hofstra Law Review
I.C.L.Q.	International and Comparative Law Quarterly
I.R.	Irish Reports
Islamic L. & Soc.	Islamic Law and Society
J. dr. int.	Journal du droit international
Jewish L. Ann.	Jewish Law Annual
J. Indian L. Institute	Journal of the Indian Law Institute
J. Leg. Hist.	Journal of Legal History
J. Soc. Comp. Leg.	Journal of the Society of Comparative Legislation
Law & Hist. Rev.	Law and History Review
La L. Rev.	Louisiana Law Review
L.Q.R.	Law Quarterly Review
L.R. Cal.	Law Reports Calcutta
McGill L. J.	McGill Law Journal
Melbourne U.L.Rev.	Melbourne University Law Review
Mich. L. Rev.	Michigan Law Review
Mod. L. Rev.	Modern Law Review
Nfld. L.R.	Newfoundland Law Reports
N. Ir. Legal Q.	Northern Ireland Legal Quarterly
N.S.R.	Nova Scotia Reports
N.Y.U.L. Rev.	New York University Law Review
O.J.L.S.	Oxford Journal of Legal Studies
O.U.C.L.J.	Oxford University Commonwealth Law Journal
P.C.	Privy Council
Pet.	Peter's United States Supreme Court Reports
Phil.	Philippine Reports
RabelsZ	Rabels Zeitschrift für ausländisches und internationales Privatrecht
R. du B.	Revue du Barreau
Rechtshistorisches J.	Rechtshistorisches Journal
Rev. crit. d.i.p.	Revue critique de droit international privé
Rev. de la common law en fr.	Revue de la common law en français

Rev. d'hist. des Fac. de droit	Revue d'histoire des Facultés de droit
Rev. hist. dr. fr. et étr.	Revue historique de droit français et étranger
Rev. int. dr. comp.	Revue internationale de droit comparé
Rev. jur. polit. indép. et coop.	Revue juridique et politique, indépendance et coopération
R.J.T.	Revue Juridique Thémis
Roma e America	Roma e America. Diritto Romane Comune
R.S.C.	Revised Statutes of Canada
S.A.L.J.	South African Law Journal
S. Calif. L. Rev.	Southern California Law Review
S. Carolina L. Rev.	South Carolina Law Review
S.C.C.	Supreme Court of Canada
S.C. Nfld.	Supreme Court of Newfoundland
S.C.N.S.	Supreme Court of Nova Scotia
S.C.R.	Supreme Court Reports
SJZ	Schweizerische Juristen-Zeitung
Stan. L. Rev.	Stanford Law Review
Syracuse J. Int'l. & Com. L	Syracuse Journal of International and Commercial Law
Tijd. v. Rechtsg.	Tijdschrift voor Rechtsgeschiedenis
TLS	Times Literary Supplement
Tul. L. Rev.	Tulane Law Review
U.B.C. L. Rev.	University of British Columbia Law Review
U. Cal. Davis L. Rev.	University of California at Davis Law Review
U. Chicago L. Rev.	University of Chicago Law Review
U. Miami Inter-American L. Rev.	University of Miami Inter-American Law Review
U. Miami Int'l. & Comp. L. Rev.	University of Miami International and Comparative Law Review
U.S.	United States Reports
Washington U. Global Studies L. Rev.	Washington University Global Studies Law Review
Willamette L. Rev.	Willamette Law Review
W.W.R.	Western Weekly Reports
Yale L. J.	Yale Law Journal
ZEuP	Zeitschrift für europäisches Privatrecht
ZgR	Zeitschrift für geschichtliche Rechtswissenschaft

ZRG GA Zeitschrift der Savigny Stiftung, Germanistische Abteilung
ZRG RA Zeitschrift der Savigny Stiftung, Romanistische Abteilung

1

THE COMMON LAWS OF EUROPE

The concept of common law comes to us from European legal history but is now of worldwide significance. The current debate within Europe on the need for a new European ius commune has implications for the world beyond Europe, since a new, pan-European law would have many consequences for the relations of the rest of the world with Europe. The common law, that of English origin, is now said to be aggressively used in the process of globalization by western lawyers from common law countries, and major questions are therefore raised as to the inherently aggressive character of the methods of the common law. Much of this debate, however, is carried out in very contemporary terms, largely those of the last century or two, and it is recognized that there are major conceptual and methodological problems in dealing with the new dynamic of laws in the world.[1] The concept of common law is thus being pressed into service yet again, raising many questions as to what it means and the implications of its use. To begin to answer these questions requires historical enquiry, since a concept which has been with us for as long as that of common law will inevitably have many historical encrustations. What can it possibly mean? What has it historically meant? The answers have been surprisingly different, though some have had far greater resonance than others. They all have current application. The Romans appear to have begun the discussion.

[1] W. Twining, *Globalisation and Legal Theory* (London/Evanston, IL: Butterworths/Northwestern Univ. Press, 2000, 2001); K. P. Berger, 'The Principles of European Contract Law and the concept of the "Creeping Codification" of Law' (2001) Eur. Rev. Pr. L. 21, at 27 (European and transnational law developing outside constraints of domestic and EU law-making processes, major questions of methodological basis); H. P. Glenn, 'A Transnational Concept of Law' in P. Cane and M. Tushnet (eds), *The Oxford Handbook of Legal Studies* (Oxford: Oxford Univ. Press, 2003) at 839.

Roman law and roman universality

Roman law is deservedly famous and deservedly controversial. It is famous for its precision, detail, and apparent timelessness.[2] It is controversial for its individualism, materialism and godlessness.[3] Roman law did little, however, for the development of the notion of common law. The reasons for this are difficult to establish, though the pattern of Roman legal thinking appears relatively clear.

Roman law was the law of an empire. We thus see here the first real indication of the expansive character of European law, as it was eventually to develop.[4] As creators of the first European empire, the Romans could not have thought out all of its potential ramifications, notably with respect to the relations of different laws. With hindsight, their structures appear rather crude and . . . imperial, compared to later models of common law. The Romans took what turned out to be a unique view of the legal relations of the world, and it has never been followed since. So while Roman law was very successful, Roman attempts to deal with legal diversity were much less so, in the judgment of those who followed them.

Roman lawyers used the expression common law in two ways. First, and the Greek influence is here evident, they stated that there is a law common to all humanity, which could be known as the ius gentium.[5] This was part of a still broader notion of natural law, which applied to the entire world, including animals, and it was distinct from a notion of civil law, which was the law of a particular state or city, applicable to its citizens. It was this civil law, or ius civile, which Roman lawyers were interested in, and the idea of a broader, universal, natural law was essentially left to wither away. No real attention was given to it, and the expressions ius naturale and ius gentium were used rather indiscriminately, whenever it

[2] A. Watson, *The Spirit of Roman Law* (Athens, Ga./London: University of Georgia Press, 1995); R. Zimmermann, *The Law of Obligations: Roman Foundations of the Civilian Tradition* (Oxford: Oxford Univ. Press, 1996).

[3] J. Whitman, 'Long Live the Hatred of Roman Law' Rechtsgeschichte 2003.40.

[4] For the influence of Roman notions of empire on subsequent European colonialization, A. Pagden, *Lords of all the World: Ideologies of Empire in Spain, Britain and France* c. *1500*–c. *1800* (New Haven/London: Yale Univ. Press, 1995), Ch. 1 ('The Legacy of Rome').

[5] Inst. I.II.1, in *The Institutes of Justinian: Text, Translation and Commentary*, J. A. C. Thomas (ed.) (Cape Town: Juta, 1975) at 4 ('All peoples who are governed by laws and customs use law which is in part particular to themselves, in part common to all men'). The text, from the early 6th century, AD, adopts language used in the earlier Institutes of Gaius (2nd century, AD). For the Greek influence, H. F. Jolowicz and B. Nicholas, *Historical Introduction to the Study of Roman Law*, 3rd ed. (Cambridge: Cambridge Univ. Press, 1972) at 104–5.

was felt necessary to do so. Buckland and Stein conclude that, here at least, 'the jurists do not tell a clear story.'[6] The argument for a universal, natural law, common to humanity, would have to await the Enlightenment, and modern times.[7]

The second use of the expression common law was internal to the civil law itself. All written laws contain general rules, and exceptions to them, and Roman lawyers recognized both the general phenomenon and particular examples of it. The jurist Paul thus defined particular law as that which runs against 'the general tenor of legal reason' (the common law) on account of particular policy reasons.[8] The example most frequently given in Roman law was the common law of wills, which admitted exceptions in the case of wills drawn by soldiers.[9] Law is here simply the general decree ('commune praeceptum'), which Bracton would have seen as 'general command,'[10] and it is common only in the sense that it is that which is applicable in the absence of exceptions. Both the common law, in this sense, and the exceptions to it, are part of a body of law derived from a single source or set of sources, so the diversity which may exist, justifying exceptions, is that which is judged permissible within a given body of law. One could quite properly speak of the law, with no qualifying adjective. There is here no notion of a duality or multiplicity of laws, or of the relations of different legal traditions.

Commentators have thus seen Roman law as lacking any specific or technical sense of common law.[11] In the Roman view it is either an ideal,

[6] W. W. Buckland and P. Stein, *A Textbook of Roman Law from Augustus to Justinian*, 3rd ed. (Cambridge: Cambridge Univ. Press, 1963) at 53; for indiscriminate use of the expressions, Jolowicz and Nicholas, supra, note 5, at 106; and for confusion as to whether the natural reason of natural law necessarily infused the ius gentium, G. MacCormack, 'Sources' in E. Metzger (ed.), *A Companion to Justinian's Institutes* (London: Duckworth, 1998) 1 at 3.

[7] Most recently, J. Finnis, *Natural Law and Natural Rights*, (Oxford: Clarendon Press, 1980).

[8] D. I.3.16, in *The Digest of Justinian*, A. Watson (ed.), vol. I (Philadelphia: Univ. of Pennsylvania Press, 1985) at 12; M.-F. Renoux-Zagamé, 'La méthode du droit commun: Réflexions sur la logique des droits non codifiés' (1990) Rev. d'hist. des Fac. de droit, Nos. 10, 11, Aspects du comparatisme 133, at 139 (for ius singulare as opposed to ordinary rule).

[9] D. XXVIIII.1 ('The Soldier's Will'), notably at s. 20 for instances nevertheless of application of 'general law,' in *Digest*, supra, note 8, at 867, 870; as to which see H. Coing, *Europäisches Privatrecht*, Band I, *Älteres Gemeines Recht (1500 bis 1800)* (Munich: C.H. Beck'sche Verlagsbuchhandlung, 1985) at 89, 90; F. Calasso, *Introduzione al diritto commune* (Milano, Giuffrè, 1970) at 48.

[10] G. Woodbine and S. E. Thorne (transl. and eds.), *Bracton on the Law and Customs of England*, vol. 2 (Cambridge, MA: Belknap Press of Harvard Univ. Press, 1968) at 22.

[11] Calasso, supra, note 9, at 48; P. Nève, '(Europäisches) Ius Commune und (nationales) Gemeines Recht: Verwechslung von Begriffen?' in G. Köbler and H. Nehlsen (eds.), *Wirkungen europäischer Rechtskultur, Festschrift für Karl Kroeschell* (Munich: C. H. Beck'sche Verlagsbuchhandlung, 1997) at 871; P. Petot, 'Le droit commun en France selon les coutumiers' Rev. hist. dr. fr. et étr. 1961.413, at 427.

of little real interest to the practice of law, or simply law itself, to the extent it is not subject to internal exception. In the absence of an operative notion of common law, as a device for reconciling different laws, how then did the Romans deal with the diversity they encountered in their expansion? They did so with a further legal technique, also known as the ius gentium, and by a further psychological technique, which was that of closure or exclusion.

The ius gentium was idealized as the law common to humanity, so to the extent that Romans actually encountered foreigners it was natural that they be subject to the ius gentium. The notion of the ius gentium thus had two distinct but related meanings. On the one hand it was an ideal law of nature which applied to everyone, including Romans themselves, though with little consequence; on the other hand it was a specific set of legal principles or rules which Romans used in dealing with non-citizens.[12] In contrast to the knowledge we have of Roman civil law, the ius civile, we appear to know very little, however, about the ius gentium. It was not recorded, which is already an indication of its place in the general order of things.[13] So we know about it only through discussion of it, and through the institutions which administered it. It is often said that the ius gentium was the law of foreign people, which the Romans would thereby have recognized. The reality appears to have been otherwise, since the practice was apparently one of extension of those parts of Roman civil law judged capable of application to non-Romans. Thus was done essentially in commercial matters, though not in matters of family law or successions,[14] or where Roman law was highly formalistic or ceremonial,[15] or where the Latin language played an important role.[16] There was thus no active engagement on the part of Roman lawyers with foreign law, or even any necessity of knowledge of it, in the generation of the ius gentium. It was essentially Roman law, which Roman lawyers considered appropriate for the world at large.[17]

[12] For this duality of the concept of ius gentium, B. Nicholas, *An Introduction to Roman Law* (Oxford: Clarendon Press, 1962) at 57, 58.

[13] F. Wieacker, 'Historical Models for the Unification of European Law' in W. Krawietz, N. MacCormick, and G. H. Von Wright, *Prescriptive Formality and Normative Rationality in Modern Legal Systems: Festschrift for R. S. Summers* (Berlin: Duncker & Humboldt, 1994) 297 at 300.

[14] H. Lewald, 'Conflits de lois dans le monde grec et romain' Rev. crit. d.i.p. 1968.419 (I), 615 (II), at 618, 619 ; MacCormack, supra, note 6, at 4.

[15] M. Kaser, *Ius Gentium*, (Köln/Weimar/Vienna: Böhlau Verlag, 1993) at 5; P. Stein, *Roman Law in European History* (Cambridge: Cambridge European History, 1999) at 12.

[16] Kaser, supra, note 15.

[17] Kaser, supra, note 15, at 6, 116, 120; and for Roman lawyers never actually conducting any investigation into the content of foreign law, but rather simply deciding themselves what was law in

The ius gentium was developed as the Romans came into direct contact with different peoples, and as the Romans felt it necessary to resolve disputes with such peoples (or in some cases disputes of such peoples), within Roman institutions. What was the status of the law of these peoples of the Empire, absent Roman intervention in its administration? That there was such law throughout the Empire, even in non-written form, is undisputed.[18] Its status has been described as a 'vexed question' since there appears to have been no developed Roman legal doctrine dealing with the question, and since it is now very difficult to find out what actually happened, in the different parts of the Empire.[19] Yet it appears necessarily to have been the case that Roman lawyers presumed the ongoing validity of local laws, since Roman law was reserved in principle to Roman citizens, and the ius gentium was of limited application. From given examples, notably the survival of Egyptian land registries, Lewald concluded that there was a general survival of local law, though Roman lawyers paid no official heed to the foreign law applicable in the provinces.[20] It could thus be said that there was a principle of application of personal laws, in the sense that different peoples continued to be governed by their own law, but this principle was not one which Roman lawyers articulated.[21] They simply did not acknowledge local law, and their method was therefore an essentially psychological one of closure or exclusion. It is not unknown elsewhere.

Jewish law thus survived under the Romans,[22] as did Greek and Egyptian law[23] and, perhaps more obviously, the law of the 'barbarian'

every jurisdiction, Ch. von Bar and P. Mankowski, *Internationales Privatrecht*, vol. I, *Allgemeine Lehren* (Munich: C. H. Beck, 2003) at 28.

[18] See infra, this Ch., *A common lex non scripta?*

[19] For the 'vexed question,' Michael E. Jones, 'The Legacy of Roman Law in Post-Roman Britain' in R. Mathisen (ed.), *Law, Society and Authority in Late Antiquity* (Oxford: Oxford Univ. Press, 2001) at 55–6, 61–2 (no record of local dispute resolution unless case referred 'upward' to Roman magistrate).

[20] Lewald, supra, note 14, at 617, 639; and see F. Pringsheim, 'Ausbreitung und Einfluss der griechischen Rechts' in E. Berneker (ed.), *Zur griechischen Rechtsgeschichte* (Darmstadt: Wissenschaftliche Buchgesellschaft, 1968) 58 at 58 (Theophrast in Greece showing an interest in comparative law and legal policy which always remained foreign to the Romans).

[21] Lewald, supra, note 14, at 623.

[22] A. M. Rabello, *The Jews in the Roman Empire: Legal Problems, from Herod to Justinian* (Aldershot: Ashgate Variorum, 2000) at I 299, 305; D. Johnston, *Roman Law in Context* (Cambridge: Cambridge Univ. Press, 1999) at 11.

[23] J. Madrzejewski, *Droit impérial et traditions locales dans l'Égypte romaine* (Aldershot: Variorum, 1980) at IX 396; L. Mitteis, *Reichsrecht und Volksrecht in den Östlichen Provinzen des Römischen Kaiserreichs* (Hildesheim: Georg Olms Verlagsbuchhandlung, 1963) at 8, 151; Lewald, supra, note 14, at 630.

peoples.[24] There was therefore a multiplicity of laws in the Roman Empire, but apparently clear boundaries between them, based on concepts of Roman citizenship and Roman judicial administration. It is unlikely that things were as precise as this. From the studies which are available, there was considerable mutual exchange and influence between Roman and local laws, such that in the field the distinction between the two became less clear.[25] The populations also tended to become less distinct,[26] as happens, while the Romans were also inclined to extend their citizenship as a means of co-opting local populations and extending the tax base.[27] When this occurred, local laws were sometimes preserved on an optional basis, or survived in the face of Roman intention.[28] The ius gentium thus declined in importance, but throughout the process no notion of a common law emerged. Identities were perceived as too distinct and formal boundaries too essential. When the boundaries became too obviously problematical, they had to be eliminated. The choice was thus between two laws, Roman and the other, both distinct from one another and having no formal relations between them, or one law. Only the

[24] A. J. Boudewijn Sirks, 'Shifting Frontiers in the Law: Romans, Provincials, and Barbarians' in R. W. Mathisen and H. S. Sivan (eds.), *Shifting Frontiers in Late Antiquity* (Aldershot: Variorum, 1996) at 149; P. Brown, *The Rise of Western Christendom: Triumph and Diversity, A.D. 200–1000*, 2nd ed. (Oxford: Blackwell Publishing, 2003) at 46, 50.

[25] For the pressure of local law and practice on Roman law, applicable to Romans in the field, Sirks, supra, note 24, at 146; Mitteis, supra, note 23, notably at 154, 156; E. Meyer, *Legitimacy and Law in the Roman World:* Tabulae *in Roman Belief and Practice* (Cambridge: Cambridge Univ. Press, 2004), notably at 205–7 (Roman practice beginning to vary further East and later in time, 'away from the extremes of enforced hierarchy;' change however not result of direct influence from local practice but Roman adjustment to new Roman priorities; Romans not overwhelmed by 'tsunami of foreign practice, instead fished happily and comfortably from the ocean'—though this far from Rome and not contributing to recognized sources of law); for specific changes to Roman law in Egypt, where 'Roman traditions of law were not so strong', A. Watson, *Legal Transplants* (Edinburgh: Scottish Academic Press, 1974) 31–5, quotation at 34. For Romanization of local law in Wales, Jones, supra, note 19, at 56.

[26] For gentle forms of merger, Brown, supra, note 24, at 45, 46; H. Elton, 'Defining Romans, Barbarians, and the Roman Frontier' in Mathisen and Sivan, supra, note 24, 126; and for the debate on the nature, and even existence, of the boundaries of Roman space, C. R. Whittaker, *Rome and its Frontiers: The Dynamics of Empire* (London/New York: Routledge, 2004) notably at 6, 28–9.

[27] Citizenship was extended throughout the Italian peninsula in the first century, BC, much more extensively throughout the Empire by legislation under Caracala in the early 3rd century, AD. For the text, Madrzejewski, supra, note 23, at 478; and for the absence of 'liberal intention', Stein, supra, note 15, at 20; with even stronger internal social divisions, Whittaker, supra, note 26, at 207. Wieacker speaks of people being 'equally exploited as subjects of an expanding coercive state.' Wieacker, supra, note 13, at 302.

[28] Mitteis, supra, note 23, passim; and for local options, J. Gaudemet, 'Les modalités de réception du droit à la lumière de l'histoire comparative' in Universita degli studi di Bari, *Le nuove frontiere del diritto e il problema dell'unificazione* (Milano: Giuffrè, 1979) 411 at 415.

Roman notions of common law are present in this landscape, either a utopian universal law or a single law subject only to its own exceptions. A poet, Prudentius, sang his praise of this way of thinking in the fourth century: 'To curb this frenzy God taught the nations everywhere to bow their heads under the same laws and become Romans/...A common law made them equals and bound them by a single name, bringing the conquered into bonds of brotherhood.'[29] Common law is here in the sense of the general, Roman, decree, but this law remained for the Romans, simply the ius civile. It was to become known as a common law only much later and amongst different peoples. Other ideas of commonality are thus possible.

A common lex non scripta?

Roman law was written law and Roman lawyers paid little attention to the content of the unwritten law of non-Roman peoples. They may well have seen it as law, however, since within Roman tradition there were notions of consuetudo and mos (or mores) which were highly normative in character. The western and current notion of 'custom,' which is that of simply repetitive behaviour under some sense of obligation, had yet to emerge. So there was at this time in the world a notion of unwritten law, or lex non scripta, which was not denigrated by use of the expression 'custom,' as is the case for all or most forms of unwritten law today.[30] The non-Roman people of Europe had their own form of law. To what extent could it be described as 'common'?

Unwritten law depended in large measure on particular circumstance, and one of the reasons for the long period required for national unification of law in Europe was that there were so many particular unwritten laws to overcome. Particular peoples thus had their particular laws, which were in large measure constitutive of the identities of these peoples. Moreover, there was no real need to know anyone else's law, since life was not characterized by over-arching forms of commerce or communication.

[29] Prudentius, 'Contra Orationem Symmachi/A Reply to the Address of Symmachus' Book II, l. 602, in *Prudentius*, vol. II, transl. H. J. Thomson (London/Cambridge, MA: William Heinemann/ Harvard Univ. Press, 1953) at 54, 55. I am grateful to John Cairns for this reference.

[30] H. P. Glenn, 'The Capture, Recognition and Marginalization of "Custom"' (1997) 45 Am. J. Comp. L. 613 at 614.

The rest of humanity did not intrude. So no notion of common law seems to have spontaneously emerged from what we know of the early legal life of the non-Roman peoples of Europe. There was no articulation of a common law of all humanity; there was no articulation of general norms which had to be recognized as such because of the number of specific and detailed exceptions made to them, as in the Roman manner. This does not mean there were no elements of commonality inherent in such law, however, since it is entirely possible, if one is able to secure a vantage point above and beyond a number of particular, unwritten laws, that many or all of them say the same thing on a particular issue. So there is here, beyond the Roman notions of the law common to all humanity, or the general precept or command, a third type of law which presents a form of commonality, here of substance or result. It too will bear some fruit in the future.

This notion of law which is common in terms of substance or result has been given new prominence because of remarkable and recent historical work by Maurizio Lupoi in Italy[31] and Patrick Wormald in England,[32] on early medieval law in the five centuries running up to the time of the Norman conquest of England. Of the two, Lupoi is the most explicit in stating that he is dealing with a 'European common law,' one which came to an end in the eleventh century and which was 'totally different' from the ius commune which was to succeed it.[33] Patrick Wormald challenges Maitland's view of the origins of the common law being best situated in the twelfth century (a view he describes as 'probably—not certainly but probably—wrong')[34] but does not make explicit use of the expression 'common law' in extending its origins back into earlier English kingships. English law, which is the expression Wormald uses, would be distinctive because it is as old as the English kingdom. Both of these authors look principally to legislation in making their claims and Lupoi's common law is also inclusive of canon law and Germanic written and unwritten law. He states explicitly that this law is common because it is based on 'shared *principia* and *regulae*.'[35] The criterion is one of substantive commonality. To the extent that Wormald would be willing to designate pre-conquest

[31] M. Lupoi, *The Origins of the European Legal Order*, transl. A Belton (Cambridge: Cambridge Univ. Press, 2000).

[32] P. Wormald, *The Making of English Law: King Alfred to the Twelfth Century* (Oxford: Blackwell, 1999).

[33] Lupoi, supra, note 31, at 4.

[34] Wormald, supra, note 32, at xi.

[35] Lupoi, supra, note 31 at 4. One instance of commonality in European common law (at p. 197) would be 'the right of a free man to apply to a judge whenever he wished and without delay'. It should be noted, for purposes of later discussion, that while sources of this early European law were different, there was by now much knowledge of commonality and a tendency therefore to advance it. Lupoi

English law as common, this would apparently be justified also by the common substance of varying pieces of legislation and by the notion of legislation as general precept. We thus find, in this most recent work, a new and very large slice of European legal history being examined in terms of commonality, ancient though differing concepts of commonality being put into play, and divergence being expressed as to the extent of pan-European common law. Much light has thus been shed on what were known as dark ages, and the subsequent debate on the common laws of Europe made much more comprehensible. Yet the notion of laws common in substance was not to play a large conceptual role in the millennium following the Norman Conquest. It was rather a new concept of common law (that which Lupoi considers 'totally different' from any which preceded it)[36] which was to emerge from the circumstances of Europe during and beyond the Renaissance of the eleventh and twelfth centuries.[37]

Mobility of people and mobility of laws

The written, affirmative forms of law described by Wormald and Lupoi were capable themselves of physical transportation and territorial displacement. They had become qualitatively different from the local unwritten laws, even if their content remained unchanged in the transition from unwritten to written. These laws have been described as 'legal and institutional blueprints or models which were easily exportable and adaptable but also resistant.'[38] They were 'vectors of expansion' which 'could be set down anywhere and still thrive.'[39] Legal horizons were thus, once again,

refers to this (at 433) as a 'guiding principle,' and cites (at 317) the movement of the writ from Frankish law to England, through the Normans, as indicative of the 'open system' of European common law. For doubts as to the level of commonality described by Lupoi, R. C. van Caenegem, *European Law in the Past and the Future: Unity and Diversity over Two Millennia* (Cambridge: Cambridge Univ. Press, 2002) at 25–6 (differences between feudal and allodial lands, urban and rural usages and privileges, edicts and customs of various places). For similar techniques in later law, leading to another version of 'common law,' see infra, this Ch., *The common law originating from France.*

[36] Lupoi, supra, note 33.

[37] As to which see H. Berman, *Law and Revolution: The Formation of the Western Legal Tradition* (Cambridge, MA: Harvard Univ. Press, 1983); H. Patrick Glenn, *Legal Traditions of the World*, 2nd. ed. (Oxford: Oxford Univ. Press, 2004) at 225–7, for islamic influence on the process.

[38] R. Bartlett, *The Making of Europe: Conquest, Colonization, and Cultural Change 930–1350* (London: Penguin, 1993) at 309.

[39] Bartlett, supra, note 38, at 310.

capable of expanding and both Christianity and the territorial needs of feudalism provided underlying reasons for expansion. This expansion, like that eventually beyond Europe, was freelance or non-governmental in character, as priests, knights, and merchants all found compelling reasons to push back the frontiers of the core area of European Christendom.[40] The prospects were enticing for all levels of the population.[41] The process was not so much intended to create colonies, within Europe, as rather to effect a kind of 'cellular multiplication' of the cultural and social forms of the European core, a process not so much of differentiation and subordination (the Roman model) but of replication.[42] A common church contributed much to this. New settlers would thus form a prosperous and largely governing elite, while the majority of the country folk could retain, in some measure and for a time, native language, culture, and social organization. The peripheries of Europe were thus in an ongoing dynamic state, as German urban laws formed a model for towns in eastern Europe, as Norman procedures were moved into Wales, as the fueros of Christian Spain were introduced into the towns of the Reconquista.[43] It had become necessary to reflect on the relations between expanding laws, eventually to become known as common, and the laws they met in the process of expansion. Nor could a simple line between the two be drawn, as in Roman law, since separation was not here the objective but rather, eventually and in some measure, commonality. The conceptualization of these relations was to take centuries. In the meantime, the process of adjustment began rapidly to take place in the field. We are no longer in a time of prelude to common laws, with earlier and differing concepts of commonality, but in a time of their rapid growth and expansion, now to be explicitly designated as such.

It is not until near the end of the 12th century, however, that the expression begins to surface in the literature in a way pertinent to the new phenomenon of expansion and commonality of laws. Professor Calasso

[40] Bartlett, supra, note 38, particularly at 5–7 on religious expansion, and 47–51 on the territorial requirements of feudalism ('the demand of vassals for fiefs and the desire of lords for fighting men'). For the process by which Christianity came to 'hold the center', Brown, supra, note 24, passim.

[41] For the attraction of new settlements as opposed to life in German villages, U. Wesel, *Geschichte des Rechts*, 2nd ed. (Munich: C. H. Beck, 2001) at 307; and for the process of recruitment, using agents or 'Locators,' H. Hattenhauer, *Europäisches Rechtsgeschichte*, 2nd ed. (Heidelberg: C. F. Muller, 1994) at 261. The Flemish were sought after for their skills in drainage.

[42] Bartlett, supra, note 38, at 306, 307, 309 ('Travelers . . . would not be aware of crossing any decisive social or cultural frontier'); and for cultural penetration or fusion ('Durchdringung') as opposed to conquest, Hattenhauer, supra, note 41, at 267 and 262 ('not by sword but by plough'). For the same concept of replication in the Spanish colonies of Latin America, infra, Ch. 2. The *derecho commún originating from Spain, in the world.*

[43] Bartlett, supra, note 38, at 310.

identifies a Lombard jurist at the end of the twelfth century as the first to speak of Roman private law as a ius commune and no longer, in the Roman way, as the ius civile.[44] A notarial document from Padua referred allusively to 'iure communi' in 1274.[45] Professor Ermini concludes that the doctrinal construction of the concept of the ius commune therefore takes place largely in the thirteenth and fourteenth centuries.[46] In England the expression appears to surface first in Richard fitzNigel's manual on the Exchequer, the Dialogus de Scaccario, written largely in 1177 and therefore remarkably parallel in time to what we know of Lombard use of the expression.[47] FitzNigel distinguished the law of the forest, dependent on particular and, he felt, arbitrary legislation of the king, from what he described as the 'common law of the realm.'[48] This would not be the earlier Roman distinction between general rules and particular rules within a given corpus of law, but rather the first attempt in the common law tradition to identify a distinct and overarching source of common law, as opposed to distinct and particular sources of law. Pollock and Maitland were of the view that the English usage was derived from the canonical, though the papal examples they cite are subsequent to the Scaccario, while the canonical legislation appears to follow the earlier Roman model.[49] By the twelfth and thirteenth centuries, however, the circumstances and ideas were changing. By 1246 a writ was able to express the king's wish that all writs of the common law ('de communi iure') which ran in England were also to run in Ireland[50] and by the end of the thirteenth century the expression had entered into judicial parlance. Paul Brand has identified a 1287 King's Bench decision in which Chief Justice Weyland asks rhetorically: 'Qei est la cause pur qoi le statut est fet?' and replies: 'En defaute de comune lei.'[51] As in Lombardy, the construction of common law in England thus begins in the late twelfth century, flourishes through

[44] Calasso, supra, note 9, at 104 ('commune lege vivant'). [45] Ibid.

[46] G. Ermini, *Corso di diritto commune* (Milan: Giuffrè, 1989) at 20.

[47] Richard, fitzNigel, *Dialogus de Scaccario/The Course of the Exchequer*, transl. C. Johnson (Oxford: Clarendon Press, 1983). [48] FitzNigel, supra, note 47, at 60.

[49] F. Pollock and F. W. Maitland, *The History of English Law before the Time of Edward I*, 2nd ed., vol. I (Cambridge: Cambridge Univ. Press, 1968) at 176; F. W. Maitland, *Roman Canon Law in the Church of England: Six Essays* (London: Methuen & Co, 1898) at 4.

[50] J. Hudson, *The Formation of the English Common Law: Law and Society in England from the Norman Conquest to Magna Carta* (London/New York: Longman, 1996) at 18.

[51] P. Brand, 'Eighteenth Century Legislation' in A. Romano (ed.) ... Collendo iustitian et iura condendo ... *Federico II Legislatore del Regio de Sicilia nell'Europa del Deucento. Per una storia comparata delle codificazione europee* (Rome: Edizione de Luca, 1997) at 344. The English lawyers spoke more of 'communis lex,' and not of 'ius commune,' since they would have been translating from the French 'commune lei.' H. MacQueen, *Common Law and Feudal Society in Medieval Scotland* (Edinburgh: Edinburgh University Press, 1993) at 2.

the thirteenth and gives rise to its full and active use by the fourteenth. Neither a continental nor an English notion of common law appears prior to the other in time, though everywhere there appears to be adaptation of earlier Roman language to contemporary circumstance.

The nature of the new common laws

The concept of common law is thus preceded by the practice, and the practice is an infinitely varied process of adjustment of expanding laws to recalcitrant local, legal resistance, everywhere in Europe. On the continent law is thought of, whether written or unwritten, Roman or Germanic, legislative or jurisprudential, in largely substantive terms, and the debate is in terms of choice of applicable substantive law. Questions of jurisdiction and procedure, or remedies, are not much part of the debate, since court structures and procedure are relatively stable. Even the development of roman-canonical procedure is consistent with underlying ideas of substantive law and the role of court procedure. It is thus a question, within existing structures, of whether the arrival of new settlers and new law could displace local forms of ordering. The overwhelming initial response to this question, on the continent, was no. The most striking example, following the Reconquista in Spain, was the guarantee by Alfonso the First of Aragon of ongoing enjoyment of Islamic law by the Muslim subjects of the new Christian king.[52] There was also little likelihood of legislative imposition of a new law elsewhere on the continent and it is clear that the principle of personality of unwritten law, and feudal law, left very little normative space. The new common laws faced difficult initial tasks of insinuation. They were of diverse origin, though writing appears to have been essential to all of them. The unwritten law of the Saxons became mobile in recorded form as the *Sachsenspiegel*.[53] Urban law, which had begun to be written in Italy by the mid-twelth century,[54] was transplanted to cities in search of renewal.[55] In Spain there were many legislative attempts, culminating with the *Siete Partidas*, to overcome local

[52] Bartlett, supra, note 38 , at 208.

[53] Infra, this Ch., *The common law (gemeine Recht) originating from Germany.*

[54] M. Bellomo, *The Common Legal Past of Europe, 1000–1800*, transl. Lydia G. Cochrane, (Washington, DC: The Catholic University of America Press, 1995) at 83–5.

[55] Infra, this Ch., *The common law (gemeine Recht) originating from Germany.*

particularity.[56] In these early circumstances of common laws, which were circumstances of normative plenty, recourse to Roman law was rare and tentative in the extreme. There are occasional references to use of Roman law in interpretation of substantive Frankish and Lombard law between the tenth and eleventh centuries, to judges using phrases of Roman law in the late eleventh century, and to development of a notion of 'mixed jurisprudence.'[57] This would all be a part, according to Charles Radding, not of a sudden rediscovery of Roman law and its sweeping over the continent, but of slowly increasing levels of technical sophistication on the part of Italian lawyers and an increasing willingness to experiment with Roman concepts, which had never disappeared entirely.[58]

In England the arrival of the Normans may be seen as part of the general European phenomenon of expansion of authority and control. The Conquest has also been seen as yielding the first European state, in terms of an effective government over a defined geographical area. Yet the Norman and Angevin kings were remarkably cautious in their attitudes to existing law. This may be due in part, as Patrick Wormald would have it, to its already distinctive features. It may even be said that the Norman kings were doubly cautious. First, in the European manner, they gave explicit guarantees for the maintenance of existing law. William I ordered all to seek 'the hundred and shire courts as our ancestors commanded,'[59] and would have ordered that Aethelric, the deposed Bishop of Selsey, 'a very old and learned man, should be brought to Penenden Heath in a cart to describe and expound the customary law of the Anglo-Saxons.'[60] The 'laga Edwardi,' the 'good old law' of the Anglo-Saxon period, was specifically confirmed[61] (though this gave rise to hundreds of claims for dispossession of land)[62] and Henry I, in 1108, again confirmed the

[56] Infra, this Ch., *The common law (derecho commún) originating from Spain.*

[57] Ermini, supra, note 46, at 9; C. M. Radding, *The Origins of Medieval Jurisprudence: Pavia and Bologna 850–1150* (New Haven/London: Yale University Press, 1988) at 85, 113–15.

[58] Radding, supra, note 57, at 10 ff.

[59] D. M. Stenton, *English Justice between the Norman Conquest and the Great Charter 1066–1215* (Philadelphia: The American Philosophical Society, 1964) at 56; A. Harding, *Medieval Law and the Foundations of the State* (Oxford: Oxford Univ. Press, 2002) at 195; and for William's struggle with the local language, in order to administer the old law, F. I. Schlechter, 'Popular Law and Common Law in Medieval England' (1928) 28 Col. L. Rev. 269 at 291.

[60] Stenton, supra, note 59, at 18; F. Pollock, *The Expansion of the Common Law* (South Hackensack, New Jersey, Rothman Reprints, 1974) at 37.

[61] F. Liebermann (ed.), *Die Gesetze der Angelsachsen*, vol. I (Halle: Max Niemeyer, 1898) at 492, for the laws preserved by William as 'les leis e les custumes . . . iceles meimes que li reis Edward sun cusin tint devant lui'; Hudson, supra, note 50, at 21.

[62] M. Chibnall, *The Normans* (Oxford: Blackwell, 2000) at 50.

preservation of shire and hundred courts, to meet in the same places and for the same terms as they met in the time of King Edward.[63] And the Norman and Angevin kings were doubly cautious in that their eventual, royal instrument of common law again did not provide any immediate menace to existing, substantive English law. It was rather a royal forum for litigation which was provided, or even perhaps simply a royal forum expanded slightly over its English predecessors, in which existing law could continue to be applied by sworn, or jurés, members of the population. The initial language of the common law is thus not the language of substantive law, as on the continent, but the language of jurisdiction, writs, and remedies. There is thus demarcation already, in terms of types of common law, all within a European cadre of accommodating expansion, on the one hand, and local sensibility on the other. The ius commune and the common law are thus distinct from one another, in important respects, and distinct from our three earlier concepts of common law—the law common to all humanity, the general precept of a given law, and the common elements of distinct laws. The beginnings of both the common law and the ius commune, are, however, striking in their modesty.

The early expansion of the ius unum and the common law

There were many expanding laws in Europe in the thirteenth century. Two of these benefited from particular political circumstances: the emerging common law of England, which benefited from the circumstance of Conquest, and the emerging ius commune of the continent, which benefited from the circumstance of Empire. However modest their beginnings, the political authorities behind them saw good reason for their further growth and expansion. This is most evident in the 'absolutist' phase of the ius commune and by the territorial expansion of the common law in the British Isles. The Faculty of Law of the University of Bologna was founded in the late eleventh century, around the time of our first records of the expression ius commune in its contemporary sense. Within decades the intellectual potential of Roman law had become evident. As a buttress to imperial legislation, and supplemented by such legislation, it

[63] Hudson, supra, note 50, at 24 for the writ.

could be seen, and was seen, as a 'unum ius.' There were some very large ideas behind this development, involving the Christian Church as a 'universal' church and the Emperor as 'dominus mundi,' and these ideas are said to have controlled notions of underlying European unity since this time.[64] It has been described as 'a matter of faith' ('un phénomène de foi').[65] In the eyes of the early glossators, custom could thus be tolerated, though just, since subject to legislation; emerging canon law should be treated with scornful indifference; and local or urban legislation could simply not be permitted to exist in conflict with the unum ius.[66] Justinian and Gaius had spoken of Roman law as the civil law of Rome, not as a ius commune, and there was therefore no textual authorization of particular laws existing in opposition to Roman law. Roman law provided a static model, not a dynamic one. There had been thoughts of the legal unity of the Carolingian empire since the ninth century; the time must have appeared ripe to the early Glossators.[67] The unum ius had much of the content of the later ius commune; it is much more aggressive in outlook.

In the British Isles the agents of commonality, the royal courts and royal writs, were functioning throughout England with increasing vigour from at least the mid-twelfth century. English people, however, (again, the European process of expansion) were settling in Scotland, Ireland, and Wales. In both of the latter two cases, the procedure of the English writs

[64] For the universality of the Empire, and the dominus mundi, Coing, supra, note 9, at 92; Calasso, supra, note 9, at 37, 40; and generally R. Folz, *The Concept of Empire in Western Europe from the Fifth to the Fourteenth Century*, transl. S. A. Ogilvie (London: Edward Arnold, 1969); and for the universal Church, and its implications both for canon law and Roman law, as universal reason, Calasso, supra, note 9, at 3; Bellomo, supra, note 54, at 72 (on popes continuing 'to pursue the idea of a body of laws for all of the Christian world; of a corpus that would have unity and provide unity'); F. Wieacker, 'Foundations of European Legal Culture' (1990) 38 Am. J. Comp. L. 1, at 12; and for the 'grand narrative' of European unity, Brown, supra, note 24 , at 4.

[65] Renoux-Zagamé, supra, note 8, at 138, and concluding that the idea has been 'prodigiously successful.'

[66] Ermini, supra, note 46, at 10, on the idea that only Imperial sources gave rise to law as such, and that Emperor legislator for humanity, and 26–7 on 'tenacious opposition' to recognition of other forms of (particular) law; Calasso, supra, note 9, at 68, on ius commune as 'closed system,' and 100 as 'unitary concept,' an 'entity'; A. Gouron, *Droit et coutume en France aux XIIe et XIIIe siècles* (Aldershot: Variorum, 1993) at 119, on impossibility of existence of medieval custom contrary to ius commune; and for alleged inability of legislation to alleviate situation of illegitimate children in matters of succession, given ius commune, T. Kuehn, 'A Late Medieval Conflict of Laws: Inheritance by Illegitimates in *Ius Commune* and *Ius Proprium*' [1997] Law & Hist. Rev. 243 at 252.

[67] Ermini, supra, note 46, at 7, on the request in 817 of Agobard of Lyon to Louis I, Charlemagne's immediate successor, for a communem legem in temporal matters. The proposal was an entirely radical one, implying the end of personal laws and creation of a 'universal Christian law for the universal Christian Commonwealth.' C. Dawson, *The Making of Europe: An Introduction to the History of European Unity* (London: Sheed & Ward, 1932) at 257. The time was then deemed not ripe, but with the inception of the Holy Roman Empire in 962, pressure for legal unity increased.

was specifically introduced by the English Crown, in Ireland in 1210 and in Wales in 1284. In Ireland there were even royal instructions that pleas in Ireland should be held and conducted 'just as they are customarily held and conducted in our realm of England, as you well know that the laws of our land of Ireland and of England are and should be identical.' [68] Wales has been taken as subject to similar initial objectives of unity.[69] Scotland appears to have been more problematical.[70]

The content of the ius commune, and the structures of the common law, were thus given initial shape, and some impetus, by the end of the thirteenth century, however modest may have been their beginnings. They were not to become, however, examples of a ius unum, a single, general law. Their identity and characteristics as common laws were to become more in evidence as the practice developed of accommodating both territorial expansion and local legal particularity, and as the slow process of conceptualization of a common law began to develop.

The essential tradition of the ius commune

The ius commune has been described as 'the essential tradition' because of its ability to preserve unity in diversity.[71] It appears to have been a growing awareness of the utopian character of the idea of 'one law' for all of Europe which led to the transition from the unum ius to the ius commune. This was the work of the later commentators, and Professor Calasso tells us they were essential in breaking up the 'iron framework' which the original glossators had given to Roman law.[72] Urban and regional legislation was being enacted, and followed, and some place for it had to be found. Such a place could not be found by virtue of Roman law itself, but eventually the idea of an implicit imperial concession, to the sources of particular law, seems to have been accepted in bringing about

[68] Bartlett, supra, note 38, at 214–15.

[69] R. R. Davies, 'The Twilight of Welsh Law 1284–1536' (1966) 51 History 143, at 146 on view of English chroniclers that Edward I had somehow abolished Welsh law in 1284.

[70] Infra, Ch. 3, *Territoires at the confluence of common laws.*

[71] Supra, Preface, note 1.

[72] Calasso, supra, note 9, at 64; and see H. Lange, *Römisches Recht im Mittelalter,* vol. I, *Die Glossatoren* (Munich: C.H. Beck, 1997) at 104–6, noting the requirement that local law had to be proved.

a 'necessary and opportune collaboration.'[73] Local statutes were also said to be analogous to pacta or agreements, since by agreement parties could derogate in some measure from Roman law.[74] The immense field of urban legislation thus received its legitimation from higher authority, and the cities could go on, with their charters and privileges, in granting freedoms and liberties to their citizens.[75] Much of western commercial and intellectual development has been said to be due to this fundamental, libertarian role of urban law ('Stadtluft macht Frei'), and the pressure for its recognition was immense. The cities said they had to legislate because the answers to many urban problems were not to be found in the Roman texts. The inadequacies of Roman law were evident in relation to other types of particular law as well, such as the personal laws (unwritten or written) of particular peoples, the feudal law of land-holding, which by now had spread across all of Europe,[76] and the canon law of the Christian Church.[77] These were the laws governing the family, land (the principal source of wealth), and religious belief. They all came to be recognized as privileges, as concessions or exceptions made in favour of particular groups or particular fields of law, allowing them to be excluded from the operation of the ius commune. We even owe our word privilege to this notion of private or particular laws (privatae leges).[78]

[73] Ermini, supra, note 46, at 27; for local or regional authorities as 'piccolo imperi entro l'Impero', Calasso, supra, note 9 , at 67; and for emergence of municipal law as ius civile, L. Mayali, '*Ius civile* et *Ius commune* dans la tradition juridique mediévale' in J. Krynen (ed.), *Droit romain* jus civile *et droit français* (Toulouse: Presses de l'Université des sciences sociales de Toulouse, 1999) 201.

[74] Calasso, supra, note 9, at 69.

[75] For the development of written urban law, originally through redaction of unwritten rules and principles particular to each urban location, Bellomo, supra, note 54, at 83–85; and for the importance of the 'free cities' (there were more than 150 in the Hanseatic League), J. M. Roberts, *A History of Europe* (New York: Allen Lane, 1997) at 142; and for the cities having 'made all the difference' in western development, D. Landes, *The Wealth and Poverty of Nations* (London: Abacus, 1999) at 240 (Russia, in contrast, tied people to land, 'a large prison'). For the freedom of cities essentially as commercial monopolies of their citizens, however, with close regulation of foreign traders, K. Kim, *Aliens in Medieval Law: The Origins of Modern Citizenship* (Cambridge: Cambridge Univ. Press, 2000) at 32–3.

[76] Professor Gouron attributes the recognition of custom contrary to the ius commune as due in part to English resistance, and by the end of the 12th century concludes that the question had shifted to the age required of valid custom. Gouron, supra, note 66, at 128. For feudal law as a concurrent common law, see infra, Ch. 3, *Common laws and feudal law*.

[77] For canon law as a privilege, at least in its initial recognition, J.- M. Carbasse, *Introduction historique au droit*, 3rd ed. (Paris: PUF, 2001) at 114. The glossators had initially refused recognition of canon law; Calasso, supra, note 9, at 65. For its subsequent recognition and elevation to fundamental status within the ius commune, see infra, Ch. 3, *Common laws and canon law*.

[78] Carbasse, supra, note 77, at 114 ; and for the notion of privilege as private law, E. Cortese, *La norma giuridica: spunti teorici nel diritto commune classico* (Milan: Giuffrè, 1964) at 43; Renoux-Zagamé, supra, note 8, at 141.

Once the theoretical possibility of a particular law, a ius proprium, was accepted, an entire field then opened of the means of conciliation of this new ius commune with its interlocutors, the multiple iura propria or particular laws of Europe. According to what principles was the conciliation to be effected? The ius unum here cast its shadow, and Professor Stein attributes to Bartolus the acceptance of the view that local statutes were to be interpreted according to methods established by the ius commune.[79] There were thus, initially at least, fields of the ius commune seen as immune to local legislative challenge, notably in imperial fiscal matters, violence, and sedition, but these appear to have declined over time.[80] Control of local law was possible, initially at least, for violation of divine or natural law or for having fallen into desuetude through non-application.[81] Lacunae of the ius commune did, however, emerge, as new needs arose, and statutes which added positively to the ius commune were interpreted affirmatively.[82] For centuries, however, statutes which were 'odious,' because of violation of the ius commune, or because of burdens or restrictions they imposed, were interpreted restrictively (though applied).[83] They could not be extended by analogy to related cases; they were barren 'mules,' incapable of further legal consequences.[84] The criteria were inescapably flexible, foreshadowing the various 'suitability' doctrines in the expansion of European common laws overseas.[85] The criteria of the ius commune were also extended to conflicts seen to exist amongst the various iura propria.[86] Interpretation of the spatial reach of

[79] Stein, supra, note 15, at 72; also B. Paradisi, 'Notes critiques sur le problème du droit commun' Rev. hist. dr. fr. et étr. 1980.423 at 438.

[80] Ermini, supra, note 46, at 30 ; Cortese, supra, note 78, at 47.

[81] Coing, supra, note 9, at 105, 109; R. Zimmermann, '*Statuta sunt stricte interpretanda?* Statutes and the Common Law: A Continental Perspective' (1997) 56 Camb. L. J. 315. For revival of the idea of control for obsolescence, G. Calabresi, *A Common Law for the Age of Statutes* (Cambridge MA: Harvard Univ. Press, 1982).

[82] Ermini, supra, note 46, at 36; M. Sbriccoli, *L'interpretazione dello statuto* (Milan: Giuffrè, 1969) at 462.

[83] Lange, supra, note 72, at 106; Zimmermann, supra, note 81, at 315; Coing, supra, note 9, at 106; P.-A. Côté, 'L'interprétation de la loi en droit civil et en droit statutaire: communauté de langue et différences d'accents' (1997) 31 R.J.T. 45 at 71 ; S. Vogenauer, *Die Auslegung von Gesetzen in England und auf dem Kontinent*, vol. I (Tübingen: Mohr Siebeck, 2001), at 448–9.

[84] Calasso, supra, note 9 , at 115; Paradisi, supra, note 79, at 437; Côté, supra, note 83, at 69.

[85] For the flexibility, L. Mayali, 'La notion de "statutum odiosum" dans la doctrine romaniste au Moyen Age' (1984) 12 Ius Commune 57, notably at 60; and for the suitability doctrines, infra, Ch. 2, *The common law as common law, in the world.*

[86] Stein, supra, note 15 , at 72, 73; P. Stein, 'Bartolus, the Conflict of Laws and the Roman Law' in P. Feuerstein and C. Parry, *Multum non Multa: Festschrift für Kurt Lipstein* (Heidelberg/Karlsruhe: C. F. Müller Verlag, 1980) at 251.

legislation has been with us ever since, as an unavoidable dimension of contemporary private international law. The various types of particular law once established, hierarchies of sources could then be developed, both in the work of the commentators and in particular laws themselves. It was essential to the recognition of particular laws that they displace the ius commune, in the absence of reasons to the contrary, such that the most particular of laws thus received the highest authority, the initial place of priority in the interpretive hierarchy. This could be variously expressed, in ascending order, as statute, custom, ius commune, or as city, region, Empire. Resort to the ius commune thus followed only in the face of the inadequacy of local, particular sources.[87] The way was thus open to increasing emphasis on local or regional law, both for reasons of local or regional particularity and to enable large and purposive interpretation of local remedial legislation.[88]

The concept of ius commune which emerged from these many debates was new and different from the notions of common law which had previously prevailed. Common law was no longer the general precept of a given law, or the law common to humanity, or substantive commonality found in different laws. It had become law common *in relation to* law which was particular, and it was the particular law which prevailed in priority. The ius commune was therefore not binding law. It was never enacted as the positive law of European nation states and never somehow repealed in its entirety, and it is even difficult to contemplate how this could occur.[89] The authority of authors, the main source of the ius commune, cannot be somehow abrogated. They did not, moreover, give definitive opinions, advising only 'saving a better opinion.'[90] Moreover, none of the content of the ius commune necessarily prevailed, though it

[87] Bellomo, supra, note 54, at 103, 151; Calasso, supra, note 9, at 230, for municipal ordonnances expressing hierarchy of sources.

[88] For French objection, by Du Moulin, to narrow interpretation of local statutes and written French customs, Stein, supra, note 15 , at 84; for French refusal to designate French law as 'odious' (it was rather 'strict' or 'rigorous'), Côté, supra, note 83, at 75; and for eventual liberal interpretation of local legislation and particular law, leading to contemporary ideas, Calasso, supra, note 9, at 172; Zimmermann, supra, note 81, at 322, citing 17th- and 18th-century Dutch authors.

[89] R. C. Van Caenegem, *European Law in the Past and the Future: Unity and Diversity over Two Millennia* (Cambridge: Cambridge Univ. Press, 2002) at 137; U. Santarelli, '*Ius Commune* e *Iura Propria*: Strumenti teorici per l'analisi di un sistema' in *Studi in Memoria di Mario E. Viora* (Biblioteca della Rivista di storia del diritto italiano) (Rome: Fondazione Sergio Mochi Onory per la storia del diritto italiano, 1990) 635 at 635. For various attempts at repeal, however, or prohibitions of citation, infra, Ch. 2, *National appropriation of common laws in Europe*.

[90] R. H. Helmholz, *The Ius Commune in England: Four Studies* (Oxford: Oxford Univ. Press, 2001) at 243.

had content which was available in case of need. So it has been referred to as a 'subsidiary common law'[91] though it is perhaps more accurate to think of it as *relational common law*, law which only survives and functions in relation to the vigour of the particular law which has priority over it. These particular laws, moreover, are not autonomous or independent or exclusive, in spite of their priority. It is presumed that they will need supplementary assistance, and the presence of that means of assistance, the ius commune, is constant in the functioning of the particular law. The application of the ius commune is thus often suspended in particular cases, but it will revive or reappear as the occasion demands. It may be useful to think of the Cheshire Cat.

The ius commune, as prototype

The literature on the ius commune is immense, and filled with contradictions. Yet the literature in its entirety has had the major effect of concentrating attention on the ius commune as a relational common law (with all of the theoretical implications this implies) and as being the single, outstanding exemplar of such a relational common law. The most widely circulated image of European law for the last millennium has thus been that of a single, European ius commune, subject to particular iura propria, which came to an end with the national codifications in the nineteenth and twentieth century. The common law of England is thus often presented as a iura propria (the frequent fury of common law lawyers) or as simply an exception, a paradox standing outside the general pattern of European law.[92] It is this concept of a single, European ius commune which is now the object of major efforts of revival in the context of the present European Union.

There is, however, another image of European law which is possible to conceive, which is that of multiple, interactive common laws, each

[91] Calasso, supra, note 9, at 73. The notion of subsidiarity thus has a long history in European law. For contemporary manifestations, G. Berman, 'Taking Subsidiarity Seriously: Federalism in the European Community and the United States' (1994) 94 Col. L. Rev. 331

[92] See, for example, Carbasse, supra, note 9, at 279 ('England remains deliberately separate, fixed since the middle ages with a national law of a jurisprudential type, also called common law, a law common to all of England and which sees itself as absolutely distinct from that of the continent,' author's transl). On the continental concept of the common law as a law 'common to all of England,' infra, this Ch., *The common law, as common law.*

radiating out from major centers of population or influence, and each variously accommodating iura propria internal to each of them. This is a more complex, non-binary understanding of European legal history, which would essentially deny the possibility of forcing all of European law into a single (monotheistic?) model of the one (major) and the many (minor). This hypothesis is present in the abundant literature of the ius commune, but has generally not been pursued.[93] It would explain, however, resistance to the ius commune not simply as a result of local particularity, but as a result of the play and interaction of common laws of generally equal or comparable standing, a hypothesis which, as will be seen in Chapter 2, becomes more plausible when the ongoing, overseas lives of the European common laws are considered. There would thus have been many iura communia in Europe in addition to the ius commune, notably canon law, feudal law, and commercial law, and then the many regional common laws radiating out, both within Europe and beyond, from major centres of England, Germany, France, Spain, the Netherlands, and so on. European history of the first millennium has been best described not as an exchange between one overwhelming centre and its periphery, but rather as a loosely spread constellation of centres, and the idea of multiple common laws in the second millennium therefore continues to acknowledge the essential diversity of European law and legal history—Europe as a geodesic dome, with interlocking modules, as opposed to a large tent hung on a single pole.[94] The model also corresponds to patterns of mobility of European populations.[95] The ius commune would thus be best seen as a prototype, along with the common law,[96] which inspired emulation in terms of its fundamental characteristics, but which inevitably declined in practical importance with the rise of its (somewhat) later derivatives. Verifying such a proposition would be a task of infinite labour, but some indications of its support can be readily found,

[93] See, for example, A. Wijffels, 'European Private Law: A New Software-Package for an Outdated Operating System?' in M. van Hoecke and F. Ost, *The Harmonisation of European Private Law* (Oxford/Portland: Hart Publishing, 2000) 101 at 114 (on different forms of common law prevailing); N. Rouland, *Introduction historique au droit* (Paris: P.U.F., 1998) at 258 (on error to speak of common law in singular, though then referring only to canon law and the common law). Professor Coing acknowledged that the expression common law was variously used, and that there were notions of regional common law in France, Italy, and Spain, though stating that further research was required on their operation. Coing, supra, note 9, at 87–8

[94] Brown, supra, note 24, at 16, 17.

[95] See supra, *Mobility of people and mobility of laws.*

[96] For the common law as earliest to 'modernize,' R. C. van Caenegem, *The Birth of the Common Law*, 2nd ed. (Cambridge: Cambridge Univ. Press, 1988) at 91, 105 ('an anomaly, a freak in the history of western civilization, less modern because it was modernized earlier'); and for parallel emergence of the expression common law in Italy and England, supra, Mobility of Peoples and Mobility of Laws.

both in terms of existing studies on the primacy of the ius commune, and in terms of our knowledge of the other iura communia.

There is, at least, widespread agreement that the ius commune was differently received in different parts of Europe and that there was great variation in time in the reception process. Professor van Caenegem thus states that the impact of Roman law ranged from close to nil in the case of England to massive in the case of the German Pandectists of the nineteenth century, with 'varying shades in between.'[97] Professor Coing, addressing what he describes as a 'core area' of reception, including Italy, the provinces of Spain, France, the Netherlands, Germany, Hungary, and Poland, pointed out that the process began in Italy in the early twelfth century, reached France and the Netherlands only in the thirteenth and fourteenth centuries, Germany in the fifteenth, and Scandinavia in the seventeenth.[98] He cautions, however, that the extent of influence of Roman law is not established with certainty and that its influence should not be exaggerated.[99] Given the state of empirical knowledge, opinions thus differ considerably on the real level of influence of Roman law, even in those territories where its reception is acknowledged.

The view most favourable to the ius commune would see it as a pervasive manner of thought, with overarching principles of substantive law and interpretation which were spread irresistibly throughout Europe through the ongoing influence of legal education. Professor Calasso is perhaps the most vigorous exponent of this view.[100] The ius commune would have thus provided a 'conceptual framework' for the work of lawyers at all levels,[101] an 'intellectual model' for 'every European legal system.'[102] It would have been present in 'every decision.'[103] There is some

[97] Van Caenegem, supra, note 35, at 25. [98] Coing, supra, note 9, at 13–14.

[99] Coing, supra, note 9, at 100; and see for a more recent view that 'Germany's experience was untypical' and that the 'Reception may therefore have had more to do with a shift towards the declaration of rules by courts than with an adoption of classical learning on its own merits . . . confining lay judges to questions of fact and turning more cases into questions of law for learned tribunals,' J. Baker, *The Oxford History of the Laws of England*, vol. VI, 1483–1558 (Oxford: Oxford Univ. Press, 2003) at 9–10, with references. A complicating factor is the extent to which parties may have renounced application of Roman law, as to which Calasso, supra, note 9, at 44–5, 116; Cortese, supra, note 78 , at 55.

[100] Calasso, supra, note 9; and for the importance of legal education as fundamental in the relations of legal traditions, Gaudemet, supra, note 28, at 434; Coing, supra, note 9, at 12.

[101] Stein, supra, note 15, at 61

[102] K. Pennington, 'Learned Law, Droit Savant, Gelehrtes Recht: The Tyranny of a Concept' (1994) 20 Syracuse J. Int'l. & Com. L. 205 at 207, citing notably the work of Richard Helmholz and Charles Donahue for Roman law influence in England, as to which see infra, Ch. 3, *The common law and the ius commune.*

[103] Bellomo, supra, note 54, at 154.

support for this view, notably in records of legal practice[104] and in some measure in records of library holdings,[105] though neither can be taken as conclusive.

A related view would have the ius commune present in much of Europe but much more susceptible to local integration and adaptation. Calasso insisted that it was not Roman law which was being applied in Europe, but a contemporary ius commune with a Roman base or origin.[106] The ius commune thus would have an ongoing flexibility,[107] and there has been vigorous debate on the possibility of manipulation on the part of the jurists and the nature of their particular loyalties.[108] The ius commune could also incorporate elements of the iura propria.[109] This view is in a number of respects consistent with the first, since all becomes a question of defining the ongoing nature of the ius commune. A shift in its recognized sources, however, from distant to local ones, will be seen as a change of laws. The movement will be away from the ius commune as a relational common law, towards a notion of substantive commonality (based on the 'old' Roman law) amongst laws recognized as different and distinct because of the differences in their sources. This would later become crucial in the appropriation of Roman law by national legislators through codification in the nineteenth century—Professor Carbonnier referred to a process of 'decanting' into national vessels—a process widely thought to have brought about the end of the ius commune.[110] So it is a subtle and important distinction when the ius commune is recognized as existing in

[104] See, for example, A. Wijffels, 'Einflüsse der Doktrin auf die gerichtle Argumentationsspraxis in der frühen Neuzeit' (1987) Ius Commune, Sonderhefte 30 Studien zur Europäischen Rechtsgeschichte 371, notably at 380 for frequency of citing of 'foreign books.'

[105] For instances of library holdings of ius commune (e.g., German author held in Portugal), H. Coing, 'The Roman Law as *Ius Commune* on the Continent' (1973) 89 L.Q.R. 505, though for the inconclusive character of such data, absent computerization of library holdings, Osler, infra, note 114.

[106] Calasso, supra, note 9, at 20, 21, qualifying Vinogradoff's explanation of second life of Roman law as more poetic than scientific.

[107] Stein, supra, note 15, at 86 ('ultimate triumph of commentary over the text'); R. H. Helmholz, *The* Ius Commune *in England: Four Studies* (Oxford: Oxford University Press, 2001) at 241, for significant change of ius commune over time.

[108] Helmholz, supra, note 107, at 242 (jurists could be too clever, law a 'nose of wax,' subject to manipulation and disfigurement); and for accusations of bias in favour of local sources of power, A. Cavanna, 'Il Ruolo del giurista nell età del diritto comune (Un'occasione di riflessione sull'identità del giurista di oggi)' (1978) 44 Studia et Documenta Historiae et Iuris 95, at 103, 106, 109.

[109] On the subtlety of the process, Paradisi, supra, note 79 at 435–7 ('la réalité contemporaine se faisait sentir sur l'interprétation des jurists . . . Tout était donc possible'); and generally L. Maruoti, *La tradizione romanistica nel diritto europeo*, vol. I (Torino: G. Giappichelli Editore, 2001) at 95.

[110] J. Carbonnier, 'Usus hodiernus pandectarum' in R. Graveson et al (eds.) *Festschrift für Imre Zajtay* (Tübingen: J.C.B. Mohr, 1982) 107 at 110.

identifiably different forms, depending on geography and the interaction with local sources of law.[111] The identification of a Roman-Dutch law, a Roman-Hispanic law, a Roman-Scottish law, a 'Bavarian form of the ius commune,'[112] or the German law of the Pandectists as 'common German private law of Roman origin'[113] is an affirmation both of the ongoing importance of Roman law and of its apparent vulnerability to local law. The question is crucial for the existence of multiple common laws across the seas (Ch. 2).

A final view is one which is least favourable to the influence, and even the existence, of the ius commune. The ius commune would thus be essentially a 'Euro-myth,' created for contemporary political purposes, the mythical character of which will become evident once computerization of law library holdings from 1500–1800 is completed.[114] The myth may be due to bias in favour of Italy (said to be its source) and Germany (said to be its main repository).[115] In any event the ius commune would never have existed; it never controlled material law, or even the interpretation of law, and the appearance of its existence would be due simply to use of Latin as a common language, as opposed to any common substance or method.[116] Since the main source of wealth in late medieval and early modern Europe was land, and since land was largely governed by feudal law, there was in any event little for the Roman law of the ius commune to do.[117] Nor does the absence of a developed, written law of obligations

[111] See, e.g., R. Zimmermann, 'Das Bürgerliche Gesetzbuch und die Entwicklung des Bürgerlichen Rechts' in M. Schmoeckel, J. Rückert, and R. Zimmermann, *Historisch-kritischer Kommentar zum BGB*, vol. I, *Allgemeiner Teil* (Tübingen: Mohr Siebeck, 2003) at 2,3; D. Ibbetson, *Common Law and* Ius Commune (London: Selden Society, 2001) at 7 (on local courts being able to establish own custom of interpretation of ius commune).

[112] Stein, supra, note 15, at 105.

[113] B. Windscheid, *Lehrbuch des Pandektenrechts*, vol. 1, 9th ed. by T. Kipp (Frankfurt am Main: Literarische Anstalt Rütten & Loenig, 1906) at 1; and for the extent of the break between the Pandectists and the ius commune, H. Coing, 'German "Pandektistik" in its Relationship to the Former "Ius Commune"' (1989) 37 Am. J. Comp. L. 9 (also at 11 on the 'creative work' of the ius commune in relation to Roman law).

[114] D. Osler, 'The Myth of European Legal History' (1997) 16 Rechtshistorisches J. 393, notably at 305 on the 'hidden continent' of legal literature in national libraries.

[115] J.-L. Halperin, 'L'approche historique et la problématique du *Jus Commune*' Rev. int. dr. comp. 2000.717, at 724.

[116] J. Schroder, 'Zur Bedeuting des "Ius Commune" für das Moderne Europäisches Privatrecht' in W. Vitzthum and M. Pena (eds.), *L'identité de l'Europe* (Aix/Marseille: Presses Universitaires d'Aix-Marseille, 2002) 65 at 66, 71; A. Leca, 'Un droit européen avant le droit européen? Note à propos du ius commune' in Vitzthum and Pena, supra, 53 at 56; and for the ius commune as a linguistic mirage, D. Heirbaut, 'Feudal Law: the Real *Ius Commune* of Property in Europe, or: Should We Reintroduce *Duplex Dominium*?' (2003) 11 Eur. Rev. Pr. L. 301 at 304, 305.

[117] Heirbaut, supra, note 116, at 306; A. Watson, *The Evolution of Western Private Law*, expanded edition (Baltimore/London: The Johns Hopkins University Press, 2001) at 243–5.

imply a necessary reception of Roman law. There are many instances of contractual relations developing in the absence of a formal, written law of contract.[118] There would thus be no real difference in Europe between a supposed group of core countries of the ius commune, and those said to have resisted the ius commune, such as England, Switzerland, and the Scandinavian countries.[119]

In the state of existing understanding of the ius commune, the hypothesis of multiple European common laws is therefore as plausible as that of a single, overarching common law. Of the countries seen as most resistant to the ius commune, it is England which has provided another version of common law, again as a potential prototype.

The common law, as common law

The arrival of the Normans in England was part of a general movement of population in Europe, which gave rise to the entire phenomenon of laws expanding outwards, as common laws, and being necessarily reconciled with the laws they encountered in this process.[120] The phenomenon of

[118] For enforcement of commercial contract in the China of the Han dynasty (of the first 2 centuries AD), in spite of Confucian resistance, H. Scogin, 'Between Heaven and Man: Contract and the State in Han Dynasty China' (1990) 63 S. Calif. L. Rev. 1326; and for the importance of mutual trust, as opposed to a law of contract, in contemporary commercial dealings, B. Kozolchyk, 'The UNIDROIT Principles as a Model for the Unification of the Best Contractual Practices in the Americas' (1998) 46 Am. J. Comp. L. 151 at 168. In Europe, commercial exchange took place outside of Roman law through a variety of devices (obligations of reciprocal gift, oaths, pledge, ceremony). There was also a developing commercial law (as to which see infra, Ch. 3, *Common laws and commercial law*). For the earlier devices, and for reliance by fourteenth-century English courts on 'the practice of merchants' (which already existed) in development of a law of contract, F. Schlechter, 'Popular Law and Common Law in Medieval England' (1928) 28 Col. L. Rev. 269 at 275 ('common customary law of contracts'); D. J. Ibbetson, *A Historical Introduction to the Law of Obligations* (Oxford: Oxford Univ. Press, 1999) at 3–6, 74.

[119] For non-reception, though influence, of Roman law in Scandinavia, D. Tamm, 'The Danes and Their Legal Heritage' in B. Dahl, T. Melchior, L. A. Rehof, and D. Tamm, *Danish Law in a European Perspective* (Copenhagen: Gadjura, 1996) 33 at 38; O. Fenger, 'L'influence du droit romain dans la Scandinavie mediévale' (1981) Pars V, 14 Ius romanum medii aevi 10; and for similar attitudes in Switzerland, J.-F. Poudret, 'L'attitude des coutumiers à l'égard du droit écrit en pays romands à la fin du moyen âge' in A. Iglesia Ferreiros, *El dret comúi Catalunya 'Ius proprium—Ius commune a Europa'* (Barcelona: Fundació Noguera, 1993) 123. For refusal of the notion of reception in countries such as Poland and Hungary said to be part of core of ius commune, though admitting as ratio scripta, K. Bukowska, 'Le droit romain en Pologne au XVIIe siècle' Rev. hist. dr. fr. et étr. 1961.76 at 89; Gaudemet, supra, note 28, at 432–3.

[120] See supra, *Mobility of people and mobility of laws.*

commons laws thus preceded their theoretical articulation. The English common law, as it developed from central royal courts, was a common law in the sense of the ius commune, that is, it was common *in relation to* the particular laws or iura propria which it encountered in the course of its expansion, first in England, then further afield. This appears not to be understood by many continental commentators today; indeed it is perhaps not understood today by many common law lawyers as well, since all have been conditioned by present understandings of the operation of state law. Yet there are statements by continental writers, of an historical nature, which nevertheless draw a sharp distinction between the historical phenomena of the ius commune and the common law. Professor Coing thus stated that the common law was not of a subsidiary nature, as was the ius commune, but was of rather 'more or less exclusive application.'[121] This would mean, of course, that the common law was not a common law, in any overarching, relational sense, as would have been the ius commune. More recently still it has been said that the ius commune of the continent was not a single law comparable to the common law of England, which disregards every form of local differentiation.[122] It is not clear why there is such widespread misunderstanding, since René David was able to state quite clearly that the English common law was common 'par opposition aux coutumes locales'[123] and the statement has been re-affirmed more

[121] Coing, supra, note 9, at 13 ('mehr oder weniger ausschliessliche Geltung'), 89 ('nicht nur subsidiär'), citing as authority J. H. Baker, *An Introduction to English Legal History* (London: Butterworths, 1971) at 21. Professor Baker however, makes, no such statement as to the exclusivity of the common law, though stating, at 21, a different proposition entirely, that 'Royal justice triumphed not because a conscious effort was made to impose it on the country, but because it was inherently better than the alternatives;' and at 20 that 'It would no longer be acceptable to regard this challenge as a deliberate attack on the local courts and on feudalism, simply because its ultimate effect was to replace them. Until 1300 at least the lesser courts were encouraged.' For the ongoing (long) life of the lesser courts, and the only relative 'triumph' of the common law, infra, text accompanying notes 142–52.

[122] Leca, supra, note 116, at 54; and see O. Beaud, 'L'Europe entre droit commun et droit communautaire' (1991) 14 Droits 3, at 4 (the common law a common law 'à sa manière,' a law applicable in a uniform manner throughout the territory); Maruoti, supra, note 109, at 123 (common law following Norman arrival 'suffocating' local laws in creation of national law); E. Bucher, Book review of Glenn, *Legal Traditions of the World*, ZEuP 2002.895 at 898, on unacceptability of proposition that common law suppletive law like the ius commune, arguing that plaintiff's choice of royal forum resulted in necessary application of royal law. Even were this latter statement correct, as to which see the subsequent discussion in the text, it would still leave the common law in some measure dependent on party choice, and far from the idea of a mandatory or imperative ius proprium. All of these statements of the exclusivity of the common law, or its character as general decree, would have the effect of leaving the ius commune as the prime and even only exemplar of a relational or subsidiary common law in Europe, which was far from being the case.

[123] R. David, 'Droit commun et common law' in *Studi in memoria di Tullio Ascarelli*, vol. I (Milano: Giuffrè, 1969) 345 at 348.

recently by R. C. van Caenegem.[124] It is possible that the misunderstanding arises from the fact that the law of England today, having gone through the same process of apparent nationalization that took place on the continent, may be seen in the form of general decree, in the Roman sense. Yet the contemporary concept of the law of England is not the same as that of the common law, which exists both within and beyond England.[125] The common law in its origin was a relational, floating common law and, particularly in its transnational dimensions, remains so today. So the common law is equally capable of being seen as a prototype of other common laws (including that of the ius commune, as it eventually developed). In current circumstances, however, it is evident that this requires some demonstration.

We left the common law with some form of structure in place, and having received some initial propulsion towards territorial expansion through its formal introduction into Ireland and Wales.[126] Scotland lay beyond. We were not dealing, however, with a substantive common law containing rules or principles of material or substantive law, as on the continent, but with structures or institutions of eventual commonality, in the form of the royal courts and system of forms of action. There is great controversy in English legal history as to the origins of these institutions. The traditional view, most visibly represented by Maitland, identifies the reign of Henry II in the late twelfth century as 'supremely important.'[127] Professor van Caenegem looks to a period of a century and a half from the time of the Conquest as that of the 'judicialization' of royal writs and hence as the 'birth' of the common law.[128] Lady Stenton saw the roots of the common law 'far back' in the Anglo-Saxon past (preceding Patrick Wormald in this) but concluded that '[g]enius was at work' in the time of Henry II, notably in the formulation of the great writs and forms of action.[129] S. F. C. Milsom tended to doubt whether the reforms of Henry II

[124] Van Caenegem, supra, note 35, at 14; and see, for a subtle appreciation from France, E. Picard, 'Common Law' in D. Alland and S. Rials, *Dictionnaire de la culture juridique* (Paris: Lamy/puf, 2003) 238 at 239 (common law seen as instrument of Crown nevertheless capable of authorizing ongoing application of customary rules, principle not one of uniformity of law), 244 (not characterized by given normative content, but by juridical attitude).

[125] Hence the title of the work edited by the late Peter Birks, *English Private Law* (Oxford: Oxford Univ. Press, 2000), which speaks not of the common law; and see the language of the former Chief Justice of Canada, Bora Laskin in B. Laskin, *The British Tradition in Canadian Law* (London: Stevens, 1969) at 62 ('the English version of the common law').

[126] Supra, *The nature of the new common laws.*

[127] Pollock and Maitland, supra, note 49, at 137.

[128] Van Caenegem, supra, note 96, at 34–6, 39–41, 50–6.

[129] Stenton, supra, note 59, at viii, 26; for P. Wormald, supra, *A common lex non scripta?* and see, for continuity evidenced by the Domesday book, R. Fleming, *Domesday Book and the law: Society*

were all that innovative.[130] Yet the expression common law appears to have emerged only in the late twelfth century,[131] so both the reality of a relational common law and the recognition of it appear to emerge only with the Normans.

Yet how is the reality of the relational character of the common law to be demonstrated? The essential feature of the common law, as a relational common law, was the optional, even subsidiary, character of the royal courts, source of the common law. In the language of the continent, parties were free to choose both the institutions and the substance of the iura propria. Thus Paul Brand concludes that the royal courts were 'limited to hearing only such litigation as they had been authorized to hear by royal writ' and that the extent of such writs was deliberately limited.[132] The existence of royal jurisdiction, moreover, did not preclude local jurisdiction. This suppletive character of royal jurisdiction was part of existing (old) law, since in Anglo-Saxon times, and thereafter, jurisdiction amongst borough, shire, and royal courts was very flexible and open to party choice.[133] Use of local courts was probably faster and cheaper.[134] Yet by the late twelfth century there were signs of growing popularity of these royal structures or institutions. Lady Stenton speaks of litigants who would 'flock' to the Chancery for writs.[135] Even amongst those who see the late twelfth century as fundamental to the emergence of the common law, however, there is agreement that this was without prejudice, at least at the time, to survival of existing law and institutions. The growth of the structures of the common law was not imposed on local particularity.[136]

and legal custom in early medieval England (Cambridge: Cambridge Univ. Press, 1998), notably at 29, 34, 39, for earlier use of writs, at least for royal finances, ongoing orality of procedure and open choice of forum.

[130] S. F. C. Milsom, *The Legal Framework of English Feudalism* (Cambridge: Cambridge Univ. Press, 1976) at 36, 37 (royal writs mechanisms for enforcing customs on lords and their courts; ultimate destructive effect on seigniorial order 'a juristic accident, altogether beyond foresight'), 66 ('Royal control sought only to keep seigniorial courts to their customs'), 185 ('Probably there was no intention to change the framework at all, not even to take jurisdiction'); S. F. C. Milsom, *Historical Foundations of the Common Law*, 2nd ed. (London: Butterworth, 1981) at 33 ('not devised as a national system of civil judicature ... an accumulation of expedients').

[131] Supra, note 47.

[132] P. Brand, *The Making of the Common Law* (London/Rio Grande: The Hambledon Press, 1992) at 96.

[133] Fleming, supra, note 129, at 39, 40 ('enormous flexibility in the choice of venue'); Hudson, supra, note 50, at 26 (no strict rules of jurisdiction).

[134] Stenton, supra, note 59, at 129.

[135] Stenton, supra, note 59, at 52.

[136] Stenton, supra, note 59, at 81 ('large field of litigation left to local representatives,' royal judges coming at irregular intervals could not take place of local courts available month in month out); Hudson, supra, note 50, at 210 (on ability of lords to claim cases felt wrongly removed or begun in wrong court); Pollock, supra, note 60, at 40, 56 (royal jurisdiction developing along 'lines of least

It is true the king retained jurisdiction over the most direct affronts to royal authority[137] and that plaintiffs in principle could, by choice of royal courts, oblige defendants to appear in them. Even here, however, there was the possibility of initial distraint of goods in a lord's court, which would force a potential tenant plaintiff to pursue locally.[138] Where the praecipe quod redat was used to initiate proceedings relating to land in a royal court, the lord could reclaim the action, and Clause 34 of the Magna Carta even limited the initial use of the praecipe.[139] The rule requiring a royal writ to challenge a freehold holding did not preclude resort to local courts, though did prevent lords from using their own courts to seize land with no royal intervention.[140] Henry II, moreover, made further specific promises for maintenance of the jurisdiction of local courts, such that the progression of the royal courts was clearly a matter of popular choice.[141] Litigants opted for effective possessory remedies for the recovery of land, notably the writ of novel disseisin, and for the use of the jury in place of older and now less favoured means of proof and adjudication. It was only by the seventeenth century that the royal courts had obtained *concurrent* jurisdiction over most important actions dealing with property and obligation.[142]

The history of the common law is dominated by questions of jurisdiction, writs, and remedies. What law was applied by English courts? In the local courts it was generally a combination of local, unwritten law and legislation, the iura propria of England. The common law literature speaks of local, particular, special, manorial, or county 'custom.' In the royal

resistance,' no jurisdiction in appeal to reverse dooms of county or hundred); F. Schlechter, 'Popular Law and Common Law in Medieval England' (1928) 28 Col. L. Rev. 269 at 279 (difficult to reconcile important growth in jurisdiction with 'hatred and fear of the royal courts,' detestation of their 'unscrupulous venality,' inhabitants fleeing into woods on arrival of Eyre of Cornwall in 1233), 283 (need to reverse modern idea of local court of limited jurisdiction, Anglo-Saxon notion of unlimited justice close at hand). F. Greer, 'Custom in the Common Law' (1893) 9 L.Q.R. 153 at 161 (local courts only courts readily accessible to greater number of people for 'long after the Conquest'); J. H. Baker, *An Introduction to English Legal History*, 4th ed. (London: Butterworths LexisNexis, 2002) at 22–5 (communal justice too deep-rooted to think of abolition; no deliberate attack on feudal jurisdiction; city and borough courts continuing until Tudor times; manorial, county, hundred courts 'finally put down in 1977').

137 Hudson, supra, note 50, at 29 (listing examples), 115 (difficult to estimate frequency).

138 Harding, supra, note 59, at 154.

139 Stenton, supra, note 59, at 77–81; Hudson, supra, note 50, at 224–5.

140 Stenton, supra, note 59, at 26, for uncertain origins of rule; Hudson, supra, note 50, at 192.

141 Hudson, supra, note 50, at 145.

142 C. Donahue, Jr., '*Ius Commune*, Canon Law, and Common Law in England' (1992) 66 Tul. L. Rev. 1745 at 1747; and for some 12,000 local courts, each with their own rolls, in the early Tudor period, and for details of these courts, Baker, supra, note 99, at 117, and Ch. 16 ('Local Courts').

courts two types of 'custom' were recognized. The first is most often described as 'general custom,' which J. G. A. Pocock explains as a conflation of true custom with the work of the judges.[143] This is what developed as the common law, a particular combination of jurisprudential and (often unwritten) doctrinal understanding, which developed spontaneously in the absence of any notion of stare decisis until the nineteenth century.[144] The royal courts also, however, applied local custom. The judges did so, to the extent their functions required and to the extent the local custom was the object of proof.[145] More importantly, the jury inevitably did so, and the jury's monopoly of decision making on the substance of a case meant that local custom could continue to prevail (in undiscernible form) until the abolition of the obligatory role of the jury in the nineteenth century.[146] As was the case on the continent, there was also mutual borrowing between suppletive common law and local custom.[147] There are long lists of the customs of the regions of England,[148] the most visible of which was that of Kent, both for its content (of gavelkind, in which succesion was amongst all of the sons and not exclusively to the eldest) and for its importance and persistence.[149] Its gavelkind was abolished only in 1925.[150] There was also

[143] J. G. A. Pocock, *The Ancient Constitution and the Feudal Law* (Cambridge: Cambridge Univ. Press, 1987) at 35; and see Pollock and Maitland, supra, note 49 at 184 ('The custom of the king's court is the custom of England, and becomes the common law').

[144] J. H. Baker, *The Law's Two Bodies* (Oxford: Oxford Univ. Press, 2001), for the unwritten tradition of the common law as its second body; and for stare decisis as a 19th-century phenomenon, J. Evans, 'Change in the Doctrine of Precedent during the Nineteenth Century' in L. Goldstein (ed.), *Precedent in Law* (Oxford: Clarendon Press, 1987) 35 at 68; and more generally G. J. Postema, 'Roots of our Notion of Precedent' in Goldstein, supra, at 9; M. Lobban, *The Common Law and English Jurisprudence 1760–1850* (New York: Oxford University Press, 1991); D. Lieberman, *The Province of Legislation Determined: Legal Theory in Eighteenth-Century Britain* (Cambridge: Cambridge Univ. Press, 1989).

[145] For questions of proof, and actual practice, A. Kiralfy, 'Custom in Mediaeval English Law' (1989) 9 J. Leg. Hist. 26, notably at 30; and for continuation of the legal category of 'particular customs' as a 'principal branch of common law, denoting the plethora of situations in which the general law of the realm was abandoned in deference to the settled usages of a particular local or a particular group of subjects,' D. Lieberman, 'Law/Custom/Tradition: Perspectives from the Common Law' in M. Philips and G. Schochet (eds.), *Questions of Tradition* (Toronto: Univ. of Toronto Press, 2004) 233 at 240.

[146] For the 'law-finding function' of the jury, which became only 'extensively tamed and restricted' and only by the 18th century, Lieberman, supra, note 145, at 240, with references.

[147] Baker, supra, note 99, at 308–10 (pleading in local courts in Tudor period following common law forms of action, local causes of action becoming recognized by royal courts).

[148] For listing, N. Neilson, 'Custom and the Common Law in Kent' (1924–25) 38 Harv. L. Rev. 482 at 484; and for content, Greer, supra, note 136, notably at 156 for complete character of customs, extending notably to contract; E. K. Braybrooke, 'Custom as a Source of English Law' (1951) 50 Mich. L. Rev. 71; Kiralfy, supra, note 145, at 33–38 and noting, at 28, similarity or commonality of many 'basic principles.'

[149] For its 'commanding' position 'hors de la ley commune', Neilson, supra, note 148, at 482, 492.

[150] Milsom, supra, note 130, at 1.

the local law of the cities, or boroughs, the equivalent of the municipal statutes or statuta of the free cities on the continent, and that of London was so well known to the judges as not to require formal proof.[151] Certainly the customs declined in influence, as they did on the continent, but the law of England today, as stated by Halsbury's, is to the effect that 'to this day a local custom is recognized by the courts as taking priority over a general rule of common law if certain strict requirements are met.'[152]

The common law in England, like the ius commune on the continent, thus achieved its commonality through local acceptance and not imposition. In both cases the common laws were suppletive to existing normativity. So the common law has been a relational common law, defining itself in relation to the particular laws with which it had constant relations. It may even be seen as a structure of maintenance of those particular laws, since the role of the jury meant in some measure the incorporation of local custom into royal procedure, and the royal courts themselves were the means of enforcement of particular legislation. Moreover, the common law was not formulated in terms of substantive rules. It rather only defined when particular questions could be put to the jury, and what remedies were available. So it essentially had no substantive content to impose over local norms, and the outcome of cases was rarely recorded through much of its history ('and so to judgment'). What mattered was the voluntary choice of forum, the influence of the remedial and general form of reasoning of the common law writs, and the effect of that reasoning on application of particular sources of law, in the form of custom or legislation. The common law of England was thus structurally different from the iura communia of the continent, in being defined in jurisdictional and remedial terms. It has been a common law in the same manner as the iura communia, however, in defining itself in relation to particular sources of law, in terms of custom and legislation. And since the common law was not a law defined in terms of its necessary content, there could be no doctrine of stare decisis in the common law until the late nineteenth century. Like the jurists of the ius commune, the judges of the common law did not give answers which they saw as definitive.[153] Gerald Postema

[151] Greer, supra, note 136, at 155; for its pleading in matters of liability for fire, Baker, supra, note 136, at 407; and for the charters of the boroughs protecting them 'against the meddling of the king's justices,' Pollock and Maitland, supra, note 49, at 186.

[152] *Halsbury's Laws of England*, 4th ed., vol 12(1) (London: Butterworths, 1998), para. 601 (also acknowledging loss of much of importance of custom since abolition of customary tenure of land in 1925).

[153] For the jurists, supra, *The essential tradition of the ius commune*; for stare decisis as a 19th-century phenomenon, supra, this section.

has recently written a philosophy of the common law in which the common law is defined not as a system of positive rules, nor as natural law (both of which would be definitions based on content) but as, in his language, a 'practised framework of practical reasoning.'[154] The common law would thus be best thought of as a common law, a framework of reasoning in ongoing relations with particular laws, the content of which has priority of application. The common law and the ius commune, in spite of their differences, are best seen as two species of a larger genus, which is that of a relational common law. This fundamental character of the common law becomes more evident in the course of its expansion, at first within the British Isles.

The common law originating from England

Until the middle of the twelfth century Welsh law was unwritten and made use of triadic verse form.[155] It began to assume written form with the development of handbooks of private lawyers, themselves purporting to state the unwritten law which had prevailed at the time of King Hywel Dda (904–50). They were, moreover, 'dynamic' law books, with no inhibitions preventing the redactors from updating as time went by.[156]

[154] G. Posterma 'Philosophy of the Common Law' in J. Coleman and S. Shapiro (eds.) *The Oxford Handbook of Jurisprudence and Philosophy of Law* (Oxford: Oxford Univ. Press, 2002) 588 at 596, and defining the reasoning of the common law as essentially 'discoursive', a 17th-century word capturing both the interlocutory and discursive nature of the process. This character is preserved by one contemporary version of the common law, that of Melvin Eisenberg, who rejects the notion of fixed rules to concentrate rather on rules 'that would be generated' by common law principles of adjudication. Yet the formulation conceives of the common law as itself occupying the entire field of law, in the modern manner, though admitting the relevance of decisions from other jurisdictions. The dialogical relation with the ius proprium is absent. M. A. Eisenberg, *The Nature of the Common Law* (Cambridge, MA: Harvard Univ. Press, 1988), notably at 154, 156 ('generative' conception of common law). Stephen Waddams rejects also the idea that the common law can have definitive statements or categorizations, since obligations arise often 'not from a single concept but from the interaction of two or more concepts in such a way as to preclude the allocation of the legal issue to a single category.' S. Waddams, *Dimensions of Private Law: Categories and Concepts in Anglo-American Legal Reasoning* (Cambridge: Cambridge Univ. Press, 2003) at 2. Here again, however, the iura propria have disappeared.

[155] P. J. Cook, 'Hywe Dda's Law-Books and the Welsh Legal Tradition' (1991) 18 Ius Commune 195 at 202.

[156] Cook, supra, note 155, at 197; R. R. Davies, 'The Twilight of Welsh Law, 1284–1536' (1966) 51 History 143, at 144; M. E. Jones, 'The Legacy of Roman Law in Post-Roman Britain' in R. W. Mathisen,

While the English writs were introduced formally into Wales in 1284,[157] they were so introduced for the English settlers. In the era before states, communities were defined otherwise than in terms of formal equality and such distinctions were regularly made. This was entirely consistent, moreover, with English authority existing as a kind of 'High Kingship of the British Isles,' exercising only indirect rule over much of the territory, and with the tentative nature of English settlement into Wales, which had begun to reverse itself by 1330.[158] So Welsh law was not abolished by the introduction of English writs and even continued to flourish thereafter, notably in matters of private law and procedure.[159] It was a particular law, in a constant state of interaction with the common law. There was a widespread process of picking and choosing between different courts and laws, in pursuit of litigation advantage,[160] while the common law assumed a distinctly local colour to the extent it came to be applied. In the Welsh marches, where the King's writ reached the outer limits of its authority, application of English law entailed a process of mediation.[161] English law eventually came to prevail because, in the language of Professor Davies, it was 'more convenient, adaptable and expeditious' in the eyes of the population, which was attracted both by the jury and by the possessory remedies for land.[162] Welsh law continued, however, well into the sixteenth century, as a ius proprium. Even with the extension of English land law and the granting of English 'laws and liberties' to the Welsh in 1536, it was acknowledged that 'reasonable local customs' were not necessarily abolished, and a case of application of Welsh law was reported in 1540.[163] Integration of court structures was not to take place until 1830.[164]

English law was also not imposed on the Irish with the arrival of the English in the twelfth century. The English writs of the common law were introduced, or at least those considered suitable for introduction, but they

Law, Society and Authority in Late Antiquity (Oxford: Oxford Univ. Press, 2001) 56 at 57, with refs (authority of Welsh law deriving from ancient custom as law of people and not as legislation associated with royal or imperial power); and generally, T. M. Charles-Edwards, *The Welsh Laws* (Cardiff: Univ. of Wales Press, 1989); D. Jenkins (trans. & ed.), *The Law of Hywel Dda* (Llandysul: Gomer Press, 1986).

157 Supra, *The early expansion of the ius unum and the common law.*

158 R. R. Davies, *The First English Empire: Power and Identities in the British Isles 1093–1343* (Oxford: Oxford Univ. Press, 2000) at 4, 178–79.

159 R. R. Davies, *Conquest, Coexistence, and Change: Wales 1063–1415* (Oxford/Aberystwyth: Clarendon Press/University of Wales Press, 1987) at 367–8; Cook, supra, note 155, at 195 ('no concerted attempt to substitute English law in general').

160 Davies, supra, note 156, at 160.

161 Davies, supra, note 158 at 161; Cook, supra, note 155, at 196.

162 Davies, supra, note 156, at 161; Davies, supra, note 158, at 159.

163 Cook, supra, note 155, at 203, 204.

164 Baker, supra, note 136, at 31.

were intended principally for the benefit of the English settlers.[165] The old Brehon law thus continued and it has been said that the failure to bring all under a single law 'prevented the consolidation of the colony.'[166] The Irish could, however, opt for English law and many did so, from the fourteenth century.[167] Conversion to the 'English way of life' was a clear objective, but there was much resistance and the 'exception of Irishry' long prevailed.[168] The two laws were in constant contact.[169] Professor Baker speaks of the common law thereafter being 'gradually absorbed'[170] and this eventual predominance was 'ultimately that of popular appeal and demand,' as in Wales.[171] The process of implantation of the common law accelerated in the seventeenth century, under the policies of Sir John Davies, but the process was a judicial and therefore a necessarily gradual one. In the famous Case of the Tanistry, the court affirmed the general principle of the survival of the law of conquered territory, though found the particular Irish practice of succession by tanistry to the 'most worthy' of an extended kin group to be invalid.[172] Even after the decision, Irish succession practices continued to be given some effect, and the case in any event could not be given effect beyond the question put to the court.[173] Other dimensions of Brehon law were left to survive as they might. The Irish Supreme Court was still enquiring as to the nature of Brehon property law in solving problems of fishing rights in tidal waters, well into the twentieth century.[174]

Within the British Isles the non-exclusive or relational character of the common law originating from England is best demonstrated by its

[165] F. H. Newark, *Notes on Irish Legal History* (Belfast: Marjory Boyd, M.A., Printer to the Queen's University of Belfast, 1960) at 12; W. J. Johnston, 'The First Adventure of the Common Law' (1920) 36 L.Q.R. 9 at 9, 22; .

[166] G. J. Hand, *English Law in Ireland 1290–1324* (Cambridge: Cambridge Univ. Press, 1967) at 215. For Brehon law, F. Kelly, *A Guide to Early Irish Law* (Dublin: School of Celtic Studies, 1988), notably at 241 for both Irish and Welsh law stemming from 'Common Celtic law' (common here in the sense of substantive commonality or general decree).

[167] J. Muldoon, *Canon Law, the Expansion of Europe, and World Order* (Aldershot: Ashgate/Variorum, 1998) at 273.

[168] Ibid; Bartlett, supra, note 38, at 215; though for the mixing of the population, R. G. Asch, 'Kulturkonflikt und Recht: Irland' in Common Law *und die* Ancient Constitution (1994) 21 Ius Commune 169 at 171.

[169] G. Mac Niocaill, 'The Contact of Irish and Common Law' (1972) 23 N. Ir. Legal Q. 16.

[170] Baker, supra, note 136, at 31.

[171] Davies, supra, note 158 at 159.

[172] (1608) Davies 28, 80 E.R. 516.

[173] H. Pawlish, *Sir John Davies and the Conquest of Ireland: A study in legal imperialism* (Cambridge: Cambridge Univ. Press, 1985) at 81.

[174] *Moore* v. *A.G. for Saorstát Éireann* [1934] I.R. 44, notably at 66–69, 88–91. Brehon law is also said to have been used in the Irish Arbitration Courts.

(partial) reception in Scotland. The process in Scotland differed radically, however, from similar processes in Ireland and Wales. In Scotland the common law encountered not simply an informally recorded law of the people but, in addition, another common law, in the form of the ius commune of the European continent. The relations between common laws, and their relations in Scotland, are the object of separate developments, in Chapter 3. There were, however, other common laws emerging in Europe, beyond the common law and the ius commune.

The common law (droit commun) originating from France

The French had their own droit commun, and it was not composed of Roman law. It was rather, originally at least, a droit commun coutumier, and the expression droit commun, in France, can be found as early as 1262, less than a century after its emergence with the common law or with the ius commune.[175] The expression may have been initially used only in the Roman sense, of general precepts of a given law, but even at the end of the thirteenth century Beaumanoir is writing of 'le droit qui est commun à tous au royaume de France,' a law which is common over the multiple customs of France.[176] So there is a very early shift from the limited Roman sense to the notion of substantive commonalities found amongst different customs. We would here be dealing with the substantive common law, in Marizio Lupoi's terms, of the early Middle Ages, now continuing through the eleventh- and twelfth-century renaissance.[177] This reliance on a droit commun coutumier in France in no way declined in importance through the subsequent centuries and even became an increasingly important conceptual instrument. The slow process of redaction of the customs

[175] Petot, supra, note 11, at 422–3, citing judicial decisions; and for subsequent use, G. Giordanengo, '*Ius commune* et "droit commun" en France du XIIIe au XVe siècle' in Krynen, supra, note 73, at 219.

[176] Petot, supra, note 11, at 414 (on possible use of Roman notion), 417 (on Beaumanoir's extension to substantive commonalities); J.-L. Thireau, *Charles du Moulin (1500–1566)* (Geneva: Librairie Droz, 1980) at 120 ; Leca, supra, note 116, at 55. For the original, Ph. De Beaumanoir, *Coutumes de Beauvaisis*, 2 vols (Paris : Alphonse Picard, 1899) ; *The* Coutumes de Beauvaisis *of Philippe de Beaumanoir*, transl. F. R. P. Akehurst (Philadelphia : Univ. of Pennsylvania Press, 1992), with refs. at xxiii, xxix, xxxii to debate on Beaumanoir's use of the expression.

[177] For this common law of the early middle ages, supra, *A common lex non scripta?*

eventually gave rise to the possibility of their comparative study. 'Families' of customs then became evident as commonalities were identified and there was talk of 'la conférence des coutumes' or bringing together and comparison of written customary law.[178] The great sixteenth-century names of French doctrine then took up the cause and Du Moulin affirmed that 'our customs are not municipal [or particular] laws. They suffice unto themselves and are our only common law.'[179]

This French movement towards a common law is of interest in definitional terms, since it went beyond a type of archeological or anthropological process of determining that there were in fact commonalities, or a common core, amongst the customs, but went some distance in formulating an overarching synthesis of those commonalities, for normative purposes. A relational and overarching common law thus emerged, which would have left the particular customs intact to live out their respective lives and which would have prevented the ius commune from achieving the status of a common law in France.[180] The passive resistance of the droit commun was also accompanied by explicit prohibitions of the teaching of Roman law[181] and ferocious doctrinal opposition, notably in the work of Hotman.[182] The overarching nature of the French droit commun was found in articulated maxims of customary law, recognized in many territories now recognized as part of France ('the seigneur must protect the rights of all of those under age', 'death seizes the living') and in doctrinal writing.[183] The Custom of Paris was also taken to be a synthesis of many other customs, a type of ideal custom against which others could be measured, and it was often the object of choice of law clauses, from as

[178] Carbasse, supra, note 77, at 119; G. Leyte, '"Le droit commun de la France". Observations sur l'apport des arrêtistes' (2003) 38 Droits 53.

[179] Du Moulin, *Commentaire de la coutume de Paris, Epitome tituli I de feudis*, § 107 and 108, éd. 1681, vol. I, pp. 22–3, as cited in Petot, supra, note 11, at 413 (author's transl.); and for Coquille to the same effect, J. Brissaud, *Manuel d'histoire du droit francais* (Paris: A. Fontemoing, 1898) at 158; V. Guizzi, 'Il diritto comune in Francia nel XVII Secolo' (1969) 37 Tijd. v. Rechtsg 1 at 5.

[180] J. H. Franklin, *Jean Bodin and the Sixteenth-Century Revolution in the Methodology of Law and History* (New York/London: Columbia University Press, 1963) at 37. For the absence of discussion of the ius commune in contemporary manuals of legal history in France, Halperin, supra, note 115, at 718, though for defence of Roman law as the droit commun of France in an 18th-century preface by Bretonnier, at a time when the Roman law of obligations was of unquestionable influence, J. Krynen, 'Le droit romain "droit commun de la France"' (2003) 38 Droits 21.

[181] J. Gaudemet, *Les naissances du droit* (Paris: Montchrestien, 1997) at 302, for prohibition in Paris in 1219, though authorization in Orléans in 1235; Guizzi, supra, note 179, at 21, with refs; Thireau, supra, note 176, at 92.

[182] As to which, D. Kelley, *François Hotman: A Revolutionary's Ordeal* (Princeton, NJ: Princeton University Press, 1973); Franklin, supra, note 180, at 40 ('the most militant of the anti-Romanists').

[183] For the maxims, Thireau, supra, note 176, at 126.

far away as Toulouse.[184] It was said to occupy the same position as the law of Justinian in other jurisdictions and its prestige grew with its reformulation and expansion in 1580.[185] It was also exported overseas, the beginning of a transnational droit commun.[186] Given such a recognized common law, private laws or privileges and legislation came to be narrowly construed, and so the same interpretive principles emerged as those of the ius commune in relation to its iura propria.[187] In 1747, just 57 years before the codification of French civil law, Bourjon published his treatise on 'the common law of France and the custom of Paris reduced to principles.'[188] We are here clearly dealing with a relational common law, defining itself against the particular customs, but the codification of 1804 largely drew an end to this development, at least in France itself. Its continuation lay beyond the seas. The French experience of common law, however, was not unique in its general outlines on the continent of Europe.

The common law (gemeine Recht) originating from Germany

While Germany was eventually a country of formal reception of the ius commune, this process occurred only from the sixteenth century and was preceded by major developments towards a German gemeines Recht, which became applicable throughout many territories in northern and north-eastern Europe. The *Sachsenspiegel* (Mirror of the Saxons) was the most visible element of this common German law ('gemeindeutsches

[184] O. Martin, *Histoire de la Coutume de la Prévôté et Vicomté de Paris*, vol. I (Paris: Editions Ernest Leroux, 1922) at 26; Gaudemet, supra, note 181, at 176.

[185] E. Chenon, *Histoire générale du droit francais public et privé des origines a 1815*, vol. 2 (Paris: Sirey, 1929) at 317, 318 ; though for resistance to it in other regions, A. Lefebvre-Teillard, 'Les différents facteurs d'unification dans l'Ancien droit' in *1804–2004 Le Code civil: Un passé, un présent, un avenir* (Paris: Dalloz, 2004) 77 at 82.

[186] Martin, supra, note 184, at 65 ('C'est même en Nouvelle France, si doucement conservatrice, que la coutume parisienne a le plus longtemps duré; elle y est morte, vraiment de sa belle morte, au milieu du XIXe siècle') ; and see the discussion, infra, Ch. 2.

[187] Supra, *The essential tradition of the ius commune*; and for the French principles of interpretation, Petot, supra, note 11, at 424–5; and for this as Du Moulin's position, Thireau, supra, note 176, at 91.

[188] F. Bourjon, *Le droit commun de la France et la coutume de Paris réduits en principes*, 2 vols (Paris: Au palais, chez Grangé, Rouy, 1747).

Recht'). It contained law which was originally the lex non scripta of the Saxons, written down as the *Sachsenspiegel* first in Latin then in German by Eike von Repgow in the early thirteenth century.[189] It has recently been produced in a new edition by the University of Pennsylvania Press.[190] The *Sachsenspiegel* contained the law of the countryside, the law of feudal relations and provincial life (Lehnrecht and Landrecht) but there were also many laws of individual cities (Magdeburg, Lübeck) which became highly influential and mobile. The *Sachsenspiegel* also served as a model for an ongoing process of redaction of local or regional unwritten laws, such that by the end of the thirteenth century many other Mirrors had come into existence.[191] This common, German law became territorially widespread, both to the west, in Holland, but more extensively to the east, with the considerable movement eastwards of German-speaking people, though it has been said that this process left no corresponding impression on European consciousness.[192] As with the English common law, it was initially reserved to German settlers,[193] and then became more widespread as a means of restrictive interpretation of local feudal privilege.[194] As the most influential legal instrument in this process the *Sachsenspiegel* was re-published in Poland[195] and at least one chair was created in Poland for its teaching.[196] The Polish jurist Zalaszowksi referred to it as the common law of the territories of north-east Europe, while still remaining a particular law or ius proprium in Germany (the law of Saxony).[197] It was still being applied in Ukraine in the nineteenth century.[198] While the *Saxonspiegel* and other Landrechte were thus widely received in the eastern

[189] Hattenhauer, supra, note 41, at 265.

[190] *The Saxon Mirror: A Sachsenspiegel of the Fourteen Century*, transl. M. Dobozy (Philadelphia: University of Pennsylvania Press, 1999).

[191] H. Lück, *Über den Sachsenspiegel: Entstehung, Inhalt und Wirkung des Rechtsbuches* (Halle an der Saale: Verlag Janos Stekovics, 1999), notably at 55 (Augsburger Sachsenspiegel, Deutschenspiegel, Schwabenspiegel).

[192] W. Ebel, *Deutsches Recht im Osten (Sachsenspiegel, Lübisches und Magdeburgisches Recht)* (Kitzingen/Main: Holzner-Verlag, undated, though post-1946) at 3, and with map at p. 2 showing spread of Saxon law to over a hundred cities in what is now Poland, Ukraine, Hungary, the Baltic States, the Czech Republic, Slovakia, and Russia.

[193] Hattenhauer, supra, note 41, at 263.

[194] K. Nehlsen-von Stryk, 'Das sächsisch-magdeburgische Recht in der Spruchtätigkeit des Oberhofs des deutschen Rechts auf der Burg zu Krakau' in G. Köbler and H. Nehlsen, *Wirkungen europäscher Rechtskultur, Festschrift für Karl Kroeschell* (Munich: C. H. Beck'sche Verlagsbuchhandlung, 1997) 829 at 831.

[195] Lück , supra, note 191, at 70–3

[196] K. Bukowska, 'Le droit romain en Pologne au XVIIe siècle' Rev. hist. dr. fr. et étr. 1961.76 at 80.

[197] I. Kwiatkowska, 'Das sächsische Recht in der polnischen juristischen Literatur des 17. Jahrhunderts' in G. Lingelbach and H. Lück, *Deutsches Recht zwischen Sachsenspiegel und Aufklärung* (Frankfurt/Bern/New York/Paris: Peter Lang, 1991) 119 at 123.

[198] Lück, supra, note 191, at 73.

countryside, the cities of Magdeburg and Lübeck became 'Mother Cities' many times over as their Stadtrechte became the models for urban law in a large number of 'Daughter Cities.'[199]

German common law was very important in the absence of any strong central authority amongst the German states. It thus received even more theoretical attention than the droit commun of France, though both displayed remarkably similar characteristics. Thus the notion of a relational or subsidiary common law was distinguished from laws common only because of substantive commonalities in their content, and it was recognized that there could be layered, relational common laws, each acting as a subsidiary law to the particular laws beneath them.[200] German common law would thus have been 'a common law beneath the common law (a 'gemeines Recht unterhalb des gemeinen Rechts').[201] As in France, the German common law had to emerge from the substantive commonalities found in regional laws, and there is a greater difference of opinion in Germany than in France as to whether this stage of higher synthesis had been reached, at least for the entire territory of what was to become Germany. Wächter and Coing expressed doubts as to the existence of a pan-German, German common law.[202] Others, particularly the Germanic law authors of the nineteenth century, were much more affirmative.[203] The debate is much affected by various forms of loyalty, particularly in relation to the role of Roman law, and will eventually be returned to.[204] Certainly the concept of a German common law was widespread, however, and continued to receive great attention up to, and well beyond, the apparent abrogation of the *Sachsenspiegel* by Prussian legislation in the late eighteenth century.[205]

[199] The Mother Cities would provide not only the initial model of urban law, but also ongoing advice in its implementation. Lück, supra, note 191, at 56–8; Hattenhauer, supra, note 41, at 264. The process was not limited to Germany. For the municipal laws of Edinburgh, Aberdeen, and London as models for other towns in Scotland and England, D. Guth, 'Law' in R. Tittler and N. Jones, (eds.) *A Companion to Tudor Britain* (Oxford: Blackwell, 2004) 77 at 91.

[200] See, for example, C. G. von Wächter, *Pandekten*, vol. I, *Allgemeiner Theil* (Leipzig: von Breitkopf und Härtel, 1880) at 15 (distinguishing 'merely factually common law' from relational common law) and 12 (layered relational common laws).

[201] R. Jacob, 'Doctrine et culture nationale. La naissance de la littérature juridique en langue populaire en France et en Allemagne' Droits 1994.5, at 18.

[202] Coing, supra, note 9, at 114; Wächter, supra, note 200, at 22 (*Sachsenspiegel* would never have been entirely generalized, as was the case for the Coutume de Paris).

[203] G. Gudian, 'Gemeindeutsches Recht im Mittelalter?' (1969) II Ius Commune 33 at 33–7, suggesting that possible and even probable that common German law, though still further research and comparison required.

[204] Infra, Ch. 3, *The ius commune and other continental common laws.*

[205] As to which, Lück, supra, note 191, at 75.

The common law (derecho commún) originating from Spain

The common laws of Europe were not limited to those of the North. In Castile royal authority had long struggled against both local particularity and imperial authority, whether Roman or Islamic. In the thirteenth century a policy of standardization of local laws, or fueros, was underway, and particular models of law were sought to be introduced in regions and towns.[206] The royal policy then became one of blocking off, to the extent possible, resort to Roman sources, while incorporating those judged acceptable into royal texts, along with indigenous material, so as to provide a general source for the kingdom. This was a difficult undertaking. Many efforts preceded the eventual drafting of the *Siete Partidas* (Seven Parts or Books) in the late thirteenth or early fourteenth centuries, under Alfonso X ('the Wise').[207] It was conceived not as legislation but as a book of teaching, yet the resistance to it (and to the measure of Roman law which it contained) was such that it was only officially adopted in 1348.[208] Thereafter it assumed great importance as a suppletive source of law, first in the Iberian Peninsula, then overseas. Already with its adoption, in the *Ordenamiento de Alcala*, a hierarchy of sources of law was established, with the *Ordenamiento* itself as the primary source, followed by the local fueros, and followed finally, as suppletive source, by the *Siete Partidas*. In subsequent statements of hierarchies, down through the centuries, the *Siete Partidas* always retained its final, ultimate place, a relational law which yielded to imperative legislation and local sources.[209]

Did the *Siete Partidas* constitute a common law? Opinions are, once again, divided. Some have been categorically affirmative.[210] Others have

[206] M. Scheppach, *Las Siete Partidas: Entstehungs- und Wirkungsgeschichte* (Pfaffenweiler: Centaurus, 1991) at 26, 34.

[207] For prior efforts, Coing, supra note 9, at 121; and for controversy on the authorship and dating, Scheppach, supra, note 206, at 44–5.

[208] Scheppach, supra, note 206, at 61, 191; for the text, in a new edition, R. I. Burns (ed.), *Las Siete Partidas*, transl. S. P. Scott (Philadelphia: University of Pennsylvania Press, 2000).

[209] J. B. Grandon, *Historia del derecho indiano del descubrimiento colombino a la codificación*, vol. I, *Ius Commune—Ius Proprium en las Indias occidentales* (Roma: Il Cigno Galileo Galilei, 2000) at 203; J. Lalinde Abadia, *Derecho histórico español*, 3rd ed. (Barcelona: Editorial Ariel, 1983) at 129–30; R. Gibert, *Historia general del derecho español* (Granada: F. Roman, 1968) at 53; Scheppach, supra, note 206, at 202, 206, 207.

[210] For Spanish authors to this effect, Grandon, supra, note 209, at 199 (citing Juan de Matienzo in the 16th century, for whom the Spanish royal texts would be common law 'equal to that of England');

preferred to speak of a 'general law' as opposed to a common law.[211] Others again settle on the idea of a ius proprium at the highest level (recalling the German notion of layered common laws).[212] The text functioned unquestionably as a relational common law, having been meant to apply not as binding legislation or general decree, but as an ultimate, supplementary source in the absence of particular royal laws or local customs. The *Siete Partidas* thus had content, but could not be defined in terms of such content, since it yielded in all cases to local law and thus existed, and had to be defined, in relation to that local law. As a common law, it was also expansive, and came to be of great influence beyond Castile, in territories now recognized as Spanish, as well as in Portugal and, eventually, in the Spanish territories overseas.[213]

Other common laws of Europe

The notion of a common law was a powerful one, appropriated or invented by the jurists of all of the major legal traditions of Europe. The traditions of common law which have been examined thus far have all gone on to assume major transnational and contemporary importance. Other European common laws remained regional in character or, having obtained some territorial expansion, declined in influence thereafter. There were thus identifiable common laws in the regions of Tuscany, Naples, and Piedmont, each with their iura propria and each providing an

C. Petit, '*Derecho comun y derecho castellano: Notas de literatura juridica para su estudio (siglos XV-XVII)*' (1982) 50 Tijd. v. Rechtsg. 157 at 169 (Spanish doctrine of 16th and 17th centuries 'near unanimous' in treating as common law); and more recently, from outside Spain, Gaudemet, supra, note 181, at 183 (expression common law used, however, both to designate Spanish texts and ius commune); Maruoti, supra, note 109, at 109–10, (*Siete Partidas* as 'Pandectas Castellanas,' 'diritto comune castigliano'); Lalinde Abadia, supra, note 209, at 49 (legal order of Castile considered as derecho común in Castile); S. Jacobson, 'Law and Nationalism in Nineteenth-Century Europe: The Case of Catalonia in Comparative Perspective' (2002) 20 Law & Hist. Rev. 307 at 314 ('The legal tradition known as the Spanish "common law," not to be confused with either the *ius commune* or the English common law, was the most dominant').

[211] Grandon, supra, note 209, at 121; Bellomo, supra, note 54, at 100; O. F. Robinson, T. D. Ferbus, and W. M. Gordon, *European Legal History: Sources and Institutions*, 2nd ed. (London/Dublin/Edinburgh, 1994) at 118.

[212] Grandon, supra, note 209, at 198; Bellomo, supra, note 54, at 100; and for the German notion, supra, *The common law (gemeine Recht) originating in Germany.*

[213] For Portugal, Coing, supra, note 9, at 122; Maruoti, supra, note 109, at 111.

overarching source of regional normativity.[214] The law of the Lombards, the Germanic people of the long beards who settled in Italy, was such a regional law, but in written form as the Liber Feudorum achieved major influence from the late twelfth century throughout much of Europe as a statement of feudal relations. It was developed academically in the law school of Pavia and provided a Latin and hence mobile source of the law of land.[215] Its influence extended north to Germany, the Netherlands and Scotland[216] but also south to Spain.[217] France, with its Custom of Paris, resisted.[218] The Constitution of Federico of Sicily in 1232 referred, on one of the rare occasions in European legal history, to common laws in the plural in describing Roman law and Lombard law as the 'iura communia' of the jurisdiction.[219] At the time, it may well have been the Lombard law which was of greatest practical significance. It eventually became seen as incorporated into the ius commune.[220]

* * * * * * * *

The common laws of Europe thus existed in great variety. Ius commune did not exist in singular but in multiple form, as iura communia, and there were vigorous relations not only between the common laws and the particular laws of each of them, but also between the common laws themselves.[221] There were also, as will be seen, common laws which were free of a territorial base, such as canon law or commercial law, which also played a vital role in the functioning of the common and particular laws examined thus far.[222] The common law which received perhaps the greatest renown was that based upon Roman law, in large measure because it was expressed in a common language, Latin, and because it was the only ius commune taught in a manner which transcended the states

[214] Calasso, supra, note 9, at 75; Gaudemet, supra, note 181, at 83.

[215] M. Ryan, 'Ius Commune Feudorum in the Thirteen Century' in A. Romano (ed.), . . . colendo iustitiam et iura condendo . . . *Federico II Legislatore del Regno di Sicilia nell'Europa del Duecento: Per una storia comparata delle codificazioni europee* (Rome: Edizioni de Luca, 1997) at 51, notably at 52 ('Despite the variety of institutions called fiefs in thirteenth-century Europe, civilians and canonists could discuss and analyse them in a *lingua franca*, in convertible and generally comprehensible terms'); and for its multiple editions, Heirbaut, supra note 116, at 311. For Lombard success in attracting adherence to their way of life in Italy, Brown, supra, note 24, at 192.

[216] Watson, supra, note 117, at 218.

[217] G. F. Margadant, *An Introduction to the History of Mexican Law* (Dobbs Ferry, NY: Oceana, 1983) at 43.

[218] Coing, supra, note 9, at 91; and see Guizzi, supra, note 179, at 24, for Custom of Paris being common law of France 'principalement en ce qui concernait les Fiefs.'

[219] Ermini, supra, note 46, at 19; Calasso, supra, note 9, at 51

[220] Infra, Ch. 3, *Common laws and feudal law.*

[221] Infra, Ch. 3.

[222] Infra, Ch. 3, *Common laws and canon law, common laws and commercial law.*

which were later to emerge. Yet the ius commune was only one example of a common genus of relational common law, which also included the common law, the droit commun coutumier of what we know today as France, the gemeine Recht of what is today Germany, the derecho común of the *Siete Partidas*, as well as what were recognized as regional common laws, such as those of Tuscany or the region of Naples. Moreover, even within any one of the major relational common laws, there were regional variations, such as that of Bavaria, as the particular local laws influenced interpretation of an overarching common law.

The most remarkable characteristic of the common laws was their relational character. Put differently, they were laws which did not define themselves in terms of their eventual territorial application, or in terms of their content. It could even be said that ultimately they demonstrated their capacity to sacrifice all of their content. None of that content *required* application. Such relational common laws thus cannot be said simply to exist, in positive form, since they are always and constantly in a process of re-definition, in relation to the claims of particular laws. They are in a constant dynamic state. All of these developments took place, moreover, in a non-conflictual and even conciliatory manner. It was in all instances a question of influence and persuasion (which did not exclude argument), and local acceptance and adoption. Differences amongst the laws which were present, in the same territory, were not seen as conflicts of laws, but as ongoing options, since no particular choice of law in a particular dispute had any influence on the ongoing collaboration between particular and common law. The notion of conflicts of laws was that of the minor problem or irritant of differences between particular laws or iura propria. The notion of common law was the most important instrument for conceptualizing legal relations in Europe for hundreds of years.

These characteristics of the common laws of Europe were to become more evident as they assumed a larger role in the world.

2

THE COMMON LAWS OF THE WORLD

The rich proliferation of the common laws of Europe has been seen, in the last century or two, as a thing of the past. The ius commune is thought to be long since deceased, hence the need for its resuscitation in Europe today. The common law has been considered by many to have disintegrated into many national laws or national legal systems, such that the designation common law would have lost any relational or transnational meaning. Other common laws are no longer designated as such. Yet the reports of the death of the common laws may have been exaggerated. To test this hypothesis, we perhaps need to examine both the alleged cause of death, as well as its real effect on the entire circumstances of the alleged victims.

How was it possible for common laws, of such large influence and application, to expire? The standard answer, on the continent, is through the effect of national codifications.[1] The equivalent in the common law world would be the nineteenth-century emergence of the concept of stare decisis, by virtue of which the effect of case law would be controlled and limited by the existence of national judicial hierarchies. There was also the effect, in the common law world, of national legislation. These answers appear to be correct, as far as they go, but they leave out almost as much as they explain and they are, if one may be permitted a single use of the word, Eurocentric. How, exactly, would national legislation and stare decisis have brought about the end of the common laws? Perhaps the best expression would be that of the national appropriation of the common

[1] H. Coing, *Europäisches Privatrecht*, vol. I, *Älteres Gemeines Recht (1500 bis 1800)* (Munich: C. H. Beck'sche Verlagsbuchhandlung, 1985) at 82 (notion of 'Endpunkt' of common European legal science); H. Coing, 'The Roman Law as *Ius Commune* on the Continent' (1973) 89 L.Q.R. 505 at 515, while acknowledging that 'one cannot deny the common background all these systems have'; A. Cavanna, 'Il Ruolo del giurista nell età del diritto comune (Un' occasione di riflessione sull'identità del giurista di oggi)' (1978) 44 Studia et Documenta Historiae et Iuris 95 at 98 on moment of 'rupture.'

laws, as their content came to be decanted into national receptacles. The process calls for a number of preliminary observations, relating first to the process in Europe, then to its pan-European nature, then to its territorial dimensions. All are closely related to one another.

National appropriation of common laws in Europe?

The process of national appropriation of law which occurred in Europe does appear to be inconsistent in some measure with the idea of a relational common law. Relational common laws float and are not defined in terms of their content, largely because there is no one to control their content and decide definitively what it is. The ius commune was an informal creation. So was the common law, and so were the other common laws. All depended on persuasion and collaboration, amongst jurists, amongst judges. Nobody gave commands. So a floating common law would die, at least a small death, somewhere, if someone (successfully) assumed the authority to state what its definitive content was, and in a mandatory or binding way. This would destroy the tension between the common and the particular. It would mean the creation of a unum ius, one law, and the nationalization of law was seen as a movement in this sense. Seen from within a zone of nationalized law, a common law or ius commune could be effectively seen as dead, and national laws, we know, did much to reinforce this impression. A number of intellectual, legislative, and judicial techniques were used. They have today lost much of their force.

At the broadest, intellectual level, it was necessary to deprive ancient, existing normativity of its persuasive force while providing a credible alternative, eventually in the form of a unum ius. This was a great intellectual movement and involved converting old law from ongoing normativity into simply old law, best seen as raw, factual material, either for jettisoning or for new legal construction. Cujas led the charge, and by the seventeenth century a major movement had developed towards the accreditation of the notion of 'facts,' amongst which were prominently included the old law of ancient or other people.[2] Outside the western world 'facts' do not exist, and the concept is today challenged within the

[2] B. Shapiro, *The Culture of Fact: England 1550–1720* (Ithaca/London: Cornell Univ. Press, 2000) (culture of fact drawn from legal origins but, notably at 11, 'matter of fact' an *issue* placed before jury,

western world as well.[3] Old law having, however, been 'historicized,'[4] the normative vacuum could be filled with modern natural law and the results rendered into contemporary, positive, national form.[5] Since both natural law and positivism are, however, very large ideas upon which reasonable people may reasonably disagree, more precise techniques were also called into play. One was the notion of 'binding' law, borrowed from religion as that which 'bound' (relegare), and which came into frequent use in the nineteenth century.[6] A second consisted of efforts of formal limitation of sources of law, as found for example in article 7 of the French *Loi du 30 ventôse an XII* (1803–04), the careful wording of which stated that Roman laws ('lois romaines'), ordonnances, general and local customs, statutes ('les statuts'), and regulations, ceased to have the force of general or particular law in matters governed by the new Civil Code.[7] Other legislation was more explicitly prohibitive, and on occasion extended to the citing of academic writing which, if it could not be somehow abolished, could at least be denied a place in the officially sanctioned list of sources.[8]

not established truth) and for the same idea behind the Roman action *in factum*, R. Dekkers, 'Le fait et le droit. Problèmes qu'ils posent' in Centre national de recherches de logique, *Le fait et le droit* (Brussels: Bruylant, 1961) 7 at 8.

[3] H. Putnam, *The Collapse of the Fact/Value Dichotomy* (Cambridge, MA: Harvard Univ. Press, 2002), notably on nature of statement that someone is cruel, though admitting, at 31, differences between 'epistemic and ethical values.'

[4] H. Hübner, 'Zum Untergang des Ius Commune' in H. Hübner, *Rechtsdogmatik und Rechtsgeschichte* (Köln: Carl Heymanns Verlag, 1997) 291 at 296.

[5] Hübner, supra, note 4, at 298; and for 'jusnaturalisation,' B. Oppetit, *Droit et modernité* (Paris: Presses universitaires de France, 1998) at 75 ; O. Beaud, 'L'Europe entre droit commun et droit communautaire' Droits 1991. 3 at 8 (on the 'meeting' of state positivism and modern natural law).

[6] For the common law, J. Evans, 'Change in the Doctrine of Precedent during the Nineteenth Century' in L. Goldstein (ed.), *Precedent in Law* (Oxford: Clarendon Press, 1987) 35 at 45–54. The nineteenth century also marked the shift in the common law from a historical notion of (non-binding) precedent to that of stare decisis.

[7] For the debate on the effect of the text, P. Morvan, *Le principe de droit privé* (Paris: L.G.D.J. 1999) at 216–22; J. Cairns, 'Comparative Law, Unification and Scholarly Creation of a New *Ius Commune*' (1981) 32 N. Ir. Legal Q. 272 at 277–8.

[8] For examples, notably the banning of opinions of law professors in the Prussian General Code of 1794, B. Grossfeld, *The Strength and Weakness of Comparative Law* (Oxford: Oxford Univ. Press, 1990) at 4; E. Bucher, 'Rechtsüberlieferung und heutiges Recht' ZEuP 2000.394 at 428; E. Huber *System und Geschichte des schweizerischen Privatrechts* vol. I (Basel: C. Detloff's Buchhandlung, 1886) at 65 (on 19th-century Swiss cantonal prohibition of foreign sources); M. Ascheri, 'A Turning Point in the Civil-Law Tradition: From *Ius Commune* to *Code Napoléon*' (1996) 70 Tul. L. Rev. 1041 at 1046–88 (notably on debate in France on whether authorities other than those abrogated could still be referred to by judges, and noting lack of prohibition of citing of authorities by counsel); F. Ranieri, 'Rezeption und Assimilation ausländischer Rechtsprechung, dargestellt am Beispiel des europäischen Einflusses der französischen Judikatur im 19. Jahrhundert' (1977) VI Ius Commune 202 at 204; R. Gibert,

A third technique consisted of the simple restatement of common law (whichever it was) in a national source, on the assumption that a change of source would bring about an understanding of a change in the type or identity of the law, such that the notion of a relational common law would disaggregate, leaving only a common core or substantive commonalities of different laws. There was also, as a fourth technique, the notion of the territoriality of law, which concentrated attention on the operation and efficacy of a single, given law in a defined area and so obviated the necessity of reference to another law which could serve as a subsidiary and auxiliary law in the same territory.[9] Indeed, the notion of two laws applying in the same territory would come to be seen as a logical impossibility. A fifth and related technique consisted of the development of the idea of a legal system, as a complete and autonomous legal construction, necessarily incompatible with any other legal system on the same territory.[10] This idea contributed greatly to the idea of an English legal system, particularly up to the late twentieth century, and was preceded by the nineteenth-century emergence of the notion of stare decisis.[11] Finally, and not least important in the rush to local jurisprudence, invective played a major role. The jurists of the common laws, or at least those of the ius commune, were treated, in their defence of an ancient and

Historia general del derecho español (Imp F. Roman Granada 1968) at 62 (for Spanish prohibition of use of Roman authors); J-L Halperin 'L'approche historique et la problématique du *jus commune*' Rev. int. dr. comp. 2000.717 at 727 (Bavarian Maximilian code (1756) prohibiting resort to *ius commune*). These prohibitions may be seen not only as designed to ensure the primacy of state law but also to overcome remaining ideas that the writings of authors on the *ius commune* prevailed over national legislation. Professor Zimmermann has concluded that the Prussian prohibitions were 'doomed to failure,' as were 'all . . . attempts to enact statutes prohibiting to comment upon, interpret and develop the law.' R. Zimmermann '*Statuta sunt stricte interpretanda?* Statutes and the Common Law: A Continental Perspective' (1997) 56 Camb. L. J. 315 at 326, with refs. On the long tradition, however, of the *Zitiergesetz*, G. Teipel, 'Zitiergesetze in der romanistischen Tradition' (1955) 72 ZRG RA 245; and on the Dutch abrogation, in 1829, of the 'legislative authority' ('gesetzliche Autorität') of Roman law, R. Zimmermann, 'Das Bürgerliche Gesetzbuch und die Entwicklung des Bürgerlichen Rechts' in M. Schmoeckel, J. Rückert, and R. Zimmermann, *Historisch-kritischer Kommentar zum BGB*, vol. I, *Allgemeiner Teil* (Tübingen: Mohr Siebeck, 2003) at 3.

[9] Thus exclusivist study of each ius proprium made it 'plausible to study a system of law as "territorial" without qualifying it as ius proprium'; M. Bellomo, *The Common Legal Past of Europe, 1000–1800*, transl. Lydia G. Cochrane (Washington, DC: The Catholic University of America Press, 1995) at 79.

[10] Joseph Raz thus explains that '[a]ll legal systems . . . are potentially incompatible at least to a certain extent. Since all legal systems claim to be supreme with respect to their subject-community, none can acknowledge any claims to supremacy over the same community which may be made by another legal system.' J. Raz, *The Authority of Law: Essays on Law and Morality* (Oxford: Clarendon Press, 1979) at 119.

[11] Supra, Ch. 1, note 144.

overarching concept of law, as 'born to the plough, not well endowed mentally...'[12]

The national appropriation of common laws was thus not an automatic, formal result of national legislation, since there were large questions as to whether, and to what extent, national legislation was capable of bringing about such a result. All depended on whether the national legislation was sufficiently rooted in large intellectual movements and other techniques of appropriation. This is borne out by the history of the common laws after the national codifications had taken place. In no instance, it seems, was there an abrupt disappearance of use and citation of the common laws. In France, in an effort to revive the 'antique fontaine' of Roman law in a 'réception discrete, mesurée—nous avons déjà tant de textes,' Professor Carbonnier has set out the early nineteenth-century jurisprudence which continued to cite Roman texts, though it was recognized by 1838 that it was more and more difficult to justify cassation for violation of Roman law.[13] The Napoleonic Code received the same non-exclusive treatment for decades in Belgium, as Belgian judges continued to refer to the ancien droit, even as a means of reconciling the old with the new.[14] Similar phenomena have been observed in Holland and Austria,[15] as well as in Germany, where the exclusivity of the German *BGB* appeared to derive more from a shift in pedagogical and academic attitudes than from any particular feature of the new legislation.[16] Most recently, the national codes are coming to be seen as historical events, even

[12] Bellomo, supra, note 9, at 207; and see P. Grendler, *The Universities of the Italian Renaissance* (Baltimore/London: Johns Hopkins Univ. Pres, 2002) at 441 (since jurists of mos italicus 'relied on consensus and expressed their disagreements politely, they recoiled from the insults and harsh attacks that were the stock in trade of the humanists').

[13] J. Carbonnier, 'Usus hodiernus pandectarum' in R. Graveson et al (ed.), *Festschrift für Imre Zajtay* (Tübingen, J.C.B. Mohr, 1982) 107 at 109–110, citing Troplong in 1838.

[14] R. Beauthier, 'Le veritable sens de l'article 2 du Code civil: L'ambition du Code civil de remplacer l'ancient droit à la lumière de la jurisprudence "belge" de la première moitié du 19e siècle' in R. Beauthier and I. Rorive (eds), *Le Code Napoléon, un ancêtre venéré? Melanges Offerts à Jacques Vanderlinden* (Brussels: Bruylant, 2004) 217.

[15] R. Zimmermann, *Roman Law, Contemporary Law, European Law: The Civilian Tradition Today* (Oxford: Oxford Univ. Press, 2001) at 3, 5.

[16] R. Zimmermann, 'Modernizing the German Law of Obligations' in P. Birks and A. Pretto, *Themes in Comparative Law: In Honour of Bernard Rudden* (Oxford: Oxford Univ. Press, 2002) 265 at 270–71, for ongoing application of the ius commune; R. Zimmermann, 'Das Bürgerliche Gesetzbuch und die Entwicklung des Bürgerlichen Rechts' in M. Schmoeckel, J. Rückert, and R. Zimmermann, *Historisch-kritischer Kommentar zum BGB*, vol. I, *Allgemeiner Teil* (Tübingen: Siebeck Mohr, 2003) 1 at 12 ff; Zimmermann, supra, note 15, at 8, 9, 48–53 (no formal abrogation of old law considered necessary).

mythical ones, surrounded by ongoing and new forms of normativity which they are fundamentally unable to control.[17] The same phenomenon has been observed in Jewish law, where the apparently radical rupture effected by the code of Maimonides was gradually overcome through the ongoing assertion of the historical character of the code and the normativity upon which it was based.[18] Even within the European codes, the notion of 'general principles of law,' or even 'general principles of the legal order of the State,' provided an ongoing invitation to the use of ancient and non-positive sources.[19]

A common, pan-European process of appropriation

However, by way of second preliminary remark, it is important to note the pan-European character of these developments, and the absence of any pan-European authority capable of bringing them about or commanding them. There were of course differences in the process, but it was everywhere essentially the same. What were the commonalities, and upon what were they based?

A standard view of European legal history would see a single European ius commune essentially nationalized by its various iura propria, in the form of national legal systems. In an extreme form, this view would even deny the existence of a ius commune in the face of dominant and controlling, though emergent, national systems.[20] There is, however, an

[17] J.-L. Halperin, 'L'historiographie du Code civil en France' in Beauthier and Rorive, supra, note 14, at 43 (for French Civil Code no longer 'universal code' but 'object of history'); D. Tallon, 'Grandeur et décadence du Code civil français' in *Mélanges offerts à Marcel Fontaine* (Bruxelles, Larcier, 2003) 279 at 289 (myth of eternal code); D. Tallon, 'L'avenir du Code en presence des projets d'unification européenne du droit civil' in Université du Panthéon-Assas (Paris II), *1804–2004 Le Code civil: un passé, un présent, un avenir* (Paris : Dalloz, 2004) 997 at 1002 ('notre Code civil a fait son temps') ; and for similar conclusions in Germany that *BGB* 'historical phenomenon' and 'historically conditioned document,' Zimmermann, supra, note 15, at 100.

[18] H. P. Glenn, *Legal Traditions of the World*, 2nd edn. (Oxford: Oxford Univ. Press, 2004) at 107.

[19] G. Ermini, *Corso di diritto comune* (Milano, Giuffrè, 1989) at 119; and for the use of general principles as forms of liaison between national European laws, R. Schulze, 'Le droit privé commun européen' Rev. int. dr. comp. 1995.7 at 21.

[20] See, e.g., D. Osler, 'The Myth of European Legal History' (1997) 16 Rechtshistorisches J. 393, and for the standard view and debate, supra, Ch. 1, *The ius commune, as prototype*. The opposition between the (single) ius commune and the national systems is perhaps inevitable if the existence of so-called regional common laws is denied.

alternative explanation, which avoids the binary opposition between a single ius commune and exclusivist national systems. The process would in reality have been one of the ascendancy of iura propria, not within the cadre of a single ius commune, but within the cadre of operative and functioning common laws, which largely precluded the existence of national legal systems until their emergence from the unification processes of the nineteenth century. The commonalities are thus found in the relations between the various common laws and the particular laws with respect to which they defined themselves.

The existence of multiple common laws in Europe was dealt with in Chapter 1. The process of their apparent appropriation was dealt with in the preceding section. If we return to France, by way of example, what was appropriated or decanted into the new cadre of the French Civil Code was not simply whatever Roman laws might be seen as still pertinent in France, but also the 'general and local customs,' i.e., the droit commun originating in France. Until this occurred there was no national French legal system. There were some royal ordonnances, themselves of relatively recent date, of application only in specific fields and which did not extend to the entire territory of France as it is now known. The same absence of a prior system characterized all of the processes of national appropriation in Europe. The *reason* for the codifications, and for stare decisis, was that there were no existing systems. The idea of a national legal system was simply embryonic until this process was completed. Even the French codifiers disingenuously denied there was any system in their work.[21] What needed to be appropriated, moreover, was not simply Roman law, but the unstructured and centrally uncontrollable, though indigenous, common laws, and this was what was attempted.

Both the standard view of European legal history and the extreme opposition to it would therefore be inadequate to reflect the complexity of the relations between the laws of Europe in the last millennium. The standard view is inadequate because it does not reflect, or at least does not adequately reflect, the multiplicity of European common laws. The extreme view is inadequate because it casts backward in time the idea of a national legal system, and also does not reflect the existence and importance of the iura communia.[22] What was happening was a dialogical and

[21] Thus Cambacérèces, 'Un système ! Nous n'avons point . . . ' ; R. Sève, 'Système et Code' in *Le système juridique* (1986) 31 Arch. phil. dr. 77 at 82.

[22] See, e.g., Osler, supra, note 20, at 401, qualifying the standard view (of Professor Coing) as 'neither European nor legal nor history' yet stating at 410 that the process of borrowing from different laws would have meaning only 'where it is patriated in one of the national legal systems with a *real*

ongoing process involving at least three, and not two, relationships. There were relations amongst the common laws (see Ch. 3), relations between the common laws and all of their respective iura propria, and relations between the common laws and a particular ius proprium in the form of an emergent source of national law. The latter could not displace the others until national laws reached the stage of proclaimed exclusivity, mainly in the nineteenth century.[23] Nor were the common laws simply emergent national systems. They certainly contributed content to the emergence of those so-called systems, but they were qualitatively different in being relational common laws, as opposed to Roman-style substantive decrees. They did not purport to be 'binding' law.

As the common laws of Europe were different from one another, though sharing the characteristics of a common law, so the process of appropriation appeared different in some respects. On the continent the process was one of sources of national iura propria gradually asserting themselves against the relational common laws, with national legislation coming to enjoy great prominence. In England, the same process took place, and national legislation has played a very large part in the process, yet in England the judiciary itself became an agent of apparent appropriation, in subscribing in the nineteenth century to a notion of binding stare decisis, enforced through a national judicial hierarchy. The common law, though retaining its name, would have converted itself into common law in the Roman sense, of binding decree, and of national application. The common law too could be the object of nationalization, if common law judges saw fit to bring this about. The idea of stare decisis, however, is much weaker today.

Why was there a nineteenth-century pan-European phenomenon of nationalization of law, or at least attempted nationalization of law? It was not the result of chance, or some sort of chaotic attraction, but the result of ongoing pan-European legal tradition, or common law, which argued

existence' (emphasis added). Even in the 20th century, when the process of national systematization had been arguably made as complete as it could ever be, Neil MacCormick has stated that '[l]egal systems are not solid and sensible entities. They are thought-objects, products of particular discourses rather than presuppositions of them.' N. MacCormick, *Questioning Sovereignty: Law, State and Nation in the European Commonwealth* (Oxford: Oxford Univ. Press, 1999) at 113.

[23] This in no way detracts from the importance of what came to be recognized as central authority in each state. From the 13th century monarchs had been said to be 'emperors in their kingdoms' (rex in regno suo est imperator); Ermini, supra, note 19, at 21; F. Calasso, *Introduzione al diritto commune* (Milano, Giuffrè, 1970), at 23. In England John Selden in the 17th century affirmed that 'everie Christian State hath its owne Common Laws, as this Kingdom hath' and in the statement one finds both an affirmation of the distinctiveness of the common law originating in England, and the idea of national law, which he was particularly contrasting with canon law. J. Selden, *The History of Tithes*, 1st ed. (London, 1618) at 478, also at 479 for 'the Common Law of England' as the 'Ius Civile Anglorum.'

for particular state structures. There may even be a good case that the only single ius commune that Europe has known is one of public law and not private law. There would thus have been not simply a common core, in the sense of common elements, in diverse and different public laws of Europe, but rather a single, relational common law which argued for, and allowed, the emergence of exclusivist national states. There was certainly this common core in the various common laws identified by private law lawyers, since all of the common laws of Europe gave priority, and space, to local, particular laws in the face of asserted, local need. Public law may have progressed further, to the point of a shared, relational common law which said the same thing, and through sources which were recognizably pan-European. There is certainly support for this view in the writings of historians of public law. Heinz Mohnhaupt has set out some of the European dimensions of the 'ius publicum' in the seventeenth and eighteenth centuries[24] and Michael Stolleis has indicated the need to examine the 'endless mass' of the data of public law from 1600 to 1800, since questions as to the end of the state raise equally fundamental questions as to its beginnings.[25] Leibniz referred specifically to a '*ius publicum commune*' and the great names of European public law and political theory, from Machiavelli on through Hobbes and Locke, were certainly more visible across geographical and linguistic barriers than their private law counterparts.[26] Brian Tierney would have the ongoing influence of medieval political thinkers extending back much further.[27]

[24] H. Mohnhaupt, '"Europa" und "ius publicum" im 17. und 18 Jahrhundert' in C. Bergfeld et al, *Aspekte europäischer Rechtsgeschichte: Festgabe für Helmut Coing* (Frankfurt am Main: Klostermann, 1982) 207, notably at 223 on 17th century, European-wide comparison of different national models; and more generally, H. Mohnhaupt, *Historische Vergleichung im Bereich von Staat und Recht: Gesammelte Aufsätze* (Frankfurt am Main: Vittorio Klostermann, 2000).

[25] M. Stolleis (ed.), *Staatsdenker im 17. und 18. Jahrhundert*, 2nd ed. (Frankfurt: Alfred Metzner Verlag, 1987) at 12.

[26] For Leibniz, H.-P. Schneider, 'Gottfried Wilhelm Leibniz' in Stolleis, supra, note 25, 197 at 219; for the influence of Roman public law in France, A. Rigaudière, *Pouvoirs et institutions dans la France médiévale: Des temps féodaux aux temps de l'État* (Paris: Armand Colin, 1998); and for the comparative work of Bodin, J. H. Franklin, *Jean Bodin and the Sixteenth-Century Revolution in the Methodology of Law and History* (New York/London: Columbia University Press, 1963).

[27] B. Tierney, *Religion, Law, and the Growth of Constitutional Thought, 1150 to 1650* (Cambridge: Cambridge Univ. Press, 1955); also A. Harding, *Medieval Law and the Foundations of the State* (Oxford: Oxford Univ. Press, 2002); M. van Creveld, *The Rise and Decline of the State* (Cambridge: Cambridge Univ. Press, 1999). For recent examination of the growth of different types of states, P. Bobbitt, *The Shield of Achilles: War, Peace and the Course of History* (London: Allen Lane, 2002); and for different types of comparative thought in state construction, H. P. Glenn, 'The National Heritage' in R. Munday and P. Legrand (eds.) *Comparative Legal Studies: Traditions and Transitions* (Cambridge: Cambridge Univ. Press, 2003) 76.

European states were thus not founded on simple facts of obedience, or presumed Basic Norms, but on the ongoing persuasive force of common, public law. Edward Shils has concluded that '[t]he free society must rest . . . on tradition' but the tradition is here in the form of this common law.[28] So there has always been in Europe what the various European treaties refer to as the 'common constitutional traditions of the member states' and perhaps even the 'principles of liberty, democracy, respect for human rights and fundamental freedoms and the rule of law, principles which are common to the member states.'[29] It is by virtue of residual, suppletive, relational common law that exclusivist state governments exist in Europe, many of whom have sought to appropriate the specific content of the common law most appropriate to them. The residual common law teaches, however, that local particularity, so prevalent in the nineteenth century, only prevails to the extent that claims are made for its application, and that the common law, by its own terms, remains constantly available. So common law can be revived, whether public or private, in accordance with the very concept of relational common law, but it should be understood that it would never have expired in its entirety. Common laws are simply self-effacing. Like the Cheshire Cat, they can reappear at any time and any place, even smiling benignly, and this process is presently occurring in Europe itself.

Territoriality and appropriation

A third preliminary remark concerns the ambit of apparent elimination of common law. To the extent that common law can be appropriated (at least for a time), by a single national authority, it is inherent in the theory

[28] E. Shils, 'Tradition and Liberty: Antinomy and Interdependence' in E. Shils (ed. S. Grosby), *The Virtue of Civility: Selected Essays on Liberalism, Tradition, and Civil Society* (Indianapolis: Liberty Fund, 1997) 103 at 110.

[29] See notably Article 6 of the Treaty of Amsterdam, and for the European Court of Justice drawing inspiration from such common constitutional traditions, CJEC, May 14, 1974, *Nolde*, 4/73, Recueil 1974, 491 at 508; and see J. Husa, 'Guarding the Constitutionality of Laws in the Nordic Countries: A Comparative Perspective' (2000) 48 Am. J. Comp. L. 345 at 345 ('the essence of the Constitutional Law can be seen as a part of a greater body of constitutional tradition that crosses national borders'). In the common law tradition, A. Mason, 'The common law in final courts of appeal outside Britain' (2004) 78 Aust. L. J. 183 at 183 ('in the common law world, the interpretation of a constitution takes its character largely from the context of common law principle and doctrine which provides the context and the foundation against which a constitution is to be read and understood').

of the state and the territoriality of national law that this can occur only within the territorial zone in which the authority exercises its power. If a common law has gone offshore, it is beyond the legislative authority of a particular state to eliminate it in its entirety. It can be made to (apparently) disappear, only within the territory of the appropriating state. So if common laws in a sense went into hiding or hibernation on the continent, this brings us to the question of their survival overseas, beyond Europe, as common laws of the world.

Common laws within Europe resulted from the expansion of European populations and the expansion of their laws, treated as common in relation to the particular laws they encountered. It is often thought today that the expansion of European peoples beyond Europe, in the process of colonization, was driven by European states. So the expansion would have been outward, from a base of a particular state, and the law of that particular state would have been transplanted in some measure into the colonies of that state. The time of colonization, however, was generally not a time by which the European states had taken shape, and certainly not in their present form. The tracing of the boundaries of France, on the ground, began in the sixteenth century, in a haphazard manner, and became systematic only in the eighteenth century.[30] Yet Cartier had arrived in what was to become New France in 1534, and had been preceded by Spanish, or rather Castilian, expansion in the south. European colonization beyond Europe was thus not later and distinct from European nation-building, but inseparably combined with it, or even perhaps exactly the same process. It was possible to speak of 'The Indian as Irishman' since the laws of both were being encountered and dealt with in comparable manner.[31] They were both inseparable elements of the same process of expansion outwards from

[30] D. Nordman, 'Problématique historique: des frontières de L'Europe aux frontières du Maghreb (19e siècle)' in *Frontières: Problèmes de frontières dans le tiers-monde* (Paris: L'Harmattan, 1982) 17 at 19; and more generally on the process, Glenn, supra, note 27, at 80–2.

[31] J. Muldoon, 'The Indian as Irishman' in J. Muldoon, *Canon Law, the Expansion of Europe, and World Order* (Aldershot: Ashgate/Variorum, 1998) 267, notably also at 267 on continuity between Spanish Reconquista and Spanish conquest of Americas, 'this tradition' forming 'a unifying theme in Spanish history'; D. Konig, 'Colonization and the Common Law in Ireland and Virginia, 1569–1634' in J. A Henretta, M. Kammen, and S. N. Katz, *The Transformation of Early American History* (New York: Alfred A. Knopf, 1991) at 70; R. Bartlett, *The Making of Europe: Conquest, Colonization and Cultural Change 950–1350* (London: Penguin, 1993) at 313–4 ('The European Christians who sailed to the coasts of the Americas, Asia and Africa in the fifteenth and sixteenth centuries came from a society that was already a colonizing society. Europe, the initiator of one of the world's major processes of conquest, colonization and cultural transformation, was also the product of one'); J. Baschet, *La civilisation féodale: De l'an mil à la colonisation de l'Amérique* (Paris: Aubier, 2004), notably at 254–5 ('l'élan qui conduit à la Conquête des Amériques est fondamentalement *le même* que

European centres of authority and influence. States in Europe formed when the boundaries of other European political entities had been compressed to the maximum extent (uti possidetis juris), and some stability set in. The same outward pressure was occurring beyond the seas, where less resistance was to be found. Feudalism was now less important in the process, but religion, commerce, and Lockean ideas of property acquired through the expenditure of labour, were adequate for the task. When French law was unified in 1804, and the French state legally united, France had already acquired, and lost, a number of overseas colonies.

European common laws were thus expanding overseas at the same time as they were expanding in Europe, and the territorial ambit of common laws simply spread outward, in the world, until limits of some kind were reached. The common laws originating in Europe thus are not, in their nature, limited to Europe. Their commonality relates to particular laws beyond Europe as much as it relates to particular laws within Europe. This has major consequences for the idea of contemporary, transnational common laws. Since the common laws of Europe were extra-European in considerable measure, the measures of appropriation of them which were taken through the nationalization measures of the nineteenth century were necessarily ineffective with respect to the worldwide dimensions of these common laws. European states, themselves coming later than the common laws, could appropriate only so much of them as could be arguably controlled. In the result, given floating, transnational common laws, appropriation of them by particular European states meant that they were placing themselves in the position of particular states with particular laws, or iura propria, in relation to them. Jhering was entirely correct in referring to the emerging pattern of '*Landesjurisprudenz*' (local or provincial jurisprudence) but the expression was not simpy an epithet critical of overly national preoccupations, but an accurate description of the place which national laws conferred upon themselves in the broader cadre of ongoing, often worldwide, common laws.[32] The same is true, on a larger scale, of the law of the European Union. The pattern of relational common laws thus plays itself out again, this time with global dimensions, but it is always the same common laws which are operative and their

celui que l'on voit à l'oeuvre depuis le XIe siècle . . . c'est la société féodale . . . qui pousse l'Europe vers le large'); and for the early development of a 'frontier movement' within Europe, D. C. North, *Structure and Change in Economic History* (New York/London: W. W. Norton, 1981) at 132.

[32] R. von Jhering, *Der Geist des römischen Rechts auf den verschiedenen Stufen seine Entwicklung*, vol. I, 7th and 8th ed. (Leipzig: Breitkopf & Hartel, 1924) at 15.

overseas characteristics are exactly those of their European characteristics. So particular European states, with their exclusivist laws, may see both a revival of common law upon which they are all based, from indigenous, historical, European sources (a common core) or may see their sources of law supplemented by resort to extraterritorial sources of law, from within the same corpus of common law from which the state law was derived. This too is happening today.

These remarks however, tend overly to the interpretative, so it would be wise to test them by what we know of the historical experience of European common laws in the world.

The identity of the common laws abroad

A first question which appears appropriate is as to the identity of European common laws which extended beyond Europe. If there was a multiplicity of common laws in Europe, which became effective abroad? Most did, though not all, and it was possible also for a local or regional law to acquire the status of a common law as a result of expansion abroad. There have also been different types of European common laws, those of colonial times and those of post-colonial times. There are further problems of identity in delineating the sources, abroad, of those laws which came to be recognized as common.

The clearest example, and most well known instance, of a European common law extending abroad is that of the common law originating in England. It was clear law[33] and 'taken for granted' that English settlers

[33] The law would appear to derive from *Calvin's Case* (1609) 7 Co. Rep. 1a, 77 E. R. 377, dealing with the allegiance of a Scottish-born subject, in which it was said (at 9b and 388) that 'the protection and government of the King is general over all his dominions and kingdoms, as well in time of peace by justice, as in time of war by the sword, and that all be at his command, and under his obedience.' For emergence of the law, and (questionable) reliance on 12th- and 13th-century practice in Ireland and Wales, where there would have been no 'overarching legal principle' and only 'working compromises,' G. Loughton, 'Calvin's Case and the Origins of the Rule governing "Conquest" in English Law' (2004) 8 Aust. J. Leg. Hist. 143, at 147. The case law is largely that of the colonies, notably as to the date of reception. For Canada, see notably *Uniaacke* v. *Dickson* (1848) 2 N.S.R. 287 (S.C.N.S.), *Young* v. *Blaikie* (1822) 1 Nfld. L. R. 277 (S.C. Nfld.); for reluctance in England to extend English jurisdiction, and in some measure English law, to the dominions, D. J. Hulsebosch, 'The Ancient Constitution and the Expanding Empire: Sir Edward Coke's British Jurisprudence' (2003) 21 Law & Hist. Rev. 439; yet for the writ of habeas corpus being received in the U.S.A. 'by the time the Colonies achieved independence,' *Rasul* v. *Bush*, 124 S. Ct. 2686 (2004), at 2692 per Stevens J.

took their English law with them.[34] This was also the case for Irish, Welsh, and even Scottish settlers, since the colonization process was seen as unmistakably undertaken under English authority and since the common law of England was common (in the measure already indicated) to England, Wales, Ireland, and even, in some measure, to Scotland .[35] There were no major difficulties in identifying the English common law, since English sources (the cases) were its foundation (though English cases may themselves have incorporated elements of other European common laws).[36] It was, however, the totality of English law, including the case law of the Court of Chancery ('Equity') and English legislation, which was in principle received abroad, and this as a matter of the common law itself. The common law thus undertook the task of determining its own geographical area of application, as well as that of other English laws. Legislation, usually of the colony, often confirmed the process, notably with respect to the date of reception. Important limits or restraints on reception also developed.[37] All the law of England, notably legislation in the form of substantive and national decree, thus assumed abroad the form of a relational common law. It was the common law of England, however, which formed the bulk of the law of England received abroad.

There has been more difficulty in identifying the common laws of the continent which expanded beyond Europe. In some cases no such expansion occurred. The German Sachsenspiegel had moved mainly eastwards, with settlers, and was still being applied in the nineteenth century, but never, sauf erreur, moved across water. So it was essentially the major centres of trade and power on the Atlantic coast, initially during the colonial period, which saw their laws assuming importance as common laws abroad. The laws were those of Holland (the province, not the later State), the region of Paris, and Castile. These were the nuclei of the later States of the Netherlands, France, and Spain, whose laws would also, later, have great resonance. Here we do encounter problems of definition and identity, relating to the sources of these common laws and their relation to the ius commune originating from Italy.

The ius commune is generally thought of as Roman law and many of the efforts to limit its application were expressly directed against Roman

[34] J. N. Matson, 'The Common Law Abroad: English and Indigenous Laws in the British Commonwealth' (1993) 42 I.C.L.Q. 751 at 751.

[35] For affirmation of English law, in spite of use of Scottish legal terminology by the parties, *Hayduk* v. *Waterton* (1968) 64 W.W.R. 641 at 653, 656–7; and for English law in Scotland, infra in Ch. 3, *Territories at the confluence of common laws.*

[36] Infra in Ch. 3, *The common law and the ius commune.*

[37] Infra, this Ch., *The common law as common law, in the world.*

sources ('les lois romaines'). Yet Professor Calasso has insisted that it was not Roman law as such which had great influence in Europe, but rather the product of the work of the Glossators and the Commentators on a corpus of law originally Roman in character.[38] As the influence of the (originally) Roman law grew, it became subject to more and more local interpretation and more and more local implementation. So regional versions of the ius commune came to be recognized, there where it was influential.[39] Roman law, as such, never expanded beyond Europe. Where it has been influential beyond Europe it is because of the reception of a European common law itself open in some measure to Roman influence. Roman-Dutch law is perhaps the best example, since its reliance on law originally Roman in character is explicitly acknowledged.

What was, and is, Roman-Dutch law? It was essentially the law of the province of Holland,[40] never itself recognized as a common law within Europe, but which assumed world importance in expanding into North and South America, southern Africa, and south and south-east Asia. It continues to thrive in the contemporary state of South Africa. What were its sources? Lee concluded that Roman-Dutch law was 'derived from two sources, Germanic custom and Roman law,' while Hahlo agreed that it was 'born of the union of Roman law with the customary law of Holland.'[41] These statements, obvious though they may appear, neglect both the work of the Glossators and Commentators, and more importantly the work of the Dutch jurists on the corpus of the (re-worked) Roman law. More

[38] Calasso, supra, note 23, at 20, 21; and for the ius commune originating from Italy as constituting both less and more than Roman law, less since much Roman law was abandoned, and more because of additions and refinements, J.-L. Thireau, 'Droit commun' in D. Alland and S. Rials, *Dictionnaire de la culture juridique* (Paris: Lamy/puf: 2003) 445 at 447.

[39] See Ch. 1, *The ius commune, as prototype.*

[40] There are, however, differences of opinion on the importance of the law of Holland. Lee affirms: 'The system of law thus described is that which obtained in the province of Holland from the middle of the fifteenth to the early years of the nineteenth century.' R. W. Lee, *An Introduction to Roman-Dutch Law*, 5th ed. (Oxford: Clarendon Press, 1953) at 2, also at 5. Hahlo similarly was of the view that 'Roman-Dutch law was the law of the province of Holland.' H. R. Hahlo and E. Kahn, *The South African Legal System and its Background* (Cape Town/Wynberg/Johannesburg: Juta, 1973) at 562 (also asserting 'no common law of the Netherlands'). Reinhard Zimmermann takes a broader view that the expression describes the law of the United (or Northern) Netherlands, though stating that each province had a separate legal system, and that Holland largely dominated. R. Zimmermann, 'Roman-Dutch Jurisprudence and its Contribution to European Private Law' (1992) 66 Tul. L. Rev. 1685 at 1687; cf. P. Nève, '(Europäisches) Ius Commune und (nationales) Gemeines Recht: Verwechslung von Begriffen?' in G. Köbler and H. Nehlsen, *Wirkungen europäischer Rechtskultur, Festschrift für Karl Kroeschell* (Munich: C. H. Beck'sche Verlagsbuchhandlung, 1997) 871 at 875 (no common private law of northern Netherlands since no unifying High Court). Reception abroad was sometimes of the law of Holland (as in South Africa), sometimes of the laws of the United Netherlands (as in Indonesia). Grotius wrote essentially on the law of Holland, which explains much of its later pre-eminence.

[41] Lee, supra, note 40 at 3; Hahlo and Kahn, supra, note 40, at 543.

recent opinions recognize that the Roman dimensions of the Roman-Dutch law which expanded beyond Europe were very much the product of Dutch writers and courts. Reinhard Zimmermann has perhaps illustrated this most extensively, in pointing to the influence of Dutch jurists in rejection of Roman contractual formality and admission of the principle of actionability on simple agreement (ex nudo pacto oritur actio), as well as in a shift from damages to specific performance as the primary contractual remedy.[42] Others concur.[43] There is perhaps now more agreement on this local re-working and re-formulation of the ius commune than there is on its overall influence, in relation to the entirely indigenous Dutch law. The ius commune has even been described as a mere 'shadowy form,' which would leave the indigenous Dutch law as the main substantive contributor to the Dutch-originated common law.[44] In the result, however, the content of Roman-Dutch law had come to be expressed in almost exclusively Dutch sources and, as was the case for the nineteenth-century codifications, a shift in sources is of crucial importance in the identification of law. Roman-Dutch law became an identifiable common law, beyond Europe, both because of its expansion overseas and because of the talent of Dutch jurists in its domestic articulation (Grotius, Pufendorf, Huber, Voet). And as was the case for the English common law abroad, it included legislation, seen as substantive decree in the jurisdiction of its creation, converted into relational common law abroad. Dutch sources were very rich and pervasive; it is not surprising they were seen as of primary importance in other jurisdictions, which saw them as common law.[45]

The people we know as French also exported a great deal of law, and French-derived rules are now present in North America (in Quebec and

[42] Zimmermann, supra, note 40, notably at 1696, 1698.

[43] See, e.g., D. Heirbaut, 'Feudal Law: the Real *Ius Commune* of Property in Europe, or: Should We Reintroduce *Duplex Dominium*?' (2003) Eur. Rev. Pr. L. 301, at 305 ('the ius commune in the Dutch Republic was not just Roman law, but Roman-Dutch law . . . the local element went further than that . . . Roman-Dutch law in Holland was different from Roman-Dutch law in Frisia or Utrecht'); A. Wijffels, 'Einflüsse der Doktrin auf die gerichtle Argumentationsspraxis in der frühen Neuzeit' (1987) *Ius Commune*, Sonderhefte 30 *Studien zur Europäischen Rechtsgeschichte* 371 at 384 (local law in Netherlands in practice in 16th century having acquired 'independent status'); and earlier Hahlo and Kahn, supra, note 40, at 581 (citing South African court that it 'administers the Roman-Dutch law and not the Roman law of Justinian'); W. R. Bisschop, 'Modern Roman Dutch Law' (1908) 24 L.Q.R. 157 at 161 ('We do not find in their books the law as it was in the time of Justinian, but the law as it was in their own days, based, however, on Roman principles').

[44] Nève, supra, note 40, at 876; and generally P. Godding, 'La Réception sélective du droit romano-canonique par la pratique coutumière: le cas des pays-bas méridionaux' in A. Iglesia Ferreiros, *El dret comúi Catalunya 'Ius proprium—Ius commune a Europa'* (Barcelona: Fundació Noguera, 1993) 92.

[45] For extensive and impressive listing of Dutch sources of Roman-Dutch law, Hahlo and Kahn, supra, note 40, at 544 ff.

Louisiana, though earlier in a much wider area), in many jurisdictions in Africa and the Middle-East, in Pondicherry in India, and in some measure in south-east Asia. Again, however, that which accompanied French settlers was not the ius commune originating from Italy, but le droit commun coutumier of what was to be France. In New France, Champlain in the seventeenth century drew his will in the form of the customary law of Saintonge, his place of origin, and when the 'diversity of customs' of New France was overcome by royal decree, in the seventeenth century, they were replaced by the Custom of Paris, as representing the general, common law of the metropolitan territory. It had been written down, twice, in the sixteenth century and was now a 'vector of expansion' in the New World.[46] There was little, if any, Roman law in it and it continued in force in what is now Quebec until the codification of 1866, remaining as a suppletive source today. It was supplemented by other sources, notably in matters ecclesiastical, commercial, and procedural, and the substance of the ius commune is here visible in some areas. The ius commune was implemented, however, to the extent it was, largely through identifiably French sources. These were notably in the form of the Royal Ordonnances of the seventeenth and early eighteenth centuries (procedure, commerce, maritime law, gifts, and wills). Again, French domestic decree became relational common law abroad. The ius commune also appeared to some extent in New France in the form of renowned French doctrinal writing. A nineteenth-century, pre-codification summary of the sources of Quebec law listed fourteen of them, beginning with the Custom of Paris and ending, in fourteenth position, with Roman law 'as it has been adapted to French law by Domat, Argou . . . and so many others.'[47] As there was Dutch Roman law, so was there French Roman law. Again, the origin of substantive law may disappear behind its re-articulation in local language and form.

Nor did the other great Atlantic power, Castile in Spain, contribute to a very recognizable dispersal of the ius commune. That which became the

[46] For written European laws as 'vectors of expansion' first within Europe, supra, Ch. 1, *Mobility of people and mobility of laws*. Adoption of the Custom of Paris for New France was by virtue of the *Édit de creation du conseil souverain du Québec, 1663*. See *Édits, Ordonnances Royaux, Déclarations et Arrêts du Conseil d'État du Roi concernant le Canada*, vol. 1 (Québec : E. R. Fréchette, 1854) 37. For the Custom of Paris in Pondicheryy, India, J.-C. Bonnan, 'Inde (Culture juridique)' in Alland and Rials, supra, note 38, 815 at 817; D. Annoussamy, *The French Legal System and its Indian Connections* (Bangalore: National Law School of India University, 1995), notably at 143, 154.

[47] For the summary, prepared for the codification commission, see J. E. C. Brierley, 'Quebec's Civil Law Codification: Viewed and Reviewed' (1968) 14 McGill L. J. 520 at 547 ff; and for the multiplicity of civilian common laws in Quebec law, residing in 'implicit norms,' 'historical fact,' and 'legislative enactment,' J. E. C. Brierley, 'Quebec's "Common Laws" (*Droits communs*); How Many Are There?' in *Mélanges Louis-Philippe Pigeon* (Montreal: Wilson & Lafleur, 1989) 109.

common law of Hispanic territories overseas was el derecho indiano, and this was characterized by a high level of metropolitan legislative intervention, such that in 1680 it was considered necessary to publish a 'Recopilación' of the law of 'las Indias.'[48] Much of this legislation was public or administrative law and the legislative technique for matters of private law was simply to adopt by reference the existing Castilian private law. Here the major residual source, eventually to be used widely in the world, was *Las Siete Partidas*, the great Castilian law book brought together by Alfonso ('the Wise') in the thirteenth century and eventually promulgated, as the residual source of law in Castile, in the fourteenth century.[49] It too contained considerable public law, as well as previously unwritten law of the Castilian people. In its third, fifth, and sixth books it contained much Roman-inspired private law (in the fields of procedure, obligations, and successions; family law would have been less influenced).[50] To the extent it was used, however, Roman law, or the ius commune originating from Italy, had lost much of its identity. Unlike the Digest, and like the nineteenth-century codifications, the *Siete Partidas* did not name its sources. In so doing, it inevitably enhanced its own importance, as well as that of the doctrine which explained it.[51] So the content of this Hispanic common law was perhaps closer to that of the ius commune than either of the common laws originating in France or Holland, yet the *Partidas* too had succeeded, through a combination of integration of local sources, successful re-articulation of prior law, and doctrinal exposition, in establishing itself as a major, over-arching source of law, beyond Europe.

[48] As to which see J. Barrientos Grandon, *Historia del derecho indiano del descubrimiento colombino a la codificación*, vol. I, Ius Commune—Ius Proprium *en las Indias occidentales* (Roma: Il Cigno Galileo Galilei, 2000); T. Herzog, 'The "Recopilaciòn de Indias" and its discourse: The Spanish monarchy, the Indies and the seventeenth century' (1993) 20 Ius Commune 143; B. Bermal, 'El derecho castellano dentro del sistema juridico indiano' (1998) Annuario Mexicano del Derecho 89; G. F. Margadant, *Introduccion à la Historia del derecho mexicano*, 11th ed. (Naucalpan, Mexico: Editorial Esginge, 1994) at 53 ff; O. Cruz Barney, *Historia del derecho en Mexico* (Mexico: Oxford Univ. Press, 1999) , notably at 191; A. Levaggi, 'La réception du système espagnol par les systèmes indigènes en Amérique' in M. Doucet and J. Vanderlinden, *La réception des systèmes juridiques: Implantation et destin* (Bruxelles: Bruylant, 1994) 331; T. Scholl, *Die Rezeption des kontinental-europäischen Privatrechts in Lateinamerika* (Berlin: Duncker & Humblot, 1999), notably at 37; G. F. Margadant, *An Introduction to the History of Mexican Law* (Dobbs Ferry, NY: Oceana, 1983), notably at 60; K. L. Karst and K. Rosenn, *Law and Development in Latin America: A Casebook* (Berkeley: Univ. of Cal. Press, 1975), notably at 33 ff.

[49] See Ch. 1, supra, *The common law (derecho commún) originating from Spain*: Grandon, supra, note 48, at 203, on its suppletive character; and generally, M. Scheppach, *Las Siete Partidas: Entstehungs- und Wirkungsgeschichte* (Pfaffenweiler: Centaurus, 1991), with references.

[50] For listing of subjects of Roman influence, J. Beneyto Pérez, *Fuentes de Derecho Histórico Español* (Barcelona: Librería Bosch, 1931) at 38.

[51] For the importance of Spanish doctrine in the expansion of Spanish law, Levaggi, supra, note 48, at 360; Margadant (1994), supra, note 48, at 58 (with listing of authors).

In the result, the multiplicity of the common laws of Europe is confirmed by the process of transplantation of European law overseas. That which was transplanted was in no case the ius commune originating from Italy. That which was transplanted was the common laws of expanding European centres of power and influence, those situated on the coast of the Atlantic. This may have been because royal European authority was greater in the colonies than at home, but it is also likely that questions of language were of great importance, since there was little Latin amongst the settlers, and if there was to be any law at all which travelled with them it would have to be a law they knew, in a language they knew. The ius commune thus declined to the point of apparent extinction within Europe, certainly as a result of various forms of nationalization of law within Europe, but also because of its inability to reach safer ground beyond Europe. Had it obtained a foothold abroad, it would have retained its status as a floating, suppletive common law, even a visible one. Absent such a safe haven abroad, however, it was fully vulnerable to the forces of nationalism at home and apparently succumbed to them, for a few centuries at least.

The common laws thus moved offshore, but to what extent did they retain the characteristics of a relational common law?

The nature of the common laws abroad

The common laws of Europe demonstrated a number of common characteristics in Europe. To the extent that their expansion beyond Europe was the same process of expansion as had occurred in Europe, it should be possible to identify these same characteristics in the operation of the common laws abroad. There will certainly be differences in operation, as the common laws differed amongst themselves in Europe. Yet the basic characteristics which identify them as common laws, in spite of differences, should remain constant within Europe and beyond.

Amongst these characteristics of common laws, the most significant is their relational character. They yield to, and define themselves in relation to, particular laws or iura propria. They thus have no obligatory or mandatory content. The construction of empires in the world would thus not have led to a unum ius within any of the Empires, in spite of imperial tendencies. The laws of metropolitan authorities, whether explicitly recognized as common laws or not, would have assumed such a relational character. Implicit also in the relational character of the common laws, within Europe, was the recognition of different groups of people to whom different laws could be applied, though the distinction between groups was not definitive and there were major possibilities of transfer between groups and expansion or contraction of the common or particular laws which were present. Communities appear to have preceded written laws, but were not given permanent or material characteristics. This differentiation amongst peoples declined radically in importance only with the major process of unification of national laws in the nineteenth century.

In the operation of the common laws in Europe it was also the case that decisions made in the process of application of the common laws, and of the iura propria, were without prejudice to the ongoing relevance of both types of laws. No source of law was recognized as having the power of displacement, or elimination, of either common or particular law. The process was an ongoing, dialogical one. The jurists of the ius commune originating from Italy did not give definitive opinions; the judges of the common law originating in England did not give their decisions the force of stare decisis, at least until the nineteenth century. Modesty in the application of laws precluded their displacement through the emergence of new sources of law, though such sources could emerge through the intervention of political authority. Finally, as the process of adjustment of common and particular laws in Europe was a massive process with many dimensions and techniques, explicitly recognized as such, so the process beyond Europe should have such a large and visible dimension. It would decline in importance, moreover, beyond Europe, only for reasons similar to those in Europe, i.e., the emergence beyond Europe of state structures comparable to those of Europe, which could give rise to the same process of national appropriation of law which had occurred in Europe. All of these hypotheses should be tested against what we know of the operation of the European common laws, abroad.

The common law as common law, in the world

The immense task of adjusting the common law to local particularity, in the world, has been made more visible recently by the publication of Jerry Dupont's *The Common Law Abroad*, with 1228 pages of bibliography drawn from the 'world's twelve most complete law libraries,' though referring neither to case law nor to the experience of the U.S.A.[52] This immense literature, dealing with some five centuries of experience, is perhaps best seen as the common law counterpart to the equally vast continental literature on the adjustment of the ius commune to its iura propria. As was the case for the ius commune, there were some initial tendencies to treat the common law as a unum ius. Where a colony was acquired by conquest or cession from a competing European sovereign there were often vigorous attempts to dislodge the prior European law. This policy appears to have been successful only in a few cases, notably those of Trinidad (with displacement of Spanish law) and Guyana (with displacement of Roman-Dutch law).[53] Even here, however, it has been said that the displacement followed, rather than preceded, a process of 'anglicization,' so that the eventual role of the common law can be seen as a matter of popular choice, as was arguably the case for both Wales and Ireland.[54] Where the common law was sought to be introduced immediately after conquest, as was the case for Quebec, the policy failed.[55] Where a colony was acquired by simple settlement and the territory was seen as 'practically unoccupied'[56] or as a terra nullius, English law was introduced apparently 'in disregard of the existence of the aboriginal peoples.'[57] It has been said that the attitudes of the time were those later

[52] J. Dupont, *The Common Law Abroad: Constitutional and Legal Legacy of the British Empire* (Littleton, CO: Fred B. Rothman Publications, 2001). For the U.S.A., see infra, this Ch., National Appropriation of Common Laws Abroad? The U.S.A. Experience.

[53] A. Kenny, 'The Reception of the Common Law System by the Civil Law System in the Commonwealth Caribbean' in Doucet and Vanderlinden, supra, note 48, 15, notably at 37–41; further on Guyana, M. C. Dalton, 'The Passing of Roman-Dutch law in British Guiana' (1919) 36 S.A.L.J. 4; J. C. Ledlie, 'Roman-Dutch Law in British Guiana and a West Indian Court of Appeal' (1917) 17 J. Soc. Comp. Leg. 210. Even here, however, Roman-Dutch law was preserved for rights in immoveable property. Kenny, supra, at 40.

[54] Kenny, supra, note 53, at 74–5 (on creation of environment favourable to acceptance). For Wales and Ireland, supra, Ch. 1, *The common law originating from England.*

[55] The attempt to introduce as much English private law as possible in *The Royal Proclamation*, 1763 (U.K.), R.S.C. 1985, Appendix II, No. 1, was followed by a boycott on the part of the French-speaking population of the English-staffed courts. See A. Morel, 'La reaction des Canadiens devant l'administration de la justice de 1764 à 1774: une forme de résistance passive' (1966) 26 R. du B. 499. The survival of the civil law was guaranteed by the *Quebec Act*, 1774 (U.K.), R.S.C. 1985, Appendix II, No. 2. On the entire debate, J. E. C. Brierley and R. Macdonald, *Quebec Civil Law* (Toronto: Emond Montgomary, 1993) at 14–17.

[56] R. French and P. Lane, 'The Common Law of Native Title in Australia' (2002) 2 O.U.C.L.J. 15 at 16.

[57] P. W. Hogg, *Constitutional Law of Canada*, 3rd ed. (Toronto: Carswell, 1992) at 28. The policy was not uniform. New Zealand would have extinguished native title rather than ignored it, and there was a widespread practice of treaty-making in North America. For the notion of Australia, however, as an 'uninhabited country,' R. Else-Mitchell, 'The Foundation of New South Wales and the Inheritance

recognizable as social Darwinism, contemplating 'indigenous people whose place in the scale of social organization was so low that their usages and conceptions of rights could not be reconciled with the institutions or ideas of civilized societies.'[58] The social contrasts were (perhaps) greater than those found in Europe. Reception of English public law and criminal law was widespread, though even here there were exceptions.[59]

Over time, however, as was the case for the ius commune, it came to be recognized that displacement of an entire corpus of prior law, and more particularly private law, was neither desirable nor possible. For conquered or ceded territories this eventually found utterance as a common law rule to the effect that prior European law remained in force.[60] This was sometimes expressed as a presumption in favour of existing laws until the Crown altered them,[61] and there were prior European laws (such as those of Scandinavia or Holland in North America) which have been said to be 'overlooked,'[62] but the notion of the common law as a bulldozing ius unum was by now entirely abandoned. The process in regard to aboriginal or chthonic people took much longer and is still very much going on today, but it is now established 'that all aboriginal customary law did not disappear at the time of European settlement, as the rule of reception for a settled British colony might imply.'[63]

of the Common Law' (1963) 49 Royal Australian Historical Society Journal and Proceedings 1 at 2; and for aboriginals of New World being 'always disregarded' in deciding whether a territory settled, J. Cote, 'The Reception of English Law' (1977) 15 Alta. L. Rev. 29 at 37–8; Cf. S. Banner, 'Why *Terra Nullius*? Anthropology and Property Law in Early Australia' (2005) 23 Law & Hist. Rev. 95 (general colonial practice of purchase of lands from aboriginals, Australia exceptional because of mistaken views of extent and nature of aboriginal population).

58 French and Lane, supra, note 56, at 16.

59 Reception of English public law was seen as a necessary element of sovereignty. For large inroads of criminal law, W. J. Mommsen, 'Introduction' in W. J. Mommsen and J. A. de Moor, *European Expansion and Law* (Oxford/New York: Berg, 1992) at 10; S. F. Moore, 'Customary Law' in J. Middleton, *Encyclopedia of Africa South of the Sahara*, vol. 2 (New York: Charles Scribner's Sons, 1997) 526 at 529 (generally no official recognizing of criminal customary law in Africa). Yet for ongoing application of indigenous criminal law on the 'reservations' of native or chthonic people in the U.S.A., *United States* v. *Wheeler*, 435 U.S. 313, 332 (1978); and generally J. W. Zion and R. Yazzie, 'Indigenous Law in North America in the Wake of Conquest' (1997) Boston College Int'l & Comp. L. Rev. 55 at 66.

60 *Campbell* v. *Hall* (1774) 1 Cowp. 204, 98 E.R. 1054.

61 See, for example, *Re Southern Rhodesia* [1919] A.C. 211 at 233 (P.C.), per Lord Sumner.

62 Yet for the idea that prior European law in what became U.S. territory had to be overcome by specific legislation, which was often enacted, infra, this Ch., *National appropriation of common laws abroad?* The U.S.A. Experience.

63 Hogg, supra, note 57, at 28. For abolition of the terra nullius rule in Australia, *Mabo* v. *State of Queensland [No. 2]* (1992) 107 A.L.R. 1, 175 C.L.R. 1 (H.C.); and for its absence in New Zealand and early recognition of Maori law, 'for the present,' N. Seuffert, 'Shaping the Modern Nation: Colonial Marriage Law, Polygamy and Concubinage in Aotearoa New Zealand' (2003) 7 Law Text Culture 186 at 192–3.

Initial impulses towards a ius unum having been restrained, attention then had to be given to a modus vivendi between common law and particular, local law, as an essential element of what came to be known as 'indirect rule.'[64] Colonial mentalities often overlooked the complexity of this process, looking resolutely forward to a time of 'cellular replication' of life in the metropolitan territory.[65] More recent historical writing, however, has recognized that there was no 'one-way street' and that the process involved 'a complex process of interaction to which the Europeans and the indigenous peoples, especially the small, westernized intellectual elites in the colonial and semi-colonial territories, contributed in their own right.'[66] In this ongoing 'hybridity,' Upendra Baxi sees the colonial subject not as 'passive recipient' of 'high-colonial law' but as its 'strategic critic and subverter . . . resisting, ambushing, waylaying, disorientating, the mega-structures.'[67] Peter Karsten observes that '[s]ome laws were scrupulously observed, others quietly ignored, still others, vigorously resisted.'[68] Those who had resisted the enclosure movement in Europe, destructive of chthonic, common title, did so again in the 'New World',[69] often in the name of their own, popular 'common law.'[70] There was 'rampant boundary crossing' with regular appeals to multiple legal authorities and actors perceiving themselves as 'members of more than one legal community.'[71] It was not the Roman model, either by design or in execution.

[64] The expression recalls the 'High Kingship' of the British Isles, with local law continuing to be applied absent negotiations leading to recognition of common law. See supra, Ch. 1, *The common law originating from England.* For 'indirect rule' and its variations, J. Simensen, 'Jurisdiction as Politics: The Gold Coast during the Colonial Period' in Mommsen and de Moor, supra, note 59, 257 at 276; K. Mann and R. Roberts, 'Introduction' in K. Mann and R. Roberts, *Law in Colonial Africa* (Portsmouth, NH/London: Heinemann/James Currey, 1991) 3 at 19–21 (on incorporating African institutions into colonial law and administration); E. Okupa, *International Bibliography of African Customary Law: Ius Non Scriptum* (Monographs from the International African Institute, London) (Hamburg: Lit Verlag, 1999) at 3.

[65] For this notion in the European context, supra, Ch. 1, *Mobility of people and mobility of laws.* Religion appears to have played a much larger role than law in the process.

[66] Mommsen, supra, note 59, at 3.

[67] U. Baxi, 'The Colonialist Heritage' in Munday and P. Legrand, supra, note 27, 46 at 60, 74; and for early realization in India that application of English law to Indians 'would lead to chaos,' W. Menski, *Hindu Law* (New Delhi: Oxford Univ. Press, 2003) at 159.

[68] P. Karsten, *Between Law and Custom* (Cambridge: Cambridge Univ. Press, 2002) at 529; and for a 'transatlantic constitution . . . not of anwers but of arguments' to be used in reconciling common and particular law in the U.S.A., M. S. Bilder, *The Transatlantic Constitution: Colonial Legal Culture and the Empire* (Cambridge, MA: Harvard Univ. Press, 2004) at 4, and notably at 110 for ongoing conciliation of the two.

[69] Karsten, supra, note 68 at 23–5 (comparing notably with Ireland).

[70] Karsten, supra, note 68, at 4, 35, 186, 498, 529.

[71] L. Benton, *Law and Colonial Cultures: Legal Regimes in World History, 1400–1900* (Cambridge: Cambridge Univ. Press, 2002) at 8, 14, for sophisticated resort to either formal or informal law, depending on the circumstances, in both North America and India.

The violence done to 'native' or 'indigenous' people[72] in the colonization process is beyond measure. Yet nowhere in the colonized world has chthonic or indigenous law disappeared as a living legal tradition. In the last half-century common law judges, consistent with their own tradition, have even become guarantors of the ongoing vitality of this lex non scripta.[73] This may be through recognition of collective forms of chthonic ownership, as in the *Calder*[74] or *Mabo*[75] decisions in Canada or Australia, or through casuistic recognition of unwritten indigenous law in matters of the family and successions. There would even appear to be an unwritten rule that, constitutional questions aside, European law is not applied in the face of proven, and contrary, indigenous law, recalling the historic place of local custom and its relation to the common law.[76] 'Indian' or 'tribal' law survives as well in the United States, and the United States Supreme Court is engaged in a constant (and much criticized) process of delineation.[77] Common laws tend to expansion, but desist in the face of ongoing resistance. Hybridity continues to prevail, even in the contemporary states of North America and Australasia profoundly committed to notions of formal equality. The South African example has recently shown that this can be done without resort to a notion of race.[78]

[72] The language is profoundly marked by colonial experience and says nothing of the people themselves.

[73] Some would even have indigenous 'customary' law as an 'invention' of European authority, and in some respects this may be true, but it generally underestimates the importance and pedigree of unwritten legal tradition.

[74] *Calder* v. *British Columbia (A.G.)* [1973] S.C.R. 313, 34 D.L.R. (2d) 145 (S.C.C.)

[75] Supra, note 63.

[76] In *Delgamuukw* v. *British Columbia* (1993) 104 D. L. R. (4th) 470, Lambert J. thus stated, at 730: 'The existence of a body of Gitksan and Wet'suwet'en customary law would be expected to render much of the newly introduced English law inapplicable to the Gitksan and Wet'suwet'en peoples, particularly since none of the institutions of English law were available to them in their territory, so that their local circumstances would tend to have required the continuation of their own laws.' See generally H. P. Glenn, 'The Common Law in Canada' (1995) 74 Can. Bar Rev. 261 at 277–8. Modern constitutions place limits on this recognition, and were preceded by various forms of 'repugnancy clause,' as to which see Moore, supra, note 59, at 527 (for African examples); A. N. Allott, 'The Judicial Ascertainment of Customary Law in British Africa' (1957) 20 Mod. L. Rev. 244; Cote, supra, note 57, at 41 (non-application of 'barbaric' rules of law); Matson, supra, note 34 , at 761 (clause of 'natural justice, equity and good conscience,' itself derived from romano-canonical law).

[77] D. Wilkins and K. Lomawaima, *Uneven Ground: American Indian Sovereignty and Federal Law* (Norman: Univ. of Oklahoma, 2001) (with robust criticism of U.S. Supreme Court).

[78] For elimination of race as a criterion in application of written and unwritten law in South Africa, and generally on the history of 'customary' laws in South Africa, South African Law Commission, *The Harmonisation of the Common Law and the Indigenous Law: Conflicts of Law* (Discussion Paper 76, Project 90)(Pretoria: South African Law Commission: 1998) at x, 18 (on 'membership in a community' observing unwritten law), 21–2 (on constitutional limits on recognition); further on non-racial criteria in L. Du Plessis, *The Future of South Africa: Perspectives of Integrating Different Cultures—Means of Law*

The common law in the world thus yielded to local, unwritten law. It also yielded generally to local circumstance, local need, and various other forms of local normativity. On the European continent the application of the ius commune and the iura propria was a matter of interpretation of each (the 'odious' vs. the 'beneficial'). In the common law world there was also a general technique which was that of determining the 'suitability' of common law (including here English statute) for local circumstance.[79] The case law on this question is vast, spread over many continents, and the 'suitability' requirement was imposed by courts even where omitted by reception legislation.[80] Results varied greatly, and the application, or not, of the common law was always a matter of judicial interpretation. The law of England, overseas, also yielded to local, colonial legislation.[81] Where there was doubt about this, it was confirmed by imperial legislation, in the form of the *Colonial Laws Validity Act* (1865).[82] So it had been with the growth of recognition of local legislation, on the European continent, under the accommodating breadth of the iura communia.

In its recognition of local laws and local need, the common law abroad thus demonstrated its relational character. It also did so through many affirmations of its non-binding character. Absent any notion of stare decisis until the nineteenth century,[83] it could only constitute 'persuasive authority.'[84] In the language of the European continent, it applied by the authority of reason (imperium rationis) or as 'raison écrite' and not by reason of authority (ratio imperii). This was often referred to as the

(Trier: Legal Policy Forum, 2002); and under new constitution, D. Visser, 'Cultural Forces in the Making of Mixed Legal Systems' (2003) 78 Tul. L. Rev. 41 at 74. For race as concept dependent not on physical characteristics but on underlying information (or as 'social construction'), Glenn, supra, note 18, at 36–7.

79 For Africa, A. Allott, 'Western Anglophone Africa' in Middleton, supra, note 59, 533 at 536; Australia, P. Parkinson, *Tradition and Change in Australian Law*, 2nd ed. (Sydney: LBC Information Services 2001) at 119; South Pacific, J. Care, T. Newton, and D. Paterson, *Introduction to South Pacific Law* (London/Sydney: Cavendish Publishing, 1999) at 69; Canada, Hogg, supra, note 57, at 32 (statutes found unacceptable more frequently than common law); Canada, Australia, and New Zealand, Karsten supra, note 68, at 128.

80 For Ontario, H. P. Glenn, 'Persuasive Authority' (1987) 32 McGill L. J. 261 at 272.

81 See, for example, B. Bawak, 'The Common Law in Cameroon' in A. Mbu, *The Common Law in Cameroon* (Limbe: Presbook, 1998) 38 at 40–1; M. N. Wabwile, 'The Place of English Law in Kenya' (2003) O.U.C.L.J. 51 at 53; and on the finding of local legislative voice, Karsten, supra, note 68, at 3. It is often said today that the common law is no longer 'uniform' since there are local variants of it, but there have always been iura propria within the ambit of common laws.

82 28 & 29 Vict., c. 63.

83 Supra, Ch. 1, *The common law, as common law.*

84 Glenn, supra, note 80.

'declaratory' theory of law, according to which common law judges would only 'declare' a law they did not make. This attracted positivist ridicule, on the grounds that the common law was thereby, in Holmes' language, some kind of 'brooding omnipresence in the sky.'[85] The expression meant of course no such thing, but was used only to indicate that judicial decisions were not meant to be definitive (except as between the parties). They were only indications of the extent thus far of judicial reasoning, which would yield, in continental language, to later and 'better opinion.' Better judgments could always be followed, regardless of their geographical provenance, and this underlying characteristic of the common law abroad has continued to prevail, over all concepts of national law, positive law, and national judicial hierarchies. The common law is beyond the reach of any given national authority, and most have not even attempted to appropriate it.[86] How does one appropriate a 'practiced framework of practical reasoning'?[87] It had no obligatory, necessary content, and this too confirmed its ultimately relational character.

The common law in its operation in the world thus demonstrated the essential characteristics of the common law in England and the British Isles, and of the common laws of the European continent. It was relational, in yielding to local law; it was tolerant of the hybridity and fluidity of populations; it did not purport to provide definitive solutions; the process of its application was vast, highly visible, and lasted over centuries. To what extent do the other common laws of Europe satisfy these criteria, in their overseas manifestations?

[85] *Southern Pacific Co.* v. *Jensen*, 244 U.S. 205 at 222 (1917). Holmes was bombarding bravely from positions largely secured by Austin and Bentham.

[86] Reception of the common law would thus be unaffected by any purported 'cut-off date' and would continue as a matter of ongoing persuasive authority. See, for example, *State Government Insurance Commission (SA)* v. *Trigwell* (1979) 142 C.L.R. 617 at 625, per Gibbs J ('It is the common law rules as expounded from time to time that are to be applied'); Matson, supra, note 34; Cote, supra, note 57, at 56; Mason, supra, note 29, notably at 186 (common law rules adopted 'as they are expounded from time to time'); Glenn, supra, note 76, noting at 284 the frequency of the treatise title following the format 'The Law of... in...,' indicating the existence of law both in and beyond a particular jurisdiction; Care et al, supra, note 79, at 72; G. S. Ram, 'Judgments on the Internet—A Malaysian Point of View' (Aug. 2003), The Commonwealth Lawyer, vol. 12, no. 2, p. 33 (on importance of electronic retrieval of judgments across jurisdictions); Wabwile, supra, note 81, at 74–5. The new Oxford University Commonwealth Law Journal is premised on such an understanding of the common law of the Commonwealth. See 'Editorial' (2001) 1 O.U.C.L.J. 1 ('shared legal history provides a common platform for fruitful ongoing discussion and debate', 'term "Commonwealth Law" interpreted widely').

[87] For the expression, supra, Ch. 1, *The common law, as common law.*

The droit commun originating from France, in the world

The common laws of Europe which were transported abroad did not in all cases designate themselves as common laws, in their overseas variants. In part this was due to metropolitan royal desire, which preferred other designations and more precise compilations. In part it was due simply to linguistic accident. In all cases, however, the European normativity transported abroad functioned as a recognizable, relational common law. All of the tests were met: the relational and suppletive character of the law; its compatibility with differentiated populations; the absence or impossibility of unifying authority; and the ongoing nature of the process of reconciliation of common and particular law. In French practice the designation droit commun seems to have fallen out of regular use in the transposition abroad, and it was the Custom of Paris which was recognized, as well as particular royal ordonnances, major doctrinal sources, and collections of jurisprudence.[88] They all functioned, however, as the droit commun, in a relational sense, of French colonial territories. It is said that the French engaged in colonial practice which was different from that of the English in that it would have constituted a form of 'direct rule' as opposed to what was recognizably 'indirect' in the case of the English model. The French model appears to have been unique in this notion of direct rule.[89] It is possible that the French made greater use of executive authority and that they were more ambitious in terms of expansion of French law, but the reality on the ground was in no way incompatible with the notion of a relational common law. There was as much resistance to French law as to English, on the part of chthonic or indigenous peoples, on the part of colonists of prior European powers, and on the part of French settlers themselves. The expansion of French law, abroad, was cautious. There was a common law, but the questions were always for whom, and to what extent?

[88] Cf., however, L. Antier, *La Survivance de la Seconde Coutume de Paris: Le droit civil du Bas-Canada* (Rouen: Imprimerie des Petites Affiches, 1923) at 15 (less than a century after its arrival Custom of Paris considered the 'droit commun' of the colony).

[89] For Belgium as explicitly following a model of 'indirect' rule, J. Vanderlinden, 'Congo, Zaire, Rwanda, and Burundi' in Middleton, supra, note 59, 551 at 551; Mommsen, supra, note 59, at 7 (though giving little leeway to local rules); F. Reyntjens, 'The Development of the Dual Legal System in Former Belgian Central Africa (Zaire–Rwanda–Burundi)' in Mommsen and de Moor, supra, note 59, 111, notably at 117.

In New France the expansion of European criminal law was the object of extensive negotiations with Iroquois, Huron, Algonquin, and other peoples.[90] Civil law was introduced essentially for the French settlers and was the object of extensive modification in the process. The French Crown even participated in the process of adaptation, prohibiting all forms of 'chicane' in the administration of justice in the colony, a prohibition taken generally to have excluded the profession of advocates. Local adaptation was more significant, and approximately ten per cent of the Custom of Paris was explicitly modified in the period 1664–1760.[91] The *Code Louis* of civil procedure was received only after alteration to accommodate local conditions (and the absence of advocates).[92] The law of marriage was adjusted to facilitate celebration.[93] As French colonial experience grew, colonial policy became more subtle and differentiated. As was the case in New France, metropolitan legislation (becoming relational common law on its exportation) would be introduced into colonies for French settlers, but also extended to local, indigenous elites ('protégés' or 'protected persons') as a form of privilege,[94] or even made available to an entire indigenous population as an option or form of renunciation of their prior law.[95] The result was a clear duality of laws, with large parts of the colonial population French subjects though not French citizens in terms of application of French law.[96] Europeanization of the law, in its entirety, was 'out of the question.'[97]

[90] R. White, *The Middle Ground: Indians, empires and republics in the Great Lakes region, 1650–1815* (Cambridge: Cambridge Univ. Press, 1991) notably at x, 52; and see *Decree of the Superior Council of Québec Subjecting Indians to the Penalty Carried by the Laws of France Concerning Murder and Rape*, 21 April 1664, in D. G. Smith (ed.), *Canadian Indians and the Law: Selected Documents 1663–1972* (Toronto: McClelland and Steward, 197) at 21–3 (submission to French criminal law proposed as counterpart to prohibition of Frenchmen, 'creditors of the Indians, from plundering and harassing them while in default of payment'). For the conciliatory attitude of Champlain, and repeated setting aside of French criminal law, M. Morin, 'La dimension juridique des relations entre Samuel de Champlain et les Autochtones de la Nouvelle France' (2004) 38 R.J.T. 389, notably at 425.

[91] A. Morel, *Histoire du droit* (Montreal: Librairie de l'Université de Montréal, 1974) at 46.

[92] J.-G. Castel, *The Civil Law System of the Province of Quebec* (Toronto: Butterworths, 1962) at 15.

[93] J. Boucher, 'L'acculturation juridique dans l'histoire du droit de la famille au Québec' (1967) 21 Rev. jur. polit, indép. et coop. 174 at 178–81.

[94] Mommsen, supra, note 59, at 5, 6. The protected persons were often engaged in commercial activity with the French.

[95] For Pondicherry, and the 'renonçants de Pondicherry,' Announssamy, supra, note 46, at 107, 129, 146.

[96] J.-L. Miège, 'Legal Developments in the Maghrib, 1830–1930' in Mommsen and de Moor, supra, note 59, 101 at 103; Benton, supra, note 71, at 154; and for the notion of 'citoyens français de statut local,' M. Grimaldi, 'L'exportation du Code civil' (2003) 107 Pouvoirs 80 at 92.

[97] J. Fisch, 'Law as a Means and as an End: Some Remarks on the Function of European and non-European Law in the Process of European Expansion' in Mommsen and de Moor, supra, note 59,

There were occasional instances of French law being introduced as a unum ius, driven by post-revolutionary élan. This occurred in Senegal in the early nineteenth century and on the Pacific island of Rapa. In both instances the effort was abandoned.[98] Resistance was either open and obstructive or silent and subversive, or combinations of both. Local norms and institutions would go underground, invisible to the non-practised eye; formal law and institutions would represent for the majority of the population an abnormal, pathological world.[99] Yet today in Senegal French legal tradition is very visible and present, at least in Dakar, a position obtained through a long process of adjustment and reconciliation of the European, relational droit commun to the particular law it could not avoid, and could not eliminate.[100]

The droit commun coutumier of France was seen in France as ending with the French Civil Code, which also would have brought about the demise of the ius commune. In the broader, transnational context of the droit commun originating from France there was no such dramatic effect of French codification. Abroad, the ancien droit (commun) simply continued. It is an indication of the importance of the French codification, however, that it is seen even today, as a matter of legal theory and legal history, as initiating a period of exclusively national laws. This again represents a view internal to a given European state which has undergone codification. In the broader, transnational context of relational common laws, however, codification provided a new impetus to their ongoing vitality. There was a new, re-invigorated ius proprium in the community of laws, which re-stated much of the old law, refined and improved it where necessary, and to which resort could be made in the ongoing

15 at 32 (also on many forms of differentiation of populations). French courts would thus apply French law to cases involving French citizens or those exercising French civil and legal rights; other courts or alternative means of dispute resolution would be used by the remainder of the population; Mann and Roberts, supra, note 64, at 12.

[98] For Rapa, A. P. Ottino, 'Juridiction française et droit coutumier à Rapa: Les enjeux d'une traduction' [2002] Droit et Cultures 153, notably at 170; and for Senegal, A. S. Sidibé, *Le pluralisme juridique en Afrique (L'exemple du droit successoral sénégalais)* (Paris : L.G.D.J., 1991) at 21–31, for re-admission of local law; Schnapper, 'Les tribunaux musulmans et la politique coloniale au Sénégal (1830–1914)' Rev. hist. dr. fr. et étr. 1961.90, notably at 103, 124 (boycotting of French courts by Islamic population, eventual re-instatement of Islamic courts); and generally E. Le Roy, 'Le Code civil au Sénégal ou le Vertige d'Icare' in Doucet and Vanderlinden, supra, note 48, 291, notably at 300 ('un transfert plus apparent que reel').

[99] C. Bontems, 'La coutume kabule et l'implantation des systèmes étrangers' in Doucet and Vanderlinden, supra, note 48, 77 at 96 ('l'enfouissement', 'le monde pathologique, l'anormal').

[100] Le Roy, supra, note 98, notably at 313 ff. ('une réception selective'), 318 (application outside of Dakar open question) and 321 (indigenous public law, however, 'ruined' by reception of French law).

process of legitimation of local decisions. As the Ordonnances of Louis XIV became relational common law abroad, so did the Napoleonic Code, preceded in many instances by older French law but often capable of persuasion in the absence of prior French presence. Imre Zatjay observed that French law and the French Civil Code played the part of a 'droit commun' of Latin countries in the nineteenth century and he was entirely correct in his conceptual description of the transnational, suppletive nature of the French codification.[101] He was less accurate in limiting the phenomenon to Latin peoples, since the Code's influence rapidly became a worldwide phenomenon, the effects of which are far from exhausted today. It is thus entirely appropriate to speak, in the full flower of nineteenth-century romantic nationalism and construction of apparently exclusivist national legal systems, of the 'intercommunicability' of the legal science of the time.[102] Common laws are beyond national destruction, and may draw their strength from many sources.

It has been said that the Civil Code of the French was not seen initially as narrowly national legislation, and it was applied shortly after its adoption to people now identified as citizens of Germany, Switzerland, Belgium, Luxembourg, Italy, and The Netherlands.[103] This was, however, the first, militaristic expansion of the Code, even perceived as a unum ius, and its true stature as a droit commun would become evident only over time, both within and beyond Europe. Common laws tend to expansion. The influence of the Code in Europe was rapid and immediate. If the time was ripe for codification, the French Code stood throughout the nineteenth century as the single, successful model. Its remarkable qualities facilitated its expansion, and codification in the French style ('à la française') came to be a widespread phenomenon. If it was not adopted integrally it could be adopted partially, or as a model of legislative style, or in terms of re-drafted substance. Even entirely new codes would be indebted to the *principle* of codification which it represented.[104] In the jurisdictions in which it was militarily introduced, it was often retained. Elsewhere it was imitated, in some measure. Within a broadly-defined European continent its influence extended east to Romania and north to Poland.[105] Nor was it only the Code which was influential abroad. The jurisprudence which

[101] I. Zatjay, 'La permanence des concepts du droit romain dans systèmes juridiques continentaux' Rev. int. dr. comp. 1966.353 at 359, as cited in Cairns, supra, note 7, at 282.

[102] Ranieri, supra, note 8, at 203 (author's transl.).

[103] J.-L. Halperin, 'Code Napoleon' in Alland and Rials, supra, note 38, 200 at 205.

[104] Grimaldi, supra, note 96, at 91–3.

[105] For Romania, Grimaldi, supra, note 96, at 83; for Poland, and Polish lawyers citing French jurisprudence while pleading in Russian, B. Lewaszkiewicz-Petrykowska, 'Code Napoléon et son

it generated was also translated, cited, and often followed elsewhere.[106] French doctrinal writing was also transnational. Beyond Europe the influence of the Code extended to at least four further continents—North America, South America, Asia, and Africa. It has been particularly important for codifications in Latin America, the Middle East (through the influence of the Egyptian Civil Code), francophone Africa, and both Quebec and Louisiana in North America.[107] Here again, French jurisprudence and academic writing have accompanied the influence of the Code.[108] So also, though it has been somehow much less visible than the Civil Code, has French administrative law.[109]

Legislation, though it has been seen recently as exclusively national in character, may therefore constitute an element of a relational, transnational common law to the same extent as any other source of law. Nor is it limited to serving as a model for foreign legislators. It may be, and is, cited

héritage en Pologne' in *Beauthier and Rorive*, supra, note 14, at 77, and generally for the Code's influence in Europe, and beyond, *Travaux de l'Association Henri Capitant*, vol. XLIV, *La circulation du modèle juridique français* (Paris: Litec, 1994); *Colloque de commemoration*, supra, note 14; *Le Code civil 1804–2004: Livre du Bicentenaire* (Paris: Dalloz/Litec, 2004 (in all cases with extent of resistance or modification); *1804–2004 Le Code civil: Un passé, un présent, un avenir* (Paris: Dalloz, 2004), notably p. 789 and f. ('Le Code civil dans le monde'); F. Wieacker, *A History of Private Law in Europe*, trans. T. Weir (Oxford: Clarendon Press, 1995) at 275.

106 Ranieri, supra, note 8, at 206.

107 See generally the works cited supra, note 105; add, for influence in the middle East, K. Bälz, 'Europäisches Privatrecht jenseits von Europa? Zum fünfzigjährigen Jubiläum des ägyptischen Zivilgesetzbuches (1948)' ZEuP 2000.51; for Quebec, Brierley, supra, note 47; Brierley and Macdonald, supra, note 55, at 106–8; H. P. Glenn (ed.), *Droit québécois et droit français: communauté, autonomie, concordance* (Montreal, Yvon Blais, 1993); for Louisiana, S. Herman, '*E Pluribus Unum*: The Paradox that Safeguards Louisiana's Mixed Legal System' (2003) 78 Tul. L. Rev. 457; V. Palmer, 'The French Connection and the Spanish Perception: Historical Debates and Contemporary Evaluation of French Influence on Louisiana Civil Law' (2003) 63 La L. Rev. 1067; V. Palmer, *The Louisiana Civilian Experience* (Durham, NC: Carolina Academic Press, 2005; for Latin America, Karst and Rosenn, supra, note 48, at 45, 46. In Asia the French tradition contributed greatly to the process of codification in Japan, though was eventually superceded by the influence of the German *BGB*. It remains, however influential, in south-east Asia as well. For recent re-codification in Vietnam, H. P. Glenn, 'The Grounding of Codification' 1998) 31 U. Cal. Davis L. Rev. 765; and for Thailand, K. Prokati, 'Die Rechtskultur und die Rolle der Rechtskreislehre in Thailand' in H. Scholler and S. Tellenbach, *Die Bedeuting der Lehre vom Rechtskreis und der Rechtskultur* (Berlin: Duncker & Humblot, 2001) 77 at 89.

108 C. Jauffret-Spinosi, 'La circulation du modèle français en Amérique latine' in *Travaux de l'Association Henri Capitant*, supra, note 105, 109 at 118 ; and for Quebec, P.-G. Jobin, 'Les réactions de la doctrine à la création du droit civil québécois par les juges : les débuts d'une affaire de famille' (1980) 21 C. de D. 257, notably at 270 (French doctrine most utilised source of law by Supreme Court of Canada for Quebec cases, after Quebec and Canadian case law).

109 For 'reception' of French administrative law in middle-eastern Islamic jurisdictions, S. Jahel, 'Les principes généraux du droit dans les systèmes arabo-musulmans au regard de la technique juridique contemporaine' Rev. int. dr. comp. 2003.105.

abroad to confirm, contrast, or supplement the law of the citing jurisdiction. When the French Court of Cassation decided in 1930 that the Code established a broad, objective form of liability for the simple control of inanimate (though potentially dangerous) things, many jurists in many countries were forced to examine, or re-examine, the language of their similarly worded texts, and to accept, or reject, this new dimension of the droit commun originating from France.[110] The place of legislation in a transnational common law is still more amply demonstrated, moreover, by the treatment the *Siete Partidas* has received abroad.

The derecho commún originating from Spain, in the world

In the Hispanic New World Castilian legislation was very visible, more so than the metropolitan equivalent in English or French colonies. This may have been because of a more active role of the Spanish Crown in the settlement process.[111] El derecho indiano was thus a recognized corpus of Castilian law governing in principle all matters in the New World and extending to both public and private law. In spite of the prominence of legislation, however, there was no direct rule in the sense of extension of metropolitan law and administration to all populations of the new territories. El derecho indiano was legislation, but it was a relational, common law. It has been said that Spanish laws in the colonies 'had a nearly imploring tone' and that the lack of Spanish coercive forces 'brought about the adoption of a persuasive politics, dependent on argument and reconciliation . . . a soft political system.'[112] Most of the substantive law

[110] Ch. Réunies, 13 Feb. 1930, arrêt *Jandheur,* D. 30,1,57, S.30.1.121. For rejection of the new interpretation in Belgium, A. Hartkamp, 'Deutsche Einflüsse auf das niederländische Privatrecht' (2000) 200 AcP 507 at 507; and in Quebec *Quebec Railway, Light, Heat, and Power* v. *Vandry* [1920] A.C. 662 (P.C.); and for judicial reaction in Egypt, Bälz, supra, note 107, at 63. Similar debates occurred in all jurisdictions of reception of the Code, which thus came to represent a major contribution to notions of stricter or more objective liability. Some jurisdictions of course rejected such an extension of liability, but the concept of liability for the control of things had become current and transnational.

[111] For the influence of Isabel of Castile and the instruments of Royal authority, Scheppach, supra, note 49, at 214–17.

[112] T. Herzog, 'The "Recopilación de Indias" and its discourse: The Spanish monarchy, the Indies and the seventeenth century' (1993) 20 Ius Commune 143 at 160–1; and for even colonial officials rejecting royal decrees as 'impossible or impolitic,' stating subtly 'I obey but do not carry it out'

was thus unwritten, or simply the residual law of Castile.[113] In this the Spanish model is really that of all European common laws, in Europe or beyond, though the model is operating under an umbrella of apparently exclusive metropolitan texts.

The Castilian texts themselves acknowledged the need for ongoing recognition of local, particular law, the iura propria of New Spain.[114] The Recopilación of the Laws of the Indias of 1680 stated expressly that the 'laws and good customs' of the existing population were to be conserved and given effect, and this is recognized as stating practice from at least 1530.[115] There was the usual reservation of public policy, here against recognition of laws contrary to 'natural law' or 'Christianity,'[116] and there was widespread ignorance of local law in the Spanish courts. Yet there were also local courts and local judges (alcaldes) in Spanish courts, who were charged with application of local law.[117] Concepts of the unwritten law became so well known they were even on occasion taken over into formal texts. This was the case for the ejido or collective form of enjoyment of land, still operative in at least Mexico today.[118] The indigenous or chthonic population thus could often choose their forum and their law, and apparently did so very effectively.[119] Populations were differentiated, but there was fluidity in the definition, and inevitably some abandonment of the local law by its traditional adherents (recalling the European objective, within Europe, of replication of the colonizing society.[120] Elements of commonality emerged. Yet in spite of difficult days in the nineteenth and twentieth centuries, the lex non scripta of the original

('acato pero no cumplo'), M. C. Mirow, *Latin American Law: A history of private law and institutions in Spanish America* (Austin: Univ. of Texas Press, 2004) at 235.

[113] Herzog, supra, note 112, at 144. ('little flesh, yet much skin').

[114] For similar Portuguese policy and recognition of the 'indigenato,' Mann and Roberts, supra, note 64, at 17; J. Penvenne, 'Lusuphone Africa' in Middleton, supra, note 59, 553 at 554.

[115] The text is cited in Levaggi, supra, note 48 at 345 (where the process is described as a 'dynamic' one); see also Margadant (1994), supra, note 48, at 36, 53, 59; Margadant (1983), supra, note 48 at 57; Cruz Barney, supra, note 48, at 28, 182; Barrientos Grandon, supra, note 48, at 352, referring to articles of capitulation of 1530; J. A. González Galván, *Derecho indígena* (México: McGraw Hill, 1997) at 19 (indigenous law even described as fuero).

[116] Barrientos Grandon, supra, note 48, at 351 (noting exclusion of polygamy, bride sale); Levaggi, supra, note 48, at 342; Margadant (1994), supra, note 48, at 53 (adding protection of interests of Crown).

[117] Benton, supra, note 71, at 32.

[118] Generally, Margadant (1994), supra, note 48, at 35; Margadant (1983), supra, note 48, at 31; and for 'indigenous tribunals' continuing to function, Mirow, supra, note 112, at 30.

[119] Benton, supra, note 71, at 32–3, 84.

[120] Margadant (1994), supra, note 48, at 36; Margadant (1983), supra, note 48 at 31; for 'replication' in Europe, supra, Ch. 1, *Mobility of people and mobility of laws*, and for the same concept in Latin America, Mirow, supra, note 112, at xiii, 11.

populations of Latin America has survived and is now increasingly protected by national constitutions.[121]

Spanish or Castilian law was therefore in general a relational or suppletive common law in the Spanish colonies. Even amongst Spanish people, moreover, in matters of private law, the *Siete Partidas* retained the same suppletive character which it had in Spain. The same hierarchy of sources enunciated for Spanish law prevailed in the colonies, with the *Siete Partidas* as last and suppletive source, after specific legislation and local or municipal rules.[122] Though local or specific rules had priority, the way was nevertheless open for the *Siete Partidas* to play a major role, since other sources were relatively undeveloped in matters of private law.[123] It eventually came to be recognized in many jurisdictions of the world, throughout Latin America as well as in Arizona, California, Florida, Louisiana, New Mexico, Texas, and the Philippines, as residual, relational common law.[124] The expression 'common law' or 'derecho común' has been explicitly used, and citation continues to the present day in spite of the contemporary abundance of local sources.[125] As important as the

[121] On survival, even contra legem, Margadant (1983), supra, note 48 at 30 ('even near the current capital of the country... An Indian of old would have understood perfectly today's practice of working collectively some plots'); Levaggi, supra, note 48, at 346–7, 377. For constitutional protection, emerging largely in the last decades, W. Assies, G. Van der Haar, and A. Hoekema, *The Challenge of Diversity: Indigenous peoples and reform of the State in Latin America* (Amsterdam: Thela Thesis, 2000) notably at 3 (listing 12 countries), 197 ff (for Andean countries).

[122] Margadant (1994), supra, note 48, at 53; Cruz Barney, supra, note 48, at 191 (listing eight sources, with *Siete Partidas* as last); Levaggi, supra, note 48, at 340; Karst and Rosenn, supra, note 48, at 33–5; Mirow, supra, note 112, at 49–52, 126.

[123] Barrientos Grandon, supra, note 48, at 219 ('amplia utilisacion'); Levaggi, supra, note 48, at 121 ('un papel muy importante... a causa de su completitud').

[124] For U.S. states, Scheppach, supra, note 49, at 231; and see H. Baade, 'The Form of Marriage in Spanish North America' (1975) 61 Cornell L. Rev. 1; P. Reich, 'Dismantling the Pueblo: Hispanic Municipal Land Rights in California Since 1850' (2001) 45 Am. J. L. Hist. 53, notably at 354–5, 369 (criticizing California judges' distortion of Hispanic law to facilitate commodification of American town commons, disregarding 'the prior, more communal legal tradition'); R. Schlesinger, H. Baade, P. Herzog, and E. Wise, *Comparative Law*, 6th ed. (New York: Foundation Press, 1998) at 16–17 (for ongoing effect of Spanish and French law in matters of land titles, mining law, water rights, and matrimonial propery, in Florida, Texas, New Mexico, Arizona, California, or states of Louisiana Purchase); and for the Philippines, Scheppach, supra, note 49, at 239; S. M. Santos, Jr., 'Common Law Elements in the Philippine Mixed Legal System' (2000) 2 Aust. J. Asian L. 34 at 35; V. Palmer, *Mixed Jurisdictions Worldwide: The Third Legal Family* (Cambridge: Cambridge Univ. Press, 2001) at 72.

[125] For 'common law' of Spain and *Siete Partidas*, citing Spanish author Murilo, L. Moreau Lislet and H. Carleton, 'Translators' Preface' in *The Laws of Las Siete Partidas which are Still in Force in the State of Louisiana*, transl. L. Moreau Lislet and H. Carleton (New Orleans: James M'Karaher, 1820) iii at xvii; for 'derecho commún' in the Philippines, *U.S.* v. *Abiog and Abiog* 37 Phil. 137 at 141 (1917), per Justice Malcolm, as cited by Santos, supra, note 124, at 38. For citations by courts in Louisiana to the mid-1990s and in Texas in 2002, Herman, supra, note 107, at 459.

Siete Partidas has been, however, as an explicit source, it has been overshadowed by the doctrine which explains it, and throughout the world of the common law originating from Spain, doctrinal writing continues to enjoy high authority and extensive citing by courts. It has even been said, in this regard, that the world of the Spanish derecho commún remains more faithful to the tradition of civil law than continental countries such as France and Germany, which by the early twentieth century had become largely places of local jurisprudence.[126]

Roman-Dutch common law, in the world

In the South American Dutch colony of Guiana the received Roman-Dutch law, from the province of Holland, was known as 'the common law.'[127] This again is an accurate description of the relational, suppletive role which was played by Dutch law in its expansion abroad. It has also been designated as the 'common law' of South Africa and the then jurisdictions of Rhodesia and South-West Africa.[128] In the frequency of use of the expression common law there appears to be reflection of the explicit Dutch policy of legal pluralism in all of its overseas possessions where, in principle, local law and common law 'were given equal weight and practiced alongside one another' (though Dutch law would prevail in case of conflict).[129] In Java the policy was facilitated, and perhaps even dictated, by an existing duality of laws, those of royal or Hindu character

[126] For the importance of doctrinal writing down to the end of the Spanish domination, Levaggi, supra, note 48, at 360 ('preponderant role'); Margadant (1994), supra, note 48, at 58 (listing authors); and for more contemporary, but continuing, practice, J. L. de los Mozos, 'Codificaciones latino-americana, tradicion juridica y principios generales del derecho' (1996) 1 Roma e America. Diritto Romano Comune 29, notably at 30–1 on use of 'general principles of law' as means of 'cultural prolongation' of Europe into latin America; Karst and Rosenn, supra, note 48, at 7, 212, 220, 453; H. P. Glenn, 'Harmony of Laws in the Americas' (2003) 34 U. Miami Inter-American L. Rev. 223; H. P. Glenn, 'The Use of Comparative Law by Courts: A View from the Americas' in G. Canivet, M. Andenas, and D. Fairgrieve (eds.), *The Use of Comparative Law by the Courts* (London: British Institute of International and Comparative Law, 2004) 217; and for the atypicality of France and Germany, in their recent hostility to foreign sources, T. Scholl, *Die Rezeption des kontinental-europäischen Privatrechts in Lateinamerika* (Berlin: Duncker & Humblot, 1999) at 21, 194, and more generally J. Merryman, *The Civil Law Tradition*, 2nd ed. (Stanford: Stanford Univ. Press, 1985) at ix.

[127] Ledlie, supra, note 53, at 210.

[128] Hahlo and Kahn, supra, note 40, at 578–9.

[129] Mommsen, supra, note 59, at 7; and see D. S. Lev, *Legal Evolution and Political Authority in Indonesia: Selected Essays* (The Hague/London/Boston: Kluwer Law International, 2000) at 14 (Dutch East-Indies Co (VOC) 'resolved to respect local law—another way of saying they could not have cared

(pradata) and those (unwritten) of the Java population (padu).[130] In all of the Dutch colonies, however, Roman-Dutch law was received, as was said for Indonesia, 'in so far as in accordance with the conditions of these lands and practicable'[131] and this general reservation gave rise to dual court structures,[132] what has been described as a system of personal laws,[133] and a necessarily differentiated population. Equality before the law was guaranteed to the populations, but 'equality does not necessarily mean that the same laws are to be applied to all elements of the population.'[134] Local law was applied by the Dutch, moreover, 'in as far as tolerable' and penal and administrative law was generally applicable.[135] There were also subtle methods of acculturation.

The influence of Dutch colonization in the world has now faded greatly, though the new Dutch Civil Code has achieved considerable prominence as a model of law reform in the world.[136] This raises the general question of how laws may function as common laws even in the absence of prior colonization. The German law of the Pandectists and the *BGB* provides an excellent example of how this may occur.

Pandectist common law, in the world

By the twentieth century European territorial expansion was drawing to a close, and the empires were shrinking. With the French Civil Code a form of expansion of European law emerged which was based not on territorial

less—except where commercial interests were at stake'); M. Daud Ali, 'The Position of Islamic Law in the Indonesian Legal System' in T. Abdullah and S. Shiddique (eds.), *Islam and Society in Southeast Asia* (Singapore: Institute of Southeast Asian Studies, 1983) 187 at 189.

130 J. Ball, *Indonesian Legal History 1602–1848* (Sydney: Oughtershaw Press, 1982) at 37, 42.

131 A. J. B. Sirks, '"In as far as in accordance with the conditions of these lands and practicable." European and native law in the Dutch East Indies' (1998) XXV Ius Commune 159; and see H. J. Leue, 'Legal Expansion in the Age of the Companies: Aspects of Administration of Justice in the English and Dutch Settlements of Maritime Asia, c. 1600–1750' in Mommsen and de Moor, supra, note 59, 129 at 133; for South Africa, Bisschop, supra, note 43, at 168; Hahlo and Kahn, supra, note 40, at 574.

132 Lev, supra, note 129, at 16 (some of the courts predating Dutch arrival, though appeals to Dutch court).

133 Sirks, supra, note 131, at 163 (Chinese, Jewish, Islamic, adat, and European laws applied, latter tending to dominate with respect to contracts, torts, commercial affairs).

134 B. Ter Haar, *Adat Law in Indonesia* (ed. and with an introduction by E. Adamson Hoebel and A. Arthur Schiller) (New York: Institute of Pacific Relations, 1948) at 10 (of the Introduction).

135 Sirks, supra, note 131 at 163.

136 See *New Netherlands Civil Code—Patrimonial Law*, transl. P. P. C. Hannappel and E. Mackaay (Deventer: Kluwer, 1990).

expansion of states, at least not exclusively, but on what can perhaps best be described as intellectual alliance.[137] The expansion of German law abroad has been almost exclusively of this kind, beginning with the expansion of the Sachsenspiegel and the law of the city of Magdeburg into eastern lands from the thirteenth century.[138] There was a brief period of German colonialism abroad (where German law was introduced into parts of Africa, though always subject to preservation of existing local law, in the manner of common laws),[139] but this came to an end with the conclusion of the First World War. In the twentieth century there has been great expansion of German law in the world, a process which has been entirely free of territorial extension and which has been due almost entirely to the intellectual qualities of the German Pandectist[140] writers of the nineteenth century and the German Civil Code, or *BGB* (*Bürgerliches Gesetzbuch*), which came into force in 1900. This has also occurred in the absence of widespread knowledge in the world of the German language, so the conceptual refinement of the work of German jurists appears the most plausible explanation of German legal influence.[141]

It is now common in German to refer to a German 'Rechtskreise' or circle or sphere of German legal influence in the world, which includes all of those jurisdictions which have aligned themselves with German law in the last century.[142] Here German law fills all of the criteria of a relational common law. It is suppletive to the law of all receiving jurisdictions, present only in a manner compatible with local law and with no obligatory content; it is tolerant of differentiated populations (now in terms of different nationalities though other differentiations remain possible); it possesses no binding or unifying authority; its reception has been a vast

[137] Supra, this Ch., *The droit commun originating from France, in the world.*

[138] Supra, Ch. 1, *The common law (gemeine Recht) originating from Germany.*

[139] Mommsen, supra, note 59, at 7 ('we find in the German colonies much the same wide variety of forms of indirect rule as elsewhere'); Okupa, supra, note 64 at 2, notably on German project of codification of unwritten local law, never brought to fruition).

[140] From the Greek 'pandektes' or 'all receiver' as an indication of the complete character of the Justininan codification. See generally Wieacker, supra, note 105, Ch. 23 at 341 ('Pandectism and Positive Legal Science').

[141] It has also been seen by many as over-refinement, and was savagely criticized within Germany by von Jhering; see, in English translation, R. von Jhering, 'In the Heaven of Legal Concepts' in M. Cohen and F. Cohen, *Readings in Jurisprudence and Legal Philosophy* (New York: Prentice Hall, 1951) at 678–89 (heaven of juridical concepts difficult to enter, Savigny nearly refused entry; heaven filled with living juridical concepts and machines—hair-splitting machine, fiction machine, dialectic-hydraulic interpretation press, dialectic drill for getting to bottom of things, dizzying path of dialectical deduction).

[142] See, e.g., A. Spickhoff, 'Das BGB in Europa' in U. Diederichsen and W. Sellert, *Das BGB im Wandel der Epochen* (Göttingen: Vandenhoeck & Ruprecht, 2001) at 169.

and highly visible process, evident in legislation, academic writing, and the work of courts, in many parts of the world.

It is possible in some measure to see different zones of expansion of this Pandectist common law in the world. A first zone would be composed of neighbouring, German-language countries, notably Austria and Switzerland, where the German influence has been considerable.[143] The expression 'genetic alliance' has even been used,[144] though it has also been pointed out that the relations are complex and that both Austrian and Swiss codes preceded the *BGB*.[145] Ongoing relations have been facilitated not only by a common language but by a certain 'circolazione di professori' and a major study of citation patterns in the Swiss Federal Court showed that of all foreign citations from 1875 to 1989, 90 per cent were to German sources.[146] Geography and history also indicate a second zone of influence, in north-eastern Europe where, as noted above,[147] German sources historically have had great influence, from the thirteenth century. So in the contemporary states of Poland, Hungary, and the Czech Republic, codes and teaching largely follow Pandectist models and there is discussion of a 'middle-European private law.'[148] Further east, Russia has been attentive to this civilian model, geographically the closest to it. The first Soviet Civil Code, of 1922, was strongly influenced by Pandectist thought[149] and in the process of drafting the new Russian Civil Code it has been said to the present writer, in Moscow, that 'We are all Pandectists here.'[150] The trust has been thus described as derived from 'absolutely alien Anglo-American approaches.'[151] Finally, within the Eurasian land mass, a number of European countries have seen in Pandectist common

[143] Ernst A. Kramer, 'Der Einfluss des BGB auf das schweizerische und österreichische Privatrecht' (2000) 200 AcP 365 at 369.

[144] E. Bucher, 'Die Entwicklung des deutschen Schuldrechts im 19. Jahrhundert und die Schweiz' ZEuP 2003.353 at 373.

[145] Kramer, supra, note 143, at 366–7.

[146] Kramer, supra, note 143, at 373, 375. Twenty-five % of the citations were to French sources, 9% to Austrian, and 6% to Italian.

[147] Supra, note 138, and accompanying text.

[148] N. Horn, 'Die Rolle des Privatrechts in der Transformation von Wirtschaft und Gesellschaft in Mittelosteuropa und Osteuropa' in N. Horn (ed.), *Die Neugestaltung des Privatrechts in Mittelosteuropa und Osteuropa* (Munich: C. H. Beck, 2002) 3, at 14, and also at 8 for historic influence of the law of German cities; for effect of a 'mighty wave' of German legal thought in Hungary, F. Mádl, 'Der Einfluss des BGB auf die Entwicklung des ungarischen Privatrechts' (2000) 200 AcP 526 at 527; and for the *BGB*-type structure of the new Estonian Civil Code, K. Leiger, 'Newest Civil Code in Europe' January 2003 Eastern European Law Forum 13.

[149] Horn, supra, note 148 at 11, also at 12 for influence on 1964 Code and at 22 for influence on Russian commercial law.

[150] For the reform process, and influences upon it, see the Special Issue on Russian Law Reform (1999) 44 McGill L. J. 255 ff.

[151] E. A. Sukhanov, 'The Right of Ownership in the Contemporary Civil Law of Russia' (1999) 44 McGill L. J. 301 at 309–10.

law the most sophisticated and modern version of private law and have simply gravitated towards it. Italy did so, after its initial attraction to the French Code,[152] and Spain also was drawn from French to German authority by the mid-twentieth century. Translated German law books (Enneccerus/Kipp/Wolff, Larenz, Medicus, Wolff, von Hedemann) have thus had great influence, notably in Spanish-annotated form; Spanish legislation has followed German legislative models; concepts of German law have been incorporated into Spanish practice even though they have not been incorporated into Spanish legislation.[153] Greece clearly belongs to the sphere of Pandectist common law, the Greek Civil Code of 1946 following the structure of the *BGB* and much of its substantive law of obligations, though showing less influence in the law of the family and successions.[154] The Netherlands is less clearly a member of the Rechtskreise, but has increasingly looked to German authority, in the drafting of its new Civil Code and on major questions such as the protection of the rights of personality (allgemeines Personlichkeitsrecht) and the interpretation of general clauses of the Code (good faith, etc.).[155] In spite of close geographical proximity, and some influence, Scandinavian countries have been selective in resort to the German model.[156]

Pandectist common law is particularly striking, however, for its extension beyond the European continent. It has greatly influenced codification and conceptual thinking in Latin America and a 'chain of tradition' has been found even linking the Prussian General Law of the late eighteenth century to the Argentinian Civil Code.[157] There was similar influence in Chile and Brazil,[158] and more recently the Brazilian Civil

[152] A. Gambaro and A. Guarneri, 'Italie' in Travaux de l'Association Henri Capitant, supra, note 105, 77 at 80; A. Gambaro and R. Sacco, *Sistemi Giuridici Comparati* (Turin: Utet, 2002) at 377–83.

[153] L. Puig Ferriol, 'Hundert Jahre deutsches Bürgerliches Gesetzbuch: Das deutsche Bürgerliche Gesetzbuch and das spanische Zivilrecht' ZEuP 2000.195 at 195–6 for textbooks, 197 for legislation, 196 for adoption of notion 'Rechtsgeschäfte' or legal transactions, General Part of teaching of general concepts of civil law (derived from General Part of *BGB*); A. Vaquer, 'Importing Foreign Doctrines: Yet Another Approach to the Unification of European Private Law? Incorporation of the *Virwirkung* Doctrine into Spanish Case Law' ZEuP 2000.301.

[154] A. Georgiades, 'Der Einfluss des deutschen BGB auf das griechische Zivilrecht' (2000) 200 AcP 493; Th. D. Macris, 'Die Grundgedanken für die Ausarbeitung des Entwurfs eines griechischen Zivilgesetzbuches' RabelsZ 1935.586; P. J. Zepos, 'Der Einfluss des schweizerischen Privatrechts auf das griechische Zivilgesetzbuch von 1946' SJZ 1960.358 (dealing also with Swiss influence).

[155] A. Hartkamp, 'Deutsche Einflüsse auf das niederländische Privatrecht' (2000) 200 AcP 507, at 508–9.

[156] U. Göranson, 'Der Einfluss des BGB auf die Entwicklung des skandinavischen Privatrechts' (2000) 200 AcP 503, notably at 504–5 (rather 'thin picture', importance for 'particular questions').

[157] R. Knütel, 'Preussisches Recht im argentinischen Código civil von 1869' in E. Jayme (ed.) *Festschrift für Hubert Niederländer* (Heidelberg: Carl Winter, 1991) 41 at 44.

[158] Knütel, supra, note 157.

Code shows clear affinity with the *BGB*.[159] The Civil Code of the Mexican State of Quintana Roo has taken the *BGB* as its primary model.[160] In Asia, Japan westernized its law as a condition of freeing the country of western colonial presence at the end of the nineteenth century. There was hesitation between French and German models. The German eventually prevailed, and it has been said, in Japan, that 'Was nicht deutsches Recht ist, ist kein Recht' ('What is not German law is not law'), this despite an inevitable process of adjustment of Pandectist common law to Japanese circumstance.[161] The Japanese Civil Code follows the *BGB* structure and German law has been generally described as a 'Treasure Chest' of concepts for Japanese lawyers.[162] Japanese judges cite German textbooks, even in German original editions.[163] German law has also been influential in matters of competition law, administrative law,[164] and civil procedure.[165] Influence in Japan resulted in influence in both Korea and China. In Korea the 1960 Civil Code is clearly Pandectist-influenced and German academic opinions and case law are cited in Korean textbooks.[166] China has relied extensively on Japanese law to the extent it has developed private law. The Pandectist influence is evident in the structure of Chinese civil law legislation[167] and in particular fields such as concepts of property and company law.[168] Thailand's Civil and Commercial Code has an initial Pandectist-type General Part and uses many Pandectist concepts, though its

[159] Knütel, supra, note 157; A. A. Soares de Camargo, 'The Revised Brazilian Civil Code' (2003) 11 U. Miami Int'l. & Comp. L. Rev. 161.

[160] Margadant (1994), supra, note 48, at 286.

[161] For the debate within Japan, Y. Noda, *Introduction to Japanese Law*, transl. A. Angelo (Tokyo: Tokyo Univ. Press, 1976) 41–58; and see generally, Z. Kitagawa, *Rezeption und Fortbildung des europäischen Zivilrechts in Japan* (Frankfurt: A. Metzner, 1970); G. Rahn, *Rechtsdenken und Rechtsauffassung in Japan* (Munich: C. H. Beck, 1990), notably at 113 ('Was nicht deutsches . . .'); I. Shiro, 'The Reception of the Occidental Systems by the Japanese Legal System' in Doucet and Vanderlinden, supra, note 48, at 239; and on yielding to local circumstance, H. Coing et al., *Die Japaniesierung des westlichen Rechts* (Tübingen: J. C. B. Mohr (Paul Siebeck), 1990).

[162] T. Kono, 'Theorierezeption und Theorienfunktion: Zum hundertjährigen Bestehen des BGB aus der japanischer Sicht' ZEuP 1999.417 at 423, though noting problems of adjustment of German concepts to general cadre of Japanese law.

[163] Rahn, supra, note 161, at 117.

[164] J. O. Haley, *The Spirit of Japanese Law* (Athens, GA/London: Univ. of Georgia Press, 1998) at 31; and see generally for the influence of German administrative law in the world, R. Schulze, 'European Legal History—A New Field of Research in Germany' (1992) 13 J. Leg. Hist. 270, at 282.

[165] J.-H. Moitry, 'Japon (Culture juridique)' in Alland and Rials, supra, note 38, 857 at 859 (Japanese Code of Civil Procedure most influenced by German law).

[166] H.-B. Kim, 'Das deutsche BGB und das koreanische Zivilrecht' (2000) 200 AcP 511, at 515.

[167] E. J. Epstein, 'Codification of Civil Law in the People's Republic of China: Form and Substance in the Reception of Concepts and Elements of Western Private Law' (1998) 32 U.B.C. Law Rev. 153, at 170; and generally for civil law influence, H. von Senger, 'Bedeutung der Lehre vom Rechtskreis und die Rechtskultur: Das Beispiel der Volksrepublik China' in Scholler and Tellenbach, supra, note 107, 55 at 57.

[168] P. B. Potter, 'Globalization and Economic Regulation in China: Selective Adaptation of Globalized Norms and Practices' (2003) 2 Washington U. Global Studies L. Rev. 119 at 127, 143, 145.

style is said to be closer to French and Swiss codes.[169] German influence on the law of Israel has been described as 'very odd given . . . the Second World War' but has nevertheless been extensive in both civil and criminal law.[170] The *BGB*'s influence has even extended beyond the law of contemporary states and considerably influenced the 1917 Code of canon law.[171]

The influence which Pandectist common law has exerted in the world is evident beyond its implementation in specific (foreign) legislative texts or in parallel case law or in reliance on German authors. It is frequently said to give rise to a 'Theorienrezeption' or reception of theory, by which is meant that it is the underlying concepts and ideas of Pandectist legal thought which have been most influential, for their abstract clarity, applicability, and reciprocal coherence.[172] It would be therefore in reality the conceptual refinement of German law which explains its influence (as has been largely the case for the French Civil Code).[173] This also reinforces the idea of Pandectist thought as relational common law. In the world it has no obligatory content and no pretention to bind. It is, however, available, and can be applied in a suppletive, differential manner which poses no obvious threat to local circumstance or to local identity. Writers have spoken of its 'metapositive' character.[174]

National appropriation of common laws abroad? The U.S.A. experience

Resistance to expanding European common laws did not come simply from non-European peoples. It also came from European settlers

[169] K. Prokati, 'Die Rechtskultur und die Rolle der Rechtskreislehre in Thailand' in Scholler and Tellenbach, supra, note 107, 77 at 90–1.

[170] C. L. Fassberg, 'Language and Style in a Mixed System' (2003) 78 Tul. L. Rev. 151 at 157.

[171] F. Roumy, 'Corpus juris canonici' in Alland and Rials, supra, note 38, 294 at 298.

[172] Spickhoff, supra, note 142, at 170 (within Europe, most influence in terms of theory and doctrine, as opposed to simple transfer of texts or institutions); Kramer, supra, note 143, at 389 (conceptual influence in Austria so great that now taken for granted, rarely acknowledged); Shiro, supra, note 161, at 242 (for theory reception in Japan); Rahn, supra, note 161, at 116; F. Mádl, 'Der Einfluss des BGB auf die Entwicklung des ungarischen Privatrechts' (2000) 200 AcP 526 at 529 (reception not mechanical or in detail but rather at level of values, methods, principles); H. Baum, 'Rechtsdenken, Rechtssysteme und Rechtswirklichkeit in Japan' RabelsZ 1995.258 at 267.

[173] As suggested supra, text accompanying note 138; and for the French Code, supra, this Ch., *The droit commun originating from France, in the world.*

[174] Kramer, supra, note 143, at 369.

themselves, who now found themselves in radically different, non-European climes. Here there appear to be two broad patterns or models of accommodation between European common laws and the particular needs and normativity expressed by European settlers. In both patterns or models the tension between the common and the particular is maintained, though in different degrees. One model may be called the general model; the other may be called the model of the United States of America.

The general model is one which we have thus far been describing, in which the European metropolitan authority, and the European settlers themselves, are in principle agreed on the maintenance of a particular European common law in the 'new' territory. This fundamental agreement gives rise to a principle of law, found in sources of both common law and local, settlers' law, that common law is received, though subject to local, particular exception. The general principle is that of reception, subject to its suitability to local conditions. From what we have seen, this model prevailed throughout the Commonwealth, with respect to the common law originating from England, and throughout the territories where continental common laws were received. The principle existed in different forms, but the underlying pattern is the same. Nineteenth-century legal nationalism here certainly had an effect, and the adoption of some measure of national stare decisis in the common law territories, and of codification in the territories of continental-derived iura communia, brought about some form of national closure of sources of law. In the Commonwealth there was also a short-lived effort to extend the notion of stare decisis throughout the Empire, to replace the notion of a relational common law with that of common law as general decree (at least for settlers themselves).[175] Relational common laws, however, clearly survived these efforts of national or supra-national closure.

The other pattern or model is that evidenced by the United States of America, though it may be seen as occurring elsewhere where European settlement failed or did not bring about a formal reception of European law. Here the general principle of reception of common law is reversed, both for legal reasons and for diverse political sentiments including those

[175] See generally Matson, supra, note 34, at 755 (on Privy Council decisions binding beyond country of origin of decision); Cote, supra, note 57, at 55–6 (no question of colonial courts rejecting common law, but rather of knowing what common law is, particularly since House of Lords no longer bound by own decisions); and for 19th-century ideas of separation of law from all questions of religion, custom, local politics, and local history, as contributing to the colonialist idea of transplanting entire 'legal systems' abroad, A. Huxley, 'The Reception of Buddhist Law in S.E. Asia (200 BCE–1860 CE)' in Doucet and Vanderlinden, supra, note 48, 139 at 233.

of what has become known as revolution.[176] The presumption is here against reception, though reception occurs nevertheless, usually by virtue of legislative measures of adoption and because western settlers remain committed to western traditions.[177] It is a question of change from within, and national appropriation of a common law is necessary for this to be brought about. Local unsuitability was therefore the test for rejection of the common law in the Commonwealth, whereas local suitability became the test for positive adoption of it in the United States. There was thus much re-enactment of English legislation in the U.S.[178] In both the U.S. and the Commonwealth, however, the common law originating in England was a recognized source of law. The eighteenth century had seen a real Anglicization of U.S. legal practice[179] and in the late twentieth century it could be said that 'Even in the United States, the common law has become part of our national mythology.'[180] The difference between the models was a question of weight, a question of the hierarchy of sources in the range between particular and common.

As the United States represented a particular model of reception of common law, moreover, so it came to represent a particular model, in the 'new' world, of appropriation of common law. The process was broadly similar to measures of appropriation of common law which were undertaken in Europe, again largely in the name of popular sovereignty. State legislation was important in this process, in some cases, such as that of California, leading to enactment of a civil code.[181] More interesting is

[176] For revolution in its original sense of revolving, or returning back, astronomically to an original point of departure and politically to the de-stabilizing thought of the Greeks, and as having relatively little effect on underlying, especially private, law, H. P. Glenn, 'Law, Revolution and Rights' (1990) Archives for Philosophy of Law and Social Philosophy, Beiheft No. 41, *Revolution and Human Rights* 9.

[177] For the necessity of formal measures of introduction of English law into U.S. states (some of them at least being seen as territories of prior occupation), E. Brown, *British Statutes in American Law 1776–1836* (Ann Arbor, MI: Univ. of Michigan Law School, 1964) at 12–22.

[178] Brown, supra, note 177, at 24–41, and 36–7 for the efforts of Jefferson to use those parts of English laws judged most suitable to local conditions, in revising the laws of Virginia.

[179] D. Lemmings, *Professors of the Law: Barristers and English Legal Culture in the Eighteenth Century* (Oxford: Oxford Univ. Press, 2000) at 236–9 for southern states sending young lawyers to Inns of Court, pretentious pleading of English cases, though U.S. lawyers better educated, more in touch with population, and less elitist than those in England; and for U.S. 'vogue' for Blackstone, in many editions, which did not occur in Canada, B. Laskin, *The British Tradition in Canadian Law* (London: Stevens, 1969) at 90.

[180] J. Gordley, 'The Common Law in the Twentieth Century: Some Unfinished Business' (2000) 88 Cal. L. Rev. 1817 at 1875; and see J. B. Elkind, *The Impact of American Law on English and Commonwealth Law* (St. Paul: West Publishing, 1978) at ix ('English Common Law is still considered to be the basis of American jurisprudence').

[181] For codification in the U.S., S. Herman, 'Historique et destinée de la codification américaine' Rev. int. dr. comp. 1995.707; and for the importance of the French Civil Code as model, though not

the more difficult task undertaken of appropriating the common law in its judicial form. The English process of nationalization of the common law was never entirely successful, though the notion of a national hierarchy of courts, bound together by stare decisis, was an indication of the path to follow. The process was taken further in the United States, with the conceptualization of case law as a purely state product. As early as 1798 Root had written an essay on 'the common law of Connecticut';[182] state judges came to be elected by local populations, and in considerable measure still are; exclusive state case reports became established; and there were some formal prohibitions of citation or pleading of English cases,[183] emulating continental prohibitions of citation of Roman authors.[184] There was much constructive borrowing and incorporation of continental legal writings, to hasten the move from common law forms of action to modern, substantive law.[185] The effectiveness of these measures is indicated by a steady decline in out-of-state citations in U.S. state courts over the century 1870 to 1970, and an even sharper decline in citation to English or Commonwealth authority.[186] So U.S. law came close to being,

in terms of actual content, for the U. S. Uniform Commercial Code, R. Sommers, 'The Napoleonic Civil Code, the Common Law, and the American Uniform Commercial Code,' in *Beauthier and Rorive*, supra, note 14, at 157. There was perhaps more German than French influence on the U.C.C., through Llewellyn, as to which, S. Riesenfeld, 'The Influence of German Legal Theory on American Law: The Heritage of Savigny and His Disciples' (1989) 37 Am. J. Comp. L. 1, notably at 6 ('The thought pattern of the modern common law architects and that of the modern Pandectists merge in Llewellyn; that is all that can be said, but it says a lot').

[182] Root argued for a 'system of jurisprudence purely American' yet in spite of this, and his title, felt that 'we ought to . . . leave ourselves open to derive instruction and improvement from the observations, discoveries and experience of the literate, in all countries and nations, respecting jurisprudence.' J. Root, 'On the Common Law of Connecticut' in 'Preface,' *Root's Reports* (1798), reproduced in D. Coquillette, *The Anglo-American Legal Heritage: Introductory Materials* (Durham, NC: Carolina Academic Press, 1999) at 428 ff.

[183] State statutes thus often prohibited citation of post-1776 English decisions, as to which J. Langbein, 'Chancellor Kent and the History of Legal Literature' (1993) 93 Col. L. Rev. 547 at 568, with refs.

[184] Supra, this Ch., *National appropriation of common laws in Europe?*

[185] R. H. Helmholz, 'Use of the Civil Law in Post-Revolutionary American Jurisprudence' (1992) 66 Tul. L. Rev. 1649, notably at 1653–4 ('The most frequently cited civilian treatises in the early American reports were those written by seventeenth and eighteenth century Continental writers . . . Grotius . . . Pufendorf . . . Domat . . . Heineccius . . . Pothier'), indicating the importance of each of the particular European common laws; and for further references to the large literature on the subject, H. P. Glenn, supra, note 80, at 277; M. Hoeflich, *Roman and Civil Law and the Development of Anglo-American Jurisprudence in the Nineteenth Century* (Athens, GA: Univ. of Georgia Press, 1997). For the results, A. von Mehren, *The U.S. Legal System: Between the Common Law and Civil Law Legal Traditions* (Rome: Centro di studi e ricerche di diritto comparato straniero, 2000).

[186] J. H. Merryman, 'Toward a Theory of Citations: An Empirical Study of the Citation Practice of the California Supreme Court in 1950, 1960 and 1970' (1977) 50 Cal. L. Rev. 381, notably at 394–400

in von Jhering's term, a 'local jurisprudence,' just as major countries of the European continent had (nearly) become.[187] Yet state private law in the U.S. never became entirely autonomous, as statements of law continued to float over borders within the U.S., and as the notion of 'an inseparable entity called Anglo-American law' continued to prevail.[188] Most recently, U.S. judges have begun to advocate use of a broader range of sources of law, including those of the European common laws,[189] and the U.S. Supreme Court has begun to cite non-U.S. authority.[190]

U. S. efforts to appropriate a common law, or common laws, could thus do no more than constitute U.S. law as a ius proprium within an ongoing body of what has now become transnational common law, or transnational common laws. As on the continent of Europe, such measures rest on an underlying principle of the primacy of local or particular law and the self-effacing character of common law, so measures of appropriation, however successful they may be at any given time, are never definitive. Common laws always reappear, depending on local need.

Common law in federations and confederations

Measures of appropriation of common law in the once-colonized world are important not only for our understanding of common law, but also for our understanding of the workings of federations and confederations, such as those of the United States, Canada, Mexico, Australia, and even,

(by late 20th-century reference to English authority less than one-half of one per cent of citations); L. M. Friedmann, et al., 'State Supreme Courts: A Century of Style and Citation' (1981) 33 Stan. L. Rev. 773, notably at 801–2.

[187] For von Jhering, supra, note 32.

[188] On so-called 'national' private law within the U.S., notably in the form of Restatements, M. Eisenberg, 'The Unification of Law' in M. Bussani and U. Mattei, *The Common Core of European Private Law* (The Hague: Kluwer Law International, 2003) 35 at 37; and for Anglo-American law, Langbein, supra, note 183, at 567.

[189] S. S. Abrahamson and M. J. Fischer, 'All the World's a Courtroom: Judging in the New Millenium' (1997) 26 Hofstra L. Rev. 273; and see A. M. Kennedy, 'Our Shared Legal Tradition' in American Bar Association, *Common Law, Common Values, Common Rights* (San Francisco: West, 2000) at xxi.

[190] *Lawrence* v. *Texas*, 539 U.S. 558 (2003), 123 S. Ct. 2472, and on the decision D. Childress III, 'Using Comparative Constitutional Law to Resolve Domestic Federal Questions' (2003) 53 Duke L. J. 193, and its background, J. Nafziger, 'International Law and Foreign Law Right Here in River City' (1998) 34 Willamette L. Rev. 4 at 19 ff.

perhaps one day, Europe. Why is common law such an important concept for federations? It appears first of all to control in large measure the type of judicial structure to be adopted in the federation. If there is an operative concept of a relational common law, in unappropriated form, then it appears entirely suitable to leave it in the hands of a single, high court-type judiciary of general, inherent jurisdiction. In a federation or confederation, these are the courts of the states or provinces, which would thus be competent for the common law (whichever one it is) and any state or federal amendment of it, according to the division of legislative powers. If the common law is seen, however, as having been appropriated by legislative authority, or as being susceptible to such appropriation, then it is proper that each legislative authority be equipped with its own judiciary. Hence the famous argument of Madison in the United States that 'a government without a proper executive *and judiciary* would be the mere trunk of a body, without arms and legs to act or move.'[191] The judiciary must therefore be federalized, and local or state judiciaries must exist alongside a federal judiciary. Appropriation of common law would be presumed to have taken place at both federal and state or provincial levels, necessitating separate judicial structures.

So there are major differences in attitude towards common law between, on the one hand, the federalized judiciaries of the United States of America and the United States of Mexico and, on the other hand the judiciaries of federations or confederations such as Canada and Australia which remain, in some measure at least, unitary in character.[192] Of course, even given a particular type of judiciary in a federation, there are ongoing tensions as to jurisdiction and sources of law, and questions of whether common law has effectively *been* appropriated. Canada, Australia, and

[191] J. Elliot (ed.), *Debates on the Adoption of the Federal Constitution at the Convention held in Philadelphia*, 1907, at 158, 159, as cited in H. A. Johnson, 'Historical and Constitutional Perspectives on Cross-Vesting of Court Jurisdiction' (1993) 19 Melbourne U. L. Rev. 45, at 51, note 32 (emphasis added).

[192] The court structure is unitary in the sense that there is a single court of general, residual jurisdiction, competent for both federal and state or provincial matters, at the state or provincial level. It will be, however, replicated in each of the different states or territories. See generally H. P. Glenn, 'Divided Justice? Court Structures in Federal and Confederal States' (1995) 46 S. Carolina L. Rev. 819. In spite of the visibility of the federal judiciary in the United States, it has been said recently that a federal court system is 'unusual in a federalism,' contrasting the U.S.A. with both Canada and the present court structure of the European Union (in both of which state or provincial court structures have general, residual competence); G. Calabresi, 'Federal and State Courts: Restoring a Workable Balance' (2003) 78 N.Y. U. L. Rev. 1293 at 1293 (arguing for significant shift to state courts in U.S.).

the European Union have all seen the emergence of some form of federal or higher-level courts. How is the jurisdiction of such courts to be determined?

In all of these political structures there are occasions in which federal or higher-level courts can be seized with questions of enacted federal or European law. There are also occasions when they may be seized with matters which involve no federal legislation, or which do not exclusively involve federal legislation. This is the case in the United States for so-called diversity cases, involving citizens of different states, or in Canada cases concerning inter-provincial undertakings. What law applies to such cases? It can only be common law, since there is no applicable federal legislation, but federal jurisdiction can be asserted only if it is based on federal law, so it must be said to be federal common law. Can common law be effectively appropriated not only at the state level, as attempted in the United States, but also at the federal level? Mexico has moved in this direction with the enactment of a federal civil code, in addition to state civil codes, though the European and Latin American experience has shown that codification does not yield definitive appropriation.[193] In the United States the response was initially favourable to federal appropriation, in the famous nineteenth-century case of *Swift* v. *Tyson* (where the language of appropriation of the common law was used by counsel)[194] but became unfavourable as a result of the still more famous twentieth-century decision of *Erie Railway* v. *Tompkins.*[195] It is now said there is no federal general common law in the United States.[196] This has always been the case in Canada and Australia (where the common law is seen as unitary), substantially curbing federal court jurisdiction in both countries. It may be, of course, that the European Union will never face these questions, and its present judiciary appears to be federalized only at the summit, the jurisdiction of the court of first instance being limited to claims against community institutions. If the movement is towards federalism, however, the question of the existence of a European federal common law might well be put, as

[193] It is true that the Federal Code was enacted primarily for the Federal District of Mexico. See *Codigo civil para el Distrito Federal, en material comun, y para toda la Republica en materia federal.*

[194] *Swift* v. *Tyson*, 41 U.S. (16 Pet.)1 (1842), notably at 11 ('Because we have used the terms, have we thereby appropriated the entire common law...?').

[195] *Erie R.R. Co.* v. *Tompkins*, 304 U.S. 64 (1938).

[196] *Erie*, supra, note 195, at 78 ('There is no federal general common law', per Brandeis J.). The U.S. debate was apparently driven by notions of competing sets of positive law, at the state and federal levels, but the result refuses to exacerbate the positivization of law, and common laws are tolerant of local, particular iura propria.

a means of nourishing federal court structures.[197] It should perhaps be added that one of the reasons advanced by the courts in Canada for refusing to countenance a federal common law was that it was impossible to decide which of Canada's common laws, the one originating in England or the one originating in France, it should be.[198]

Influence within the commons laws of the world

The common laws of Europe radiated out from major centres of influence in Europe, but have inevitably given rise to major development outside of Europe, now in the form of independent states within an ongoing cadre of shared common laws or iura communia. There have always been reciprocal relations between common laws and their diverse iura propria,[199] but it is now the case that common laws have become less controlled by a single source and are rather the result of multiple contributions by different sources, as legislators, judges, and jurists from different national states are influential beyond their state of origin and particularly within an ongoing, transnational common law. Jurisdictions which have originated a common law thus find they no longer enjoy a monopolistic position as source of common law; there is a tendency towards equality and partnership, though relations remain very diverse across the world. This process of re-equilibrating is a very old phenomenon, captured in the Talmudic story of the Oven of Akhnai, in which Rabbi disputes with a Heavenly Voice and God eventually replies, laughing with joy, 'My

[197] For the debate in Europe see, e.g., W. Snijders, *Building a European Contract Law; five Fallacies and two Castles in Spain* (Ius Commune Lectures on European Private Law 9) (Maastricht: Ius Commune Research School, 2003) at 13 ('It seems worthwhile to investigate the possibility of setting up a real European judiciary for European private law cases'); M. Hesselink, 'The Politics of European Contract Law: Who has an Interest in What Kind of Contract Law for Europe?' (2002) Global Jurist Frontiers, Article 3, at section 1 ('Moreover, if the EU were to adopt a similar judiciary to the US, then "federal" cases would be administered by a network of European federal courts spread all over the Union which would also reduce the power of the lower national... courts').

[198] *Quebec (City of)* v. *R.* (1894) 24 S.C.R. 420, notably at 428; for rejection of a federal common law in Canada, *North Shore Paper Co.* v. *Canadian Pacific Ltd.* (1976), [1977] 2 S.C.R. 1054, 71 D.L.R. (3d) 111; J.-M. Brisson, 'Le Code civil, droit commun?' in *Le Nouveau Code civil: interprétation et application* (Les Journées Maximilien-Caron 1992) (Montréal: Editions Thémis, 1993) 295, notably at 298 ('il ne peut donc pas y avoir, en droit privé, de droit commun fédéral sans texte').

[199] See Ch. 1, supra, *The ius commune, as prototype* (for incorporation of elements of iura propria into the ius commune) and Roman Law and Roman Universality (for even Roman law, not conceived as a common law, being affected by content of local laws).

children have defeated me. My children have defeated me.'[200] Post-colonial theorists today conclude that 'the balance of power is slowly changing... along with [a] shift from formal to informal empire.'[201] So there is here really no possibility of declaring winners and losers but only understanding slow shifts in influence over time, as sources of law gain, and eventually decline, at least in some measure, in influence.

The process of growth of influence within ongoing common laws is best evidenced by the increasing role which the law of the United States (drawn from many common laws) has played in the world. There has been discussion of 'reception' of U.S. law in Europe and, at least in discussion, of the U.S. as the 'Mother Law' ('*Mutterrecht*') of the contemporary law of products liability.[202] The influence of U.S. law is unquestionable, and itself demonstrates that the operation of common law is not inevitably unidirectional. The real question, forever unanswerable, is whether U.S. law exercises an influence proportionate to the economic and political significance of the U.S. in the world.[203] U.S. influence extends across all of the different European common laws, in both public and private law, but the same phenomenon of reciprocal or returning influence is evident within the cadre of each of the common laws. It has been said recently by a senior Commonwealth judge that 'the common law of England is becoming gradually less English,' notably because of Commonwealth and U.S. influences.[204] The Commonwealth influence is evident not only in

200 Baza Metzia 59a–b.

201 R. Young, *Postcolonialism: A Very Short Introduction* (Oxford: Oxford Univ. Press, 2003) at 2.

202 W. Wiegand, 'The Reception of American Law in Europe' (1991) 39 Am. J. Comp. L. 229; D. Tamm, *Roman Law and European Legal History* (Copenhagen: DJØF, 1997) at 264 (for influence in commercial contracts of leasing, factoring, franchising); and for influence of U.S. law on English law and the Commonwealth, Elkind, supra, note 180 (in areas of public law, race relations, consumer protection, product liability, restitution, company law, divorce law). For a general assessment, U. Mattei, 'Why the Wind Changed: Intellectual Leadership in Western Law' (1994) 42 Am. J. Comp. L. 195, with further refs; and for the House of Lords use of U.S. case law in matters of liability for asbestos (along with Roman, German, Canadian, French, and Australian material), *Fairchild* v. *Glenhaven Funeral Services Ltd.* [2003] 1 A.C. 32. 'American common law' was also received in U.S. colonies in the South Pacific; M. Ntumy (ed.), *South Pacific Islands Legal Systems* (Honolulu: Univ. of Hawaii Press, 1993) at 105, 470.

203 See, e.g., D. A. Westbrook, 'Corporation Law after Enron: The Possibility of a Capitalist Reimagination' (2003) 92 Georgetown L. J. 61 at 127 ('It is not clear that [U.S.] academic corporation law has had much influence on the institutions of the corporation in the United States or worldwide'); M. Langer, 'From Legal Transplants to Legal Translations: The Globalization of Plea Bargaining and the Americanization Thesis in Criminal Procedure' (2004) 45 Harv. Int. L. J. 1, notably at 3 ('strong thesis' of Americanization not supportable, because of 'structural differences', 'differing legal culture[s],' with refs).

204 R. Cooke, 'The Road Ahead for the Common Law' (2004) 53 I.C.L.Q. 273 at 274.

case law in England but also, though less frequently, in legislation.[205] Common law thus circulates from an originating jurisdiction, and back, but also amongst the original receiving jurisdictions. So the courts of Western Samoa, which have received 'English law,' now see it as a 'type of law' and use New Zealand precedent as well as English.[206] Nineteenth-century belief in closed national judicial hierarchies brought about a number of refusals in the Commonwealth to hear citation of U.S. material, but the refusals were neither consistent nor ultimately to prevail.[207] Nearly a century ago Indian courts had indicated a willingness to follow U.S. authority rather than English;[208] citation of U.S. decisions amounted to some 25 per cent of the decisions cited to the Supreme Court of Canada during the first years of its existence, though there were later restrictions, since abandoned;[209] Australia and New Zealand are open to both Commonwealth and U.S. case law.[210] There is also a phenomenon of circulation of legislative models.[211]

Amongst the civilian common laws, there is a similar phenomenon of influence back (to an originating jurisdiction) and across (to other receiving jurisdictions). U.S. influence counts here again, as it returns re-worked civil law to civilian jurisdictions. Swiss and Austrian codifications prior to the *BGB* influenced its drafting.[212] Within the European Union there is a constant assessment of different national traditions in the work of the European courts, and through them in the work of the

[205] For recent House of Lords citation of decisions of the Supreme Court of Canada, *Lister* v. *Hesley Hall Ltd.* [2002] 1 A.C. 215; *R.* v. *A.* [2002] 1 A.C. 45; and for English legislation following that of New Zealand in matters of family maintenance of testators, Matson, supra, note 34, at 759.

[206] Ntumy, supra, note 202, at xxi.

[207] See, for example, *Re Missouri Steamship Co.* (1889) 42 Ch. D. 321 at 330 ('The practice . . . of quoting American decisions as authorities . . . is wrong,' per Lord Halsbury). For the Judicial Committee of the Privy Council discouraging reference to U. S. constitutional law as a means of interpretation of the Canadian constitution, *Bank of Toronto* v. *Lambe* (1887) 12 App. Cas. 575 at 587 ('It is quite impossible to argue from the one case to the other,' per Lord Hobhouse).

[208] *Ramratan Kapali* v. *Aswini Kumar Dutt* (1910) 1 L.R. 37 Cal. 559 (joint tortfeasors), as cited in Matson, supra, note 34, at 761–2.

[209] J. M. MacIntyre, 'The Use of American Cases in Canadian Courts' (1966) U.B.C. L. Rev. 478 at 486; Glenn, supra, note 80, at 290–2.

[210] See generally Karsten, supra, note 68, at 449–51 (though also noting skill in 'distinguishing, obfuscating and selectively citing'); P. Finn, *The Common Law in the World: the Australian Experience* (Rome: Centro di studi e ricerche di diritto comparato e straniero, Saggi, Conferenze e Seminari, 43, 2000) at 8, 9.

[211] Ram, supra, note 86, at 33 (for Malaysia); Matson, supra, note 34, at 758; J. Finn, 'Australasian Law and Canadian Statutes in the Nineteenth Century: A Study of the Movement of Colonial Legislation Between Jurisdictions' (2002) 25 Dal. L. J. 169.

[212] E. Bucher, 'Die Entwicklung des deutschen Schuldrechts im 19. Jahrhundert und die Schweiz' ZEuP 2003.353 at 373.

national courts.[213] In spite of reticence in the citing of other than national legislation, the courts of the continent make widespread use of comparative authority in the course of pleadings and in their internal deliberations.[214] The Louisiana codification had great influence in countries in Latin America and, by way of return, in Spain and Europe.[215] There is speculation in France on the influence of the world's new codifications on the French Civil Code.[216]

The mutual influence which occurs within common laws, however, is a variant of a larger process of mutual influence which takes place between common laws, and to this large theme it is now appropriate to turn.

213 For increasing exchange of legal information in the context of the EU, Kramer, supra, note 143, at 370.

214 See generally the continental reports in G. Canivet, M. Andenas, and D. Fairgrieve, *Comparative Law before the Courts* (London: British Institute of International and Comparative Law, 2004); and for France, R. Legeais, 'L'utilisation du droit comparé par les tribunaux—Rapport français' in U. Drobnig and S. van Erp, *The Use of Comparative Law by Courts* (The Hague/London/Boston: International Academy of Comparative Law/Kluwer Law International, 1999) 113 at 121; M. Lasser, 'Judicial (Self-) Portraits: Judicial Discourse in the French Legal System' (1995) 104 Yale L. J. 1325 at 1370.

215 S. Herman, 'Louisiana's Contribution to the 1852 Projet of the Spanish Civil Code' (1982) 42 La. L. Rev. 1509; R. Knütel, 'Influences of the Louisiana Civil Code in Latin America' (1996) 70 Tul. L. Rev. 1445; and for French attention to the new Quebec Civil Code, R. Cabrillac, 'Le nouveau code civil du Québec' D. 1993.I.267.

216 C. Witz, 'L'influence des codifications nouvelles sur le Code civil de demain' in *Le Code civil 1804–2004, Livre du Bicentenaire* (Paris : Dalloz-Jurisclasseur, 2004) 687.

3

ON THE RELATIONS OF COMMON LAWS

The two preceding chapters have been concerned with the relations between common laws and the particular laws which they encountered. In an era of state laws, this subject was neglected, since attention tended to be directed to the development of the particular laws of the states, the iura propria. There was corresponding further neglect of the relations between common laws themselves. As has been seen, common law was perceived in singular form ('the' common law, 'the' ius commune, etc.)[1] and essentially as a source for state law. Relations between common laws were perceived, to the extent they were perceived at all, in static form and in terms of differences or similarities of legal 'families,' relevant primarily for purposes of taxonomic categorization of national legal systems. This scientific or academic activity, which borrowed heavily from notions of the physical sciences, played no role in legal practice and only a very minor role in legal education. It is the object of contemporary criticism.[2] It is true that the relations between common laws diminished greatly during the period of state construction, since all of the relational common laws were engaged in a large process of self-effacement, at least in Europe. In their transnational forms, however, they never disappeared or died, and there was an ongoing dynamic in their relations. This has now become more evident with the acceleration of contemporary communication and the decline in the importance of individual state structures.

The relations between common laws and particular laws may already tell us a great deal about the relations between common laws. Since common laws are tolerant of particular laws it should follow that they are tolerant of other common laws as well. There should notably be nothing about any common law which would prevent the emergence of other common laws,

[1] Supra, Preface.

[2] J. Husa, 'Classification of Legal Families Today: Is it Time for a Memorial Hymn?' Rev. int. dr. comp. 2004.11.

since this might well be the result of a process of growth, and eventual expansion, of what was seen initially as a particular law. The ius commune originating in Italy would thus have been no obstacle to the emergence of the common law originating in England, and may even have assisted in the process of its development. Nor would the common law have been an obstacle to the emergence of the ius commune. Since common laws do contain information, but declare none of it as obligatory or binding, they are sources of information for other common laws as well as for particular laws. So the relations between common laws would be best conceived in terms of exchange of information and not as anything more sinister. A common law in itself is not aggressive.[3] Where it is used for aggressive purposes, in a binding or imperialistic way, those who use it appropriate it for their own purposes. In converting relational common law into a unum ius, it is not simply other laws, particular or common, which may be affected, but the individual common law of which use is made, since its fundamental relational character is thereby denied. If sufficiently aggressive use is made of it, it may be seen as having expired entirely, as was the case for the ius commune in nineteenth- and twentieth-century Europe.

To the extent there is exchange of needed information between common laws, their relations would thus best be seen as those of interdependence. The information they contain is of high value, which is why they have obtained the status of common laws, but necessarily incomplete, since it is derived from particular historical circumstance. Common laws are thus identifiable, as are their adherents in the form of particular communities, but there are no precise boundaries to their identity. Relational common laws define themselves *in relation to* other, particular bodies of law; they have no obligatory content; there is a constant dynamic in their relations with particular laws. The same characteristics must hold for relations with other common laws, except that here the self-effacement would be mutual. Persuasion would be the only means of implementation of relational common law.

Since the historical record indicates a multiplicity of common laws in Europe, and the world, there must be at least some record of their relations, as common laws. And since the common laws of Europe have been present everywhere in the world, they have had relations with other major legal traditions which cannot be seen simply as iura propria. All of this bears examination, however briefly.

[3] Cf. N. Rouland, *Introduction historique au droit* (Paris: P.U.F., 1998) at 268 who speaks of Roman law as 'juridical armature,' though this would be for forces of centralization and state construction.

The common law and the ius commune

The common law originating in England and the ius commune originating in Italy are today the two most well-known common laws in the world, if only because they have retained their original designation. They may also have been the most influential of the common laws, though there is of course no means of measuring such influence. As very influential bodies of law, initially within a single continent, it was inevitable that relations would develop between them, whether this was considered desirable or not. There is even a substantial body of literature on the subject, which is not the case for all of the relations amongst common laws. Yet an important contributor to the literature has recently expressed his 'dissatisfaction with the lack of agreed results,' pointing out that some have 'emphasized and perhaps exaggerated the extent of the influence . . . Others have done the reverse. There is no agreement.'[4] There does appear to be reason for dissatisfaction with the debate, since it appears to be driven very largely by modern and recent ideas which conceive of laws as commands, or as systems, or as means of territorial aggrandizement, or as being themselves somehow in 'conflict' or in 'competition' with one another. There is here as well a reflection of ideas of the physical sciences, and notions of competing and reciprocally aggressive natural systems.[5] To the extent that relational common laws are mutually self-effacing, however, these ideas are here misplaced. It is possible, moreover, to discuss the reciprocal relations of common laws in non-aggressive terms, in asking, for example, when and for what reasons collaboration has occurred, and when and for what reasons it has not occurred. The discussion would assume a basic condition of interdependence, as well as ongoing relations between essentially equal participants in a very large process which is controllable by no one, anywhere.

Most if not all of the literature on the relations between the common law originating in England and the ius commune originating in Italy is in terms of the influence of the latter upon the former. This in itself is interesting, since influence in the other direction, or its absence, could be

[4] R. H. Helmholz, *The* Ius Commune *in England: Four Studies* (Oxford: Oxford Univ. Press, 2001) at 6, 7.

[5] See, for the idea that in confrontation of biological systems, it is the richest in information which will prevail, R. Margalef, *Perspectives in Ecological Theory* (Chicago: Univ. of Chicago Press, 1968) at 16–17.

just as instructive in terms of the relations of the common laws. Some attention will have to be given to it.[6] If one examines the literature, however, it soon becomes evident why there are grounds for dissatisfaction in the concentration on influence of the ius commune on the common law. Some authors, not necessarily English, have been remarkably negative, exhibiting what has been described as an 'enemy theory' towards the ius commune.[7] The most developed position in this regard has been that of J. G. A. Pocock, in his *Ancient Constitution*, in which the notion of an ancient and indigenous common law is given mythical proportions, largely through the existence of an insular, even deliberately ignorant, 'common law mind.'[8] The limitations of English thought would have arisen from its having been 'compelled to contemplate the national past through one system of law alone' and while other laws within England could be acknowledged they were best regarded as 'systems borrowed from abroad and confined within limits by the common law.'[9] The argument flies in the face of the historical multiplicity of laws within the British Isles and the nature of a relational common law, and Pocock has subsequently withdrawn from this position in some measure.[10] There have been similar views expressed, however, by continental legal historians. André Gouron has written of the 'originality of the English school' in raising a 'non-Roman ensemble' to the highest rank of sources of law;[11] Raoul van Caenegem has written of the common law

[6] Infra, this section.

[7] D. Seipp, 'The Reception of Canon Law and Civil Law in the Common Law Courts before 1600' (1993) 13 O.J.L.S. 388 at 389, with further examples of hostility shown in different historical treatments of common law lawyers.

[8] J. G. A. Pocock, *The Ancient Constitution and the Feudal Law—A Study of English Historical Thought in the Seventeenth Century: A Reissue with a Retrospect* (Cambridge, Cambridge Univ. Press, 1987), notably at 264, on the 'common law mind (I shall not readily be persuaded that there was no such thing).' For a more recent echo, P. Legrand, 'European Legal Systems are not Converging' (1996) 45 I.C.L.Q. 52, notably at 63 ('the common law *mentalité* is not only different but is actually *irreducibly* different'). On the non-mythical character of pre-Conquest English law, however, Wormald, supra, Ch. 1, *A common lex non scripta?*; and for the absence even of the idea of legal systems in the period discussed by Pocock, in spite of his use of the concept, supra, Ch. 2, *A common, pan-European process of appropriation*.

[9] Pocock, supra, note 8, at 30, and see at 58 on English 'ignorance of any law but their own' and at 63 to effect that 'Civil law was an exotic; Scots law too little unified and articulate for the purpose; Irish law the product of a wild and uncomprehended society.'

[10] Pocock, supra, note 8, at 281, in the *Retrospect*, that he had not 'contended that common lawyers knew no civil law . . . but that they were not obliged to compare the two in such a way as to duplicate the French realization that civil and customary law had been agencies in one another's history.' On active forms of comparison within English law, however, see infra this and the next section.

[11] A. Gouron, *Droit et coutume en France aux XIIe et XIIIe siècles* (Aldershot: Variorum, 1993) at 128.

as 'essentially autochthonous';[12] Norbert Rouland excludes the common law from discussion of European common laws (in the plural) because of its very different characteristics, 'even if one cannot deny to England the quality of a European nation.'[13] The English judiciary has also not been unsympathetic to the idea of a local product.[14]

Yet there is no lack of support for a radically opposed conclusion which would see the common law as simply a local law under a broad umbrella of the ius commune, which would thereby have brought about a type of legal unity to Western Europe. This view is best represented by those who present the common law, often with little historical justification, as a unum ius or simple uniform decree, in the Roman manner, within England. It has already been noted how this denial of the relational character of the common law deprives it of its most fundamental characteristic, converting it automatically into local jurisprudence incapable of wider influence.[15]

Between these two extreme points of view, of the common law as entirely autochthonous or entirely overshadowed, there is much distinguished research in particular fields of law which tracks the extent of influence and which is more, or less, coloured by this dichotomous and assertive view of the question. If one attempts to set aside the conclusory views and simply appreciate the form and manner of influence, it seems clear enough that the common law has been influenced in major ways by the ius commune. Already in the thirteenth and fourteenth centuries the writing of Glanvill and Bracton followed obvious Roman models, and there has been a persistent recurrence of Roman doctrinal structures in English legal writing thereafter.[16] There has been obvious influence in particular fields of law, notably with respect to obligations,

[12] R. C. van Caenegem, *The Birth of the English Common Law*, 2nd ed. (Cambridge, Cambridge Univ. Press, 1988) at 91.

[13] Rouland, supra, note 3, at 258.

[14] Lord Bingham of Cornhill, 'A New Common Law for Europe' in B. Markesinis, *The Clifford Chance Millenium Lectures: The Coming Together of the Common Law and the Civil Law* (Oxford/ Portland OR: Hart, 2000) 27 at 27 (though tempting 'to yearn for a golden age . . . when the ius commune prevailed throughout western Christendom, such yearning has a tenuous historical foundation . . . England from an early date developed its own judge made and largely indigenous common law').

[15] Supra, Ch. 1, *The common law, as common law.*

[16] T. E. Scrutton, *The Influence of the Roman Law on the Law of England* (Cambridge: Cambridge Univ. Press, 1885), notably at 92; C. Güterbock, *Bracton and his Relation to the Roman Law: A Contribution to the History of the Roman Law in the Middle Ages*, transl. Brinton Coxe, (Littleton, CO: Fred B. Rothman & Co., 1979); C. Donahue, Jr., 'Ius Commune, Canon Law, and Common Law in England' (1992) 66 Tul. L. Rev. 1745 at 1751–3, and 1763 (on deriving influence from non-universal character of Roman models); P. Brand, *The Making of the Common Law* (London/Rio Grande: The Hambledon Press, 1992) at 73; P. Stein, *Roman Law in European History* (Cambridge: Cambridge Univ. Press, 1999) at 64; D. J. Ibbetson, *A Historical Introduction to the Law of Obligations* (Oxford: Oxford Univ. Press, 1999) at 16–19, 74–5. For Blackstone, J. W. Cairns, 'Blackstone, an English Institutist: Legal Literature

bailment, easements and servitudes, wills, water rights, and legislative interpretation.[17] Much work has also been done tracking the means of acquisition by common law lawyers of knowledge of law other than their own and the techniques of its deployment by them.[18] The process of exchange of information continued, moreover, through the nineteenth-century period of nationalization of law.[19] There has also been a major shift in common law institutions and a re-alignment of them in a way largely compatible with continental institutions. In the nineteenth-century the common law thus abandoned its forms of action, accepted the necessity of substantive law, and instituted a Court of Appeal.[20]

and the Rise of the Nation State' (1984) 4 O.J.L.S. 318; and for the general pattern of doctrinal influence, D. Ibbetson, *Common Law and* Ius Commune (London: Selden Society, 2001) at 13–14; J. Gordley, 'The Common Law in the Twentieth Century: Some Unfinished Business' (2000) 88 Cal. L. Rev. 1817 at 1821; R. Zimmermann, 'Der europäische Charakter des englischen Rechts' ZEuP 1993.4 at 10–19. Most recently, P. Birks (ed.), *English Private Law* (Oxford: Oxford Univ. Press, 2000) at xxxvi ('The five-part structure is based on a threefold division of private law . . . The essentials are simple . . . Continental lawyers will recognize them as derived from the same Roman root as their civil codes').

[17] For obligations, Ibbetson (1999), supra, note 16, J. Gordley, *The Philosophical Origins of Modern Contract Doctrine* (Oxford: Clarendon Press, 1991), Donahue, supra, note 16 at 1764 ff; bailment, M. Graziadei, 'Changing Images of the Law in XIX Century English Legal Thought (The Continental Impulse)' in M. Reimann (ed.), *The Reception of Continental Ideas in the Common Law World 1820–1920* (Berlin: Duncker & Humblot, 1993) 114 at 135 ff; easements and servitudes, O. W. Holmes, Jr. *The Common Law* (Boston: Little, Brown and Company, 1881) at 366–7, H. P. Glenn, 'Le droit romain de la propriété et le droit anglais' in E. Hermon (ed.) La question agraire à Rome: Droit romain et société, Biblioteca di Athenaeum, vol. 44 (Como, Italy: Edizioni New Press, 1999) 133; wills, R. H. Helmholz, 'Der Usus Modernus Pandectarum und die Ursprünge des eigenhändigen Testaments in England' ZEuP 1995.769; water, J. Getzler, *A History of Water Rights at Common Law* (Oxford: Oxford Univ. Press, 2004), notably at 65, 98 ('not unusual . . . for common lawyers to borrow directly . . . without openly avowing their intellectual debts') and with bibliography on general influence of Roman law, also at 98; legislative interpretation, S. Vogenauer, Die Auslegung von Gesetzen in England und auf dem Kontinent (Tübingen: Mohr Siebeck, 2001) (also raising the interesting question of the extent to which attitudes towards legislation, a source of the iura propria, is conditioned generally by the nature of a relational common law).

[18] Seipp, supra, note 7, notably at 390–1 (200 cases citing ius commune over period 1300–1600), 406 (learning through personal contact with 'the doctors'), 420 ('channels of influence were open'); J. L. Barton, 'Roman Law in England' (1971) Pars V, 13a, Ius romanum medii aevi 3, at 96 ('a mistake to regard the common lawyers as totally ignorant of the other systems. They saw something of the work of the ecclesiastical courts in the ordinary course of practice, and many of them pleaded on occasion before the Chancellor'); Helmholz, supra, note 4, at 74 (consulting of ius commune by common law lawyers in matters of sanctuary); R. H. Helmholz, 'Magna Carta and the ius commune' (1999) 66 U. Chicago L. Rev. 297 at 359; and for increasing numbers of university educated (in civil law) members of the Bar, Ibbetson (2001), supra, note 16, at 11; D. Lemmings, *Professors of the Law: Barristers and English Legal Culture in the Eighteenth Century* (Oxford: Oxford Univ. Press, 2000) at 113, 118.

[19] M. Reimann (ed.), *The Reception of Continental Ideas in the Common Law World 1820–1920* (Berlin: Duncker & Humblot, 1993), passim, and notably, for English law, Graziadei, supra, note 17.

[20] H. P. Glenn, 'La civilisation de la common law' Rev. int. dr. comp. 1993.596, English version in A. Rabello (ed.), *Essays on European Law and Israel* (Jerusalem: Sacher Institute, 1996) 65, though

The pattern of influence from ius commune to common law is thus consistent with the notion of relational common laws, and inevitable exchange of information between them. What of influence of the common law on the development of the ius commune? The subject has received 'little academic attention'[21] but there must be reasons for this. The common law was 'an anomaly, a freak in the history of western civilization because it was modernized earlier,'[22] so it must have provided an example of how an (early) modern law could develop. Why would its influence on the ius commune have been reduced? The answer must lie in questions of relative need and compatibility of solutions. It has already been observed that the common law and the ius commune, in their early forms, were particular exemplars of a common genus of relational common law, but that there were important differences between them.[23] The common law was a law of writs, of remedies, of limited access to an extremely small number of ambulatory, non-resident judges, with the jury acting as final, decision-making authority on the substance of the case. None of this was compatible with the underlying structures which the ius commune took for granted. Both the unwritten law of the European continent, and the learned law of the ius commune, assumed open adjudicative structures in which some notion of substantive law could be directly applied to established circumstances by an adjudicative authority master of both law and factual allegations. The case load was immense, the judiciary vast. The formulary procedure of Roman law, said by Pringsheim to establish an 'inner relationship'[24] between English and Roman law, had long since been abandoned. There could be no borrowing by the ius commune from the common law without fundamental challenge to the basic institutions and assumptions of the entire tradition. Large numbers of judges (who in large measure owned their offices) would have to be eliminated; those who remained would have to be persuaded to go on circuit, by horse; authors would see their massive and skillful commentaries on the substance of private law converted to historical artifacts; the emerging University teaching of law would be shut down. It was not simply a

warning at 65 that paper 'presupposes no stable states of legal traditions; no process of movement directly from one fixed state to another; and no criteria for establishing relative states of advancement, or progess,' proposing only 'to describe a slow, informal process by which the common law tradition has begun to share major components of the civil law tradition,' and indicating that '[t]he process is complex . . . and not at all one-way.'

[21] Donahue, supra, note 16, at 1768, remarking that 'I can hear some of you saying that the topic does not exist.'

[22] Van Caenegem, supra, note 12, at 105.

[23] Supra, Ch. 1, *The common law, as common law.*

[24] F. Pringsheim, 'The Inner Relationship Between English and Roman Law' (1935) 5 Camb. L. J. 347.

different vocabulary and a different set of legal ideas which distinguished the common law from the ius commune, but an entirely different understanding of the role of law and legal institutions. The two were not incommensurable. Lawyers from each could understand the other. The two were, however, largely incompatible at a basic level.[25] This did not prevent common law lawyers from flirting with the concepts of the ius commune, since this could be done at a conceptual level with no implicit challenge to existing institutions. Citations of the ius commune by common law lawyers may thus well have been 'ornamental make-weights' and the use of civilian learning to define legal concepts 'only marginally less pointless.'[26] Use of the common law by civilians would not have been ornamental; it would have been unthinkable.

In spite of these basic problems of exchange, however, the common law does not appear to have been uninfluential at a European level. The influence does not appear to have been in the highly visible books, in Latin, of substantive law. It would have rather occurred where it was institutionally possible, and even desirable, in terms of either geography or institutional need. The institutions of the ius commune would thus have been subtly modified, in England, in the courts in which it was applied in England.[27] Much more significantly, the common law would have seen one of its most important instruments taken up on the continent, as a necessary element of modern law. Roman law had no case reports; nor had the European 'common lex non scripta.'[28] Yet the common law early in its history had introduced parchment records, in roll form, as a means of tracking judicial activity.[29] They may have been derived from 'Arab practice.'[30] The earliest of these plea rolls which have survived in England date from 1194, and the practice may therefore have emerged considerably earlier.[31] The Normans were also using rolls in Normandy, and the earliest known records of these date from 1180.[32] An Anglo-Norman practice of case reporting thus existed at least by the late twelfth century, though it is

[25] Following the arrival of the English in New France there were efforts to introduce a writ system into existing French institutions, with their accompanying concepts of substantive law. The efforts failed entirely; J.-M. Brisson, La formation d'un droit mixte: L'évolution de la procedure civile de 1774 à 1867 (Montreal: Thémis, 1986) and review H. P. Glenn (1987) 32 McGill L. J. 733.

[26] Ibbetson (2001), supra, note 16, at 17.

[27] Infra, this Ch., *Common laws and canon law.*

[28] Ch. 1, *A common lex non scripta?*

[29] J. Baker, *The Common Law Tradition* (London/Rio Grande: The Hambledon Press, 2000) at 133–5.

[30] M. Clanchy, *From Memory to Written Record: England 1066–1307*, 2nd ed. (Oxford: Blackwell, 1993) at 140.

[31] Baker, supra, note 29, at 134.

[32] J. Dawson, *The Oracles of the Law* (Ann Arbor: Univ. of Michigan Press, 1968) at 290.

impossible to locate its precise origin. By the second quarter of the fourteenth century reports of cases heard in the Roman Rota began to appear, kept by English members of the court and notably by one Thomas Fastolf.[33] They spread from there to all jurisdictions of the ius commune. In the result the common law practice appears to have provided that which the ius commune needed, and could tolerate.

At a very large level each of the ius commune and the common law appears to have provided to the other essential institutions or concepts, substantive law moving in some measure to the common law, case reports moving to the ius commune. The level of traffic would have been more intense in the first situation but both would have been of fundamental importance. Moreover, since the nineteenth century the incompatibility between continental and common law structures has been greatly reduced, with the result that the common law, having moved structurally closer to the model of the ius commune, will now find it more receptive to common law ideas. The thousand-year history of the relations between these interdependent relational common laws may therefore continue in a still more equilibriated manner in the future.

The common law and other continental common laws

Much of what has been said of the relations between the common law originating in England and the ius commune originating in Italy is also applicable to the relations between the common law, on the one hand, and the various common laws originating in France, Holland, Spain, and Germany. Since all of the latter, though composed of varying elements of custom, legislation, and doctrine, shared with the ius commune the basic ideas of substantive law and an open adjudicative structure, transfer of English notions of writs and forms of action was difficult if not impossible. Some English concepts did move, but in most instances this was relatively late in the development of the common law. English lawyers were able, however, to the extent that language barriers could be overcome, to experiment with these other continental ideas to the same extent they were able to do so with the ius commune.

[33] Baker, supra, note 29, at 111, 117–18; Donahue, supra, note 16, at 1771; Stein, supra, note 16, at 93.

Of course, the common laws originating in France, Germany, Holland, and Spain all developed their own forms of case reporting, so in this sense there was an early adoption, in different manners, of an Anglo-Norman common law idea. By 1600 the Parlement of Paris had developed 'a working system of case law,' which by 1750 had even 'far outstripped' in volume that which prevailed in England.[34] Other English ideas or practices which made the difficult journey across the Channel are said to include, almost always in some modified form and without prejudice to origins even beyond England, the check, mortgage of ships, the justice of the peace, the jury (at least for criminal cases, and subject to closer forms of judicial control), probation, and many specific rules of company law and maritime law.[35]

Some continental common laws were more influential in England than others. In no case, however, does it appear there was an absence of contact and exchange. The French influence on the common law was perhaps the greatest. There is a widespread though contested view that the holograph will arrived in England from French customary law.[36] Pothier was translated into English in the first decade of the nineteenth century, in both England and the U.S.A., thus traversing the language boundary. He eventually became the most cited source in English practice, next to English case law itself.[37] The Napoleonic Code was perhaps the greatest stimulus to the nineteenth-century reforms of the common law.[38] Pandectist common law became very influential in English legal thought in the late nineteenth century and following the enactment of the *BGB*. On his appointment to a chair at the University of London, John Austin immediately left for a year's study at Bonn, there to develop much of his positivist theory of English law.[39] The Dutch writers Grotius, Pufendorf,

[34] Dawson, supra, note 32, at 316, 337.

[35] M. Ancel, *Utilité et méthodes de droit comparé* (Neuchatel: Ides et Calendes, 1971) at 61; R. Rodière, 'Le renouvellement du droit commercial français par le droit comparé' in *Livre du centenaire de la Société de législation comparé* (Paris : LGDJ, 1970) 109 at 114.

[36] Helmholz, supra, note 17, at 771.

[37] *Cox v. Troy* (1822) 5 B & Ald. 474, 106 E.R. 1264 (Best J.); and see Ibbetson (1999), supra, note 16, at 154, 251.

[38] D. B. Walters, 'L'image du Code dans le contexte de la Common Law en Grande-Bretagne et dans le Commonwealth britannique,' in R. Beauthier and I. Rorive, Le Code Napoléon, un ancêtre vénéré? Mélanges Offerts à Jacques Vanderlinden (Brussels: Bruylant, 2004) 135, notably at 145 on 19th-century English legislation (Bills of Exchange, Sale of Goods, Marine Insurance) entitled. 'An Act to codify the law relating to . . .'.

[39] J. Austin, *Lectures on Jurisprudence*, 5th edn., ed. R. Campbell (New York: James Cockcroft, 1875) at vi, vii (Austin already had conceived a 'profound admiration' for great jurists of Germany).

Huber, and Voet all became well known in England, and contributed greatly to common law notions of both public and private international law, in both England and abroad. The influence of Hispanic common law in England is harder to trace, but Edward the First, the 'English Justinian', was a cousin and brother-in-law of Alfonso the Wise, whose sister he married in Castile and with whom he maintained relations for a long period of time.[40] The *Siete Partidas* would have been one of the models behind important instances of English law-making. Throughout the common law world, moreover, the writings of the Second Scholastic legal scholars de Vitoria and de las Casas have been fundamental in the formulation and recognition of land claims of chthonic peoples.[41]

The ius commune and other continental common laws

The ius commune originating from Italy was written in Latin and had influence well beyond Italy, as was seen in Chapter 1. It therefore made a substantial contribution to other European laws, but the process was very much a dynamic one, as local, reciprocal influence had its effect on the ius commune, often supplanting it with a local product, a local common law, to the development of which the ius commune had contributed.[42] Each of the relations between the ius commune and the other common laws of the continent was different, yet exchange and interaction is common to all of them.

Roman-Dutch law came about as Roman law was integrated into legal and judicial practice in Holland. The substance of it changed in this process, as did its sources, which became predominantly Dutch.[43] The Dutch 'elegant school' is often presented as somehow continuing the refinement of a single corpus of law, a pan-European ius commune,[44] but it was essentially involved in adapting the ius commune originating from Italy (which, as Calasso has reminded us, was not simply Roman law but the product of the commentators and glossators[45]) to the circumstances

[40] M. Radin, 'Introduction,' M. W. Nichols, 'Las Siete Partidas' (1932) 20 Cal. L. Rev. 260, at 261.

[41] See, e.g., P. Cumming and N. Mickenberg, *Native Rights in Canada*, 2nd edn. (Toronto: General Publishing, 1972) at 14.

[42] Supra, Ch. 1, *The ius commune, as prototype.*

[43] Supra, Ch. 2, *The identity of the common laws abroad.*

[44] D. Osler, 'The Myth of European Legal History' (1997) 16 Rechtshistorisches J. 393 at 394.

[45] Supra, Ch. 1, *The ius commune, as prototype.*

of Holland. There was thus a dynamic process by which the ius commune originating from Italy was taken note of in Holland and re-worked, with the resulting body of Dutch common law expanding both overseas to Dutch colonies and within Europe to other compatible jurisdictions. It thus had a 'lasting effect' on German Pandectist thought[46] and enjoyed great prestige in all jurisdictions of the ius commune.

In France, or more precisely in the northern part of France, the pays des coutumes, there was great resistance to the ius commune.[47] The French monarchy was also unsympathetic. By the sixteenth century a French droit commun coutumier had been developed and it had begun its expansion overseas.[48] Yet the French droit commun could not be somehow closed to the influence of the ius commune, and there appear to have been no prohibitions of its citation in the course of pleadings in the courts, as occurred elsewhere. Even Du Moulin, the great Breton nationalist, used it in his articulation of the common law of France and by the sixteenth century it was being stoutly defended in the Parlement of Paris.[49] Its influence, as written reason or *ratio scripta*, was important in the law of obligations, which had been neglected by the coutumes.[50] Yet throughout there was disagreement as to its role, the same form of disagreement which has bedeviled the historical debate on the roles of the common law and the ius commune.[51] French common law thus made use of the ius commune where it needed it, subjecting it inevitably to the same process of re-working and re-stating as occurred in Holland. The French did not seem interested in whether their view of Roman law was viewed with approval elsewhere in Europe; the debate within France was all-consuming. Yet the great French writers (Domat, Pothier) were known abroad in

[46] R. Zimmermann, 'Roman Dutch Jurisprudence and its Contribution to European Private Law' (1992) 66 Tul. L. Rev. 1685 at 1719; and further R. Zimmermann, *The Law of Obligations: Roman Foundations of the Civilian Tradition* (Cape Town: Juta, 1990) at 567 ('Grotius, Pufendorf and Wolff').

[47] J. Gaudemet, 'Les modalités de réception du droit à la lumière de l'histoire comparative' in Università degli studi di Bari, Le nuove frontiere del diritto e il problema dell'unificazione (Milano: Giuffrè, 1979) 411 at 423; V. Guizzi, 'Il diritto comune in Francia nel XVII Secolo' (1969) 37 Tijd. v. Rechtsg. 1 at 4.

[48] Supra, Ch. 2, *The droit commun originating from France, in the world.*

[49] J.-L. Thireau, *Charles du Moulin (1500–1566)* (Geneva: Librairie Droz, 1980) at 100, and 93 for the support of the Premier President of the Parlement of Paris, Pierre Lizet.

[50] For its importance, E. Chenon, Histoire générale du droit francais public et privé des origines a 1815, vol. 2 (Paris: Sirey, 1929) at 329; O. Martin, Histoire de la Coutume de la Prévôté et Vicomté de Paris, vol. I (Paris: Editions Ernest Leroux, 1922) at 59; J. Brissaud, Manuel d'histoire du droit français (Paris: A. Fontemoing, 1898) at 159; and for 18th-century defence of its status as a 'droit commun,' J. Krynen, 'Le droit romain "droit commun de la France"' (2003) 38 Droits 21.

[51] Brissaud, supra, note 50, at 157 ('On discuta jusqu'au dernier jour, sans pouvoir s'entendre'); and for the common law/ius commune debate, supra, *The common law and the ius commune.*

Europe, even across the obstacle of language.[52] As has been seen in Chapter 2, the process greatly accelerated with the French codification in 1804 when French law, with the Roman law which had been 'decanted' into it, began to serve as a relational common law for a large number of continental territories, including those of the ius commune, as well as for many jurisdictions abroad.[53]

Hispanic common law was also informed in considerable measure by the ius commune, in spite of formal measures in the fourteenth and sixteenth centuries prohibiting the citation of Italian authors, and even apparently edicting capital punishment as a sanction for doing so.[54] The *Siete Partidas*, as noted in Chapter 2, contained many Roman-derived texts in matters of procedure, obligations, and successions,[55] and Spanish lawyers continued to make extensive use of the ius commune, particularly in doctrinal writing and from the fifteenth century.[56] Hispanic common law has not been seen as reciprocally playing a large role in the 'North European' representations of the ius commune,[57] but the writers of the Second Scholastic have been seen by some as superior to (even more elegant than) the Dutch,[58] and Michel Villey credited them (or perhaps more accurately discredited them) with much of the development of the modern doctrine of rights.[59]

Pandectist common law drew heavily on the ius commune, in a way described by van Caenegem as 'massive,'[60] yet no one can dispute the enormous conceptual contribution made by the Pandectist writers, chiefly amongst them by Savigny, to the body of law developed by the Italian writers. Savigny could thus claim to write on a system of *contemporary*

[52] Thus for the place of Domat and Pothier in re-formulation of contract law in Europe, Zimmermann (1990), supra, note 46, at 566–7.

[53] Supra, Ch. 2, *The droit commun originating from France, in the world.*

[54] J. Barrientos Grandon, Historia del derecho indiano del descubrimiento colombino a la codificación, vol. I, Ius Commune—Ius Proprium *en las Indias occidentales* (Roma: Il Cigno Galileo Galilei, 2000) at 126, 136–7; G. Teipel, 'Zitiergesetze in der romanistischen Tradition' ZRG RA 72 (1955) 245 at 270; and for ongoing anti-Romanist measures into the 17th and 18th centuries, C. Petit, 'Derecho comun y derecho castellano: Notas de literatura juridica para su estudio (siglos XV–XVII)' (1982) 50 Tijd. v. Rechtsg. 157 at 190; H. Coing, *Europäisches Privatrecht*, Vol. I, *Älteres Gemeines Recht (1500 bis 1800)* (Munich: C. H. Beck, 1985) at 98.

[55] Supra, Ch. 2, *The identity of the common laws abroad.*

[56] Petit, supra, note 54, at 160 ff, 194; and for use of concepts of the ius civile in Spanish legislation, Grandon, supra, note 54, at 131.

[57] Osler, supra, note 44, at 400 ('the old nationalistic, North European, translatio-studii-Endstation-Deutschland itinerary').

[58] Osler, supra, note 44, at 398 (citing Meerman in 1751).

[59] M. Villey, La formation de la pensée juridique moderne (Paris: Montchretien, 1975) at 351 ('le rayonnement de Salamanque'), 364 (subjectivization of notion of right by Vitoria) and 381–2 (also by Suarez, contrary to *ius civile*).

[60] Supra, Ch. 1, *The ius commune, as prototype.*

Roman law,[61] but the work of the Pandectists was not only in terms of systematization but also in terms of historical reconstruction of original Roman law.[62] They thus represented a remarkable combination of historical research and contemporary sophistication. As elsewhere in Europe, there was enormous resistance to Roman influence[63] and eventually to codification, but the coming into force of the *BGB* in 1900 represented an enormous testimonial to the conceptual work which had been accomplished. As was seen in Chapter 2, the Pandectist common law has been influential around the world, and also on the ius commune from which it derived.[64]

All of the common laws of the continent thus had demonstrable relations with all of the others, and all of them had demonstrable relations with the common law. Moreover, given the inevitable inadequacy of historical records, that which is today demonstrable must be only a part of the rich process of oral and written exchange which took place, over centuries, amongst the adherents to these complex and varied forms of normativity. There were, however, other forms of common law in Europe, and abroad.

Common laws and canon law

The relations between canon law and secular law have often been seen as stormy, but the difficulties of canon law have more frequently been with royal or state laws than with relational common laws. For centuries after the origins of the Christian religion the Catholic Church was highly de-centralized, and its normative structure was fragmentary and often informal. Canon law assumed its present identity, as did the civil and common laws, in the eleventh and twelfth centuries, notably with the synthesizing work of Gratian in compiling his *Concordance of Discordant Canons*, around 1140.[65] The Church then assumed a much more distinct

[61] F. C. von Savigny, System des heutigen römischen Rechts 8 vols. (Berlin: Veit, 1840–9).

[62] Notably F. Bluhme, 'Die Ordnung der Fragmenten in der Pankektentiteln (1820) 4 ZgR 257.

[63] G. Strauss, *Law, Resistance and the State: the Opposition to Roman Law in Reformation Germany* (Princeton: Princeton Univ. Press, 1986).

[64] Supra, Ch. 2, *Pandectist common law, in the world.*

[65] For computer-assisted detective work on its origins, which were closely related to growing awareness of Roman law, A. Winroth, *The Making of Gratian's Decretum* (Cambridge: Cambridge Univ. Press, 2000), noting at 1 that Gratian 'only lawyer authoritatively known to be in Paradise.' On

and centralized identity, and Harold Berman has concluded that canon law became 'the first modern Western legal system.'[66]

Did canon law itself become a relational common law? In purporting to govern a specific institution, and in a binding manner, it would appear more appropriate to see it as a ius proprium, or as a common law only in the Roman sense of binding decree.[67] There appears to be little doubt that the Pope was recognized as having legislative authority, a major development, and that such papal legislation was regarded as binding.[68] Maitland is generally regarded as correct in affirming that this was the case for England as well as elsewhere, in spite of the opposition of Stubbs.[69] There was also Church opposition to recognition of custom. While there was inevitable flexibility in local administration, and even local legislation,[70] in Church matters the law of Rome could thus scarcely be regarded as simply suppletive, or as in any way self-effacing. Relational common laws are laws of influence, however, and not constraint, and it was entirely possible for canon law to exercise influence beyond the Church and even in matters entirely secular. The extent it would do so depended in considerable measure on the relations it would develop with other laws, both particular and common.

Within Italy the relations between the jurists of the ius commune and the jurists of the Church were initially those of mutual ignorance and

canon law generally, R. Helmholz, *The Spirit of Canon Law* (Athens, Ga.: Univ. of Georgia Press, 1996); F. Roumy, 'Corpus juris canonici' in D. Allard and S. Rials, Dictionnaire de la culture juridique (Paris: Lamy/puf, 2003) 294, notably at 297 for impetus of Justinian's Digest in 11th, 12th centuries; though for canon law already being 'the cement that held Europe together' in the early middle ages, M. Lupoi, *The Origins of the European Legal Order*, transl. A. Belton (Cambridge: Cambridge Univ. Press, 2000) at 281.

[66] H. Berman, *Law and Revolution* (Cambridge, MA: Harvard Univ. Press, 1983) at 530.

[67] See Ch. 1, *Roman law and roman universality*.

[68] C. Duggan, *Twelfth-century Decretal Collections and their importance in English history* (London: The Athlone Press, 1963) at 27; and generally R. Helmholz, *The Oxford History of the Laws of England*, vol. I, *The Canon Law and Ecclesiastical Jurisdiction from 597 to the 1640's* (Oxford: Oxford Univ. Press, 2004) at 148 ff.

[69] F. W. Maitland, 'Church, State and Decretals' in F. W. Maitland, *Roman Canon Law in the Church of England* (London: Methuen, 1898) at 51; and see C. Donahue, 'Roman Canon Law in the Medieval English Church: Stubbs vs. Maitland Re-Examined After 75 Years in the Light of Some Records from the Church Courts' (1974) 72 Mich. L. Rev. 647 at 700; W. Holdsworth, *A History of English Law*, vol. I (London: Methuen & Co., 1956) at 582, with further refs.; J. Martínez-Torrón, *Anglo-American Law and Canon Law: Canonical Roots of the Common Law Tradition* (Berlin: Duncker & Humblot, 1998) at 46–8.

[70] R. C. van Caenegem, *European Law in the Past and the Future: Unity and Diversity over Two Millennia* (Cambridge: Cambridge Univ. Press, 2002) at 140; C. R. Cheney, *The English Church and its Laws 12th–14th centuries* (London: Variorum Reprints, 1982) at 1, 194, 202; Helmholz, supra, note 68 at 161–8 on 'supplementary' character of English canonical legislation.

hostility,[71] then of growing acceptance and collaboration. In spite of obvious levels of collaboration, however, there is reason for dissatisfaction (once again) with the present state of discussion of the relations between the two laws. There are those who affirm that canon law became fused with the ius commune of Roman origin, such that both together formed a single body of law of still greater influence.[72] Others resist the fusion and insist on separation, citing distinct teaching in the universities, different sources and fields of application and even entire treatises devoted to the differences between the two.[73] There was also the non-negligible circumstance of the canon law considering itself as binding law within the Church and therefore as qualitatively different from the suppletive character of the work of the Glossators and Commentators of the Roman texts.[74]

We thus encounter here the same pressures or patterns of thought in favour of uniformity or radical separation that we encountered in the discussion of the relations between the common law and the ius commune.[75] Relations between the ius commune and canon law became so intense, however, that more fruitful efforts have been made to seize their reciprocal relations. J. A. Brundage has described the two laws as 'interdependent' and while he was referring to the practical reality of lawyers having to study them both to earn a living, the expression exactly captures the reciprocal and mutually supportive relations of common laws.[76] Lauren Benton has also referred to the 'interdependence yet separateness'

[71] F. Calasso, Introduzione al diritto comune (Milano, Giuffrè, 1970) at 58 ('scornful indifference,' no attempt to define relations between two laws); Gouron, supra, note 11, at 47–8 ('identical ignorance').

[72] See notably Calasso, supra, note 71, at 108 (ius commune not only re-worked Roman law but Roman and canon law together, and since two common laws logically inadmissible within a single order, logical to regard them as single system); G. Ermini, *Corso di diritto comune* (Milano, Giuffrè, 1989) at 31 (canon law other branch of law of 'universal monarchy'), 146–7 (union of the two laws, though each its own field of application). For both laws relying on a 'central conceptual nucleus' which was the 'very idea of imperium,' M. Bellomo, *The Common Legal Past of Europe, 1000–1800*, transl. Lydia G. Cochrane, (Washington, DC: The Catholic University of America Press, 1995) at 74; and for tendency of common law lawyers to 'lump it all' into one 'civil law,' perhaps suggesting 'paranoia about civilians lurking under every bed,' Seipp, supra, note 7, at 396.

[73] B. Paradisi, 'Notes critiques sur le problème du droit commun' Rev. hist. dr. fr. étr. 1980.423 at 431–2, asking what fusion of two could mean; P. L. Nève, '(Europäisches) Ius Commune und (nationales) Gemeines Recht: Verwechslung von Begriffen?' in G. Köbler and H. Nehlsen, *Wirkungen europäscher Rechtskultur, Festschrift für Karl Kroeschell* (Munich: C. H. Beck'sche Verlagsbuchhandlung, 1997) 871 at 877 (two laws based on different basic fundamentals). On the 'Differentiae' literature, Ermini, supra, note 72, at 148; W. Bassett, 'Canon Law and the Common Law' (1978) 29 Hastings L. J. 1383 at 1410.

[74] Supra, text accompanying notes 67–70.

[75] Supra, this Ch., *The common law and the ius commune.*

[76] J. A. Brundage, *Medieval Canon Law* (London: Longmans Ltd., 1995) at 59, 63.

of the two laws[77] and Richard Helmholz has rejected the idea of a 'battlefield' between the two, preferring to speak of both opposition and 'productive interchange.'[78] The Latin expression of the utrumque ius also captures the subtlety of these relations. Often loosely translated as 'both laws'[79] or 'the two laws,' it is more accurately thought of as referring to 'the one and the other law' or still better as 'both laws, but each thought unto themselves.' Each law is in need of the information of the other, and the ongoing exchange between them blurs but does not eliminate the sources, field of application and identity of each.

In general the ius commune, by its nature, yielded to canon law where it claimed application.[80] In some instances it is said that the canon law brought about changes to the ius commune, notably in giving greater influence to equity in the interpretation of laws (the growth of the iura propria) but also in specific areas of law such as family relations.[81] Canon law unquestionably borrowed from the ius commune, however, notably in its early stages, since Gratian explicitly endorsed its use in case of silent or incomplete canons.[82] More generally canon law would incorporate into itself laws to which it would defer, such as the secular, civil law of contract, to the extent this was put in issue in a religious forum.[83] This process of 'canonization' will also be seen with respect to other explicitly religious laws.[84]

The relations between the canon law and the ius commune are instructive in terms of the relations between canon law and other common laws. Canon law is today said to 'canonize' the laws of every country in matters of contract,[85] thus deferring to all of them and denying to itself the character of a uniform ius unum. There have also been specific instances of other continental common laws contributing directly to canon law, as in the 1917 Code of Canon Law borrowing from the

[77] L. Benton, *Law and Colonial Cultures: Legal Regimes in World History, 1400–1900* (Cambridge: Cambridge Univ. Press, 2002) at 36.

[78] R. H. Helmholz, supra, note 4, at 25.

[79] See, e.g., H. Coing, 'The Roman Law as *Ius Commune* on the Continent' (1973) 89 L.Q.R. 505 at 508.

[80] Calasso, supra, note 71, at 65; Ermini, supra, note 72, at 151–2; Coing, supra, note 54, at 104; Bassett, supra, note 73, at 1410.

[81] For equity, Coing, supra, note 54, at 41; for family law (rights of women, freedom of choice in marriage, rights of widows to remarry, marriage between slaves, duty of parents to care for children born out of wedlock), Bassett, supra, note 73, at 1410.

[82] Helmholz, supra, note 4, at 38.

[83] J. A. Conden, T. E. Green and D. E. Heintschel, *The Code of Canon Law: A Text and Commentary* (New York: Paulist Press, 1985) at 32 (Canon 22 and Commentary).

[84] Infra, this Ch., *Common laws and Talmudic law, common laws and Islamic law.*

[85] Conden et al., supra, note 83, at 38 (secular law of contract binding not only citizens but even ecclesiastical juridical persons dealing with one another).

German *BGB* the idea of a General (or introductory) Part.[86] Castilian law is also said to have been suppletive to canon law, this confirming the former as the common law of the kingdom.[87] As a suppletive common law, canon law has also contributed enormously to western legal thought beyond the Church. The list of contributions is long and impressive, and includes at least the general theory of contract, civil, and criminal procedure and both public and international law.[88]

The common law of England was a common law different from those of the continent, in its use of national judges as a primary source of the common law, and in its concentration on writs and remedies, as opposed to substantive law. This influenced its relations with canon law, but the relations were nevertheless reciprocal. Already at the time of the Norman Conquest, William I guaranteed the existence of ecclesiastical authority as well as those of the customs of the land.[89] Thereafter the relations between the judges and courts of common law and canon law have been described as those of 'restraint, tolerance, and compromise,' conflicts of jurisdiction appearing primarily as a result of self-serving individual litigants rather than as claims of allegiance or profession.[90] This should have been the case, common law and common law judges in principle yielding to claims of canonical particularity (as did the ius commune) and ecclesiastical law and judges in principle yielding to state authority.[91] They were two self-effacing, relational common laws. It was also helpful that there was much overlapping of judges between the two types of courts, though this may perhaps best be seen as an effect, and not a cause, of the harmonious underlying relations.[92]

As the ius commune influenced the common law, so did canon law, which was as present in England as elsewhere in Europe. The fields of influence correspond in large measure to those in which canon law

[86] Roumy supra, note 65, at 298 (General Part continued also into 1983 Code).

[87] Petit, supra, note 54, at 175–6.

[88] H. Coing, 'Kanonisches Recht und Ius Commune' (1985) Monumenta Iuris Canonica, Series C: Subsidia, vol. 7, 507 at 508–9.

[89] Helmholz, supra, note 68, at 108 (for William's ordinance on separate jurisdictions) and 128, 134–5 (on later and gradual emergence, by 13th century, of formal ecclesiastical courts).

[90] W. R. Jones, 'Relations of the Two Jurisdictions: Conflict and Cooperation in England during the Thirteenth and Fourteenth Centuries' in (1970) 7 Studies in Medieval & Renaissance History (Old Series), (Lincoln, Nebraska: University of Nebraska Press) 77 at 81, 87, 205.

[91] Though canon law would enquire as to compatibility of local law with divine law and reasonableness, while recognizing that canon law could be amended by custom; Helmholz, supra, note 68, at 171–2.

[92] For the nomination of ecclesiastics as royal judges in the first centuries of the common law, Holdsworth, supra, note 69, at 584.

influenced the ius commune and some have even extended the list.[93] The influence was far from pervasive, however, and even in areas of overlap of the two jurisdictions, common law courts did not simply import or automatically have resort to a more fully developed canon law.[94] Moreover, there could be no question of 'fusion' of the common law with canon law, as allegedly occurred between the ius commune and canon law. The common law, again, was different, and in large measure incompatible with the substantive bias of both the ius commune and canon law. It has already been noted, however, that it could lend what was perhaps its most fundamental idea, that of case reports, to canon law, and from there generally to continental jurisdictions.[95] As elsewhere, canon law in England also received, or 'canonized' the common law, to the extent necessary for its purposes.[96]

In one important respect the experience of the common law has been similar to that of the ius commune and the other continental common laws. In all European jurisdictions there were canonical or ecclesiastical tribunals, exercising jurisdiction over a much larger range of cases than is today the case. In all secular tribunals the law primarily applicable was the ius proprium of the place, supplemented by a common law. The secular laws tended to rigour, if not downright sclerosis. It was canon law, as a common law, which offset the rigour of the ius commune and opened the way for liberal interpretation of local legislative intent.[97] Canon law in England could not exercise the same direct influence on the substance of the common law, and in England an entire equitable jurisdiction thus developed, the Court of Chancery. Until the sixteenth century, nearly all of the Chancellors were ecclesiastics and many were bishops or archbishops. It was inevitable that canonical teaching here would have been influential, though again impossible to measure or even to demonstrate, given the state of the written records.[98] Common laws are not complete unto themselves. They require both further substance, and relief from the

[93] Bassett, supra, note 73, at 1412–3 (the theory of corporations, judicial standards of objectivity and impartiality, wills and probate, trusts, rehabilitative theories of penal law, the distinction between negligence and intentional harm); and Martínez-Torrón, supra, note 69 ('Part III: The Influence of Canon Law on the Different Areas of English Law').

[94] See, in matters of sanctuary, Helmolz, supra, note 4, at 57, 69 ('augmented and diverged . . . in ways that would have mattered to the church') 245.

[95] Supra, this Ch., *The common law and the ius commune.*

[96] *Halsbury's Laws of England*, 4th ed., vol. 14 (London: Butterworths, 1974). 'Ecclesiastical Law', para. 303, at 138 ('The ecclesiastical law which forms part of the law of England . . . consists of statute law and common law').

[97] Calasso, supra, note 71, at 172.

[98] Martínez-Torrón, supra, note 69, at 62 ff.

substance they already have. This is evident also in the fields of commercial and feudal law.

Common laws and commercial law

For about a millennium there has been debate as to the status of commercial law. Claims for its autonomy are today increasing. There are reasons for the debate, since the autonomy of commercial law has tended to vary over time, depending on its needs and those of the other laws with which it is most closely related. Like the civil and common laws, modern commercial law is usually seen as having its origins in the renaissance of the eleventh and twelfth centuries. As has been noted, the cities, with their charters and private laws (privileges), contributed greatly to this, in both intellectual and commercial life.[99] In the context of all of the common laws of Europe, commercial law thus was seen initially at most as a ius proprium, in the form of procedural privileges, written commercial law particular to given cities, or as commercial custom.[100] There was, however, great fluidity.[101] The debate centred on the autonomy of commercial law, in relation to the common laws. Some would have denied to commercial law even the status of a ius proprium, preferring to see it only as a disparate collection of still more local and fragmented rules.[102] Others defended it as a 'specialized law' as early as the thirteenth century, though admitting that it would have no standing without reference to the

[99] Supra, Ch. 1, *The essential tradition of the ius commune.*

[100] For procedural privileges (rapidity of treatment) attaching to merchants in the 10th and 11th centuries, J. Hilaire, *Introduction historique au droit commercial* (Paris: P.U.F., 1986) at 28; for urban charters and privileges, Hilaire, supra, at 25, 31 ('derogating from *droit commun* in commercial matters'); M. E. Basile, J. F. Bestor, D. R. Coquillette, and C. Donahue, Jr., Lex Mercatori *and Legal Pluralism: A Late Thirteenth-Century Treatise and its Afterlife* (Cambridge: The Ames Foundation, 1998) at 21, 47 (also 'custom of London'); L. Trakman, *The Law Merchant: The Evolution of Commercial Law* (Littleton, Col.: Fred B. Rothman, 1983) at 8; and for commercial custom, Gouron, supra, note 11 at 185 (*mos mercatorum*); E. K. Braybrooke, 'Custom as a Source of English Law' (1951) 50 Mich. L. Rev. 71 at 85 (custom of merchants received into English law was law already applied to commercial instruments in courts of continent).

[101] Basile et al., supra, note 100, at 35 (absence of any definition of market, lack of any systematic treatment of relation of courts to markets, inconsistent definitions of merchants, ambiguity of claims of reach of mercantile law and competent courts).

[102] K. Scherner, 'Lex mercatoria—Realität, Geschichtsbild oder Vision' (2001) 118 ZRG GA 148, notably at 154–6, 167 (only particular sources, idea of overarching commercial law product only of 18th century).

common law.[103] The two would have had the relations of 'mother and daughter.'[104]

Commercial law has grown greatly in importance in the world, however, since the eleventh and twelfth centuries. This has occurred largely through the weakening of the influence of the canonical prohibition of interest (a shift in loyalty away from one common law to another in the course of emergence)[105] and as a result of the growth of corporate structures. Few would today challenge the existence of commercial law as a distinct field of study, research, and practice. The recognition of this status appears to have been from the seventeenth century, and to have been evidenced both by claims to its universal or transnational character, and by a massive process of its incorporation, as a distinct subject, into national or state laws.[106] Not only common laws were susceptible to national appropriation but also iura propria. It would have thus become 'nation-wide like the common law, and yet also other to it.'[107] The mother and daughter would have become 'unfriendly sisters.'[108]

National commercial law having come into existence, it became much more possible to identify substantive commonalities (a common core)[109] and to use national law, notably its principle of freedom of contract, to construct a body of transnational commercial practices based on an appreciation of the best of local practices. This process had always existed, even extending to borrowing from Talmudic and Islamic law,[110] but it greatly accelerated in the modern world.[111] It continues to accelerate today,

[103] Basile et al., supra, note 100, at 33; and for recognition as a *ius singulare*, A. Cordes, 'Auf der Suche nach der Rechtswirklichkeit der mittelalterlichen Lex mercatoria' (2001) 118 ZRG GA 168, at 177. For 'general maritime law' as a common law, however, and from the 8th or 9th century B.C., W. Tetley, 'The General Maritime Law—The Lex Maritima (With a Brief Reference to the Ius Commune in Arbitration Law and the Conflict of Laws)' (1994) 20 Syracuse J. Int'l. L. & Com. L. 105, at 108, 109.

[104] For the expression in England, Basile, et al., supra, note 100, at 27.

[105] Hilaire, supra, note 100, at 29; and for the authorization of interest, H. P. Glenn, *Legal Traditions of the World*, 2nd ed. (Oxford: Oxford Univ. Press, 2004) at 184, note 78.

[106] For universality, Hilaire, supra, note 100, at 39 ('L'ébauche d'un système de vocation universelle'); and for incorporation, Trakman, supra, note 100, at 24–8; J. Baker, 'The Law Merchant and the Common Law Before 1700' (1979) 38 Camb. L. J. 295 at 296 (common law courts taking over business of borough and piepowder courts, through development of assumpsit).

[107] Basile et al., supra, note 100, at 24 (though lacking the institutionalized authority of canon law).

[108] Cordes, supra, note 103, at 175.

[109] For the growth of relational common law from study of substantive commonalities, supra, Ch. 1, *A common lex non scripta?, The common law (droit commun) originating from France, The common law (gemeine Recht) originating from Germany.*

[110] Glenn, supra, note 105, at 119, 225, 232.

[111] For cross-European influences on French law, Hilaire, supra, note 100, at 40–2 (Italian, Dutch, English); and on English law, notably from Italian mercantile law as early as the 15th century,

and many affirm that there is today a *lex mercatoria* which transcends the law of individual cities, states, and regions to constitute a contemporary common law of international trade.[112] This would be composed not simply of rules of international law applicable to trade, as is sometimes mooted,[113] but of the ensemble of principles and rules which effectively governs the transnational commercial practices of individuals and firms, placing national commercial law already in a residual category.[114] Moreover, this contemporary transnational commercial law would be clearly suppletive in character, yielding notably to imperative national law where this would intrude into transnational practice.[115] From fragmented local practice, through a status of jus proprium and eventual discovery of substantive commonalities, commercial law would have reached the status of a relational common law, in its particular field.

Common laws and feudal law

Few people in today's world occupy themselves with the intricacies of feudal law, with the exception perhaps of first-year law students in jurisdictions of unreformed common law. They know it as an intellectual challenge, and worse. Yet it seems unquestionably the case, in the common law tradition, that feudal law is part of the common law. One does not own land in the common law, one holds a fee simple, and the language of a fee, or fief, or feudorum, dates in England from the time of the Norman Conquest. At the time of the Conquest 'every acre of land' was

T. F. T. Plucknett, *A Concise History of the Common Law*, 5th ed. (London: Butterworth & Co., 1956) at 663.

[112] For theoretical justification, R. Goode, 'Usage and its Reception in Transnational Commercial Law' (1997) 46 I.C.L.Q. 1; R. Goode, *Commercial Law in the Next Millenium* (London: Sweet & Maxwell, 1998); H. P. Glenn, 'A Transnational Concept of Law' in P. Cane and M. Tushnet (eds.), *The Oxford Handbook of Legal Studies* (Oxford: Oxford Univ. Press, 2003) 839 at 854–5. Classic modern articles include C. Schmitthoff, 'International Business Law: A New Law Merchant' (1961) 2 Current L. & Soc. Probs. 129; B. Goldman, 'La lex mercatoria dans les contrats et l'arbitrage international: réalités et perspectives' J. dr. int., 1979.475; and for transnational commercial law as a 'droit de synthèse,' M. Salah, *Les contradictions du droit mondialisé* (Paris: Presses Universitaires de France, 2000) at 90.

[113] See, e.g., J. H. Weiler, *The EU, the WTO and the NAFTA: Towards a Common Law of International Trade* (Oxford: Oxford Univ. Press, 2000).

[114] For its content, J. Dalhuisen, *Dalhuisen on International Commercial, Financial and Trade Law* (Oxford and Portland, OR: Hart Publishing, 2000)(also at 6 for national law only of residual application); and for a transnational law database, <www.tldb.de>.

[115] Trakman, supra, note 100, at 20–1, for cosmopolitan, suppletive character.

brought within the scope of feudal tenure and England became 'the most perfectly feudalized' of lands.[116] As a law of writs and remedies, however, the common law could be seen as lacking any notion of a substantive law of property which could actually explain entitlements to land. So the common law courts simply incorporated into the common law all of the feudal practices which had grown up, as a matter of royal grant, legislation, custom, and seigneurial jurisprudence. They did add to it, in the form of a possessory remedy (novel disseisin) but in general feudal law became 'just the common law,' in the language of Pollock and Maitland.[117] The same observation may be largely true for France, where the droit commun was essentially of customary derivation.

A sharper distinction was made in the jurisdictions of the ius commune, where the Pandects in principle included (already) everything, including a Roman-derived law of property quite distinct from feudal notions of land-holding. Roman notions were eventually the most persuasive on the continent (though there is ongoing debate about the loss of the trust), but were quite inadequate in terms of existing enjoyment of land from the eleventh century.[118] The Langobards appear to have been the first to set down their forms of land-holding, in the early twelfth century, in a private collection describing the various fees or fiefs of the north of Italy, the *Libri feodorum*. By the end of the century the civilians had 'calmly incorporated' it into the fifth volume of the Corpus iuris, where it essentially remained, now a suppletive and 'ideal' feudal law, until the nineteenth century.[119] Its influence extended to the north of Europe, less to the west and south, so that what was initially clearly a 'special' or particular law became largely integrated into the ius commune.[120] It never

[116] F. Pollock and F. W. Maitland, *The History of English Law*, vol. I, 2nd ed. (Cambridge: Cambridge Univ. Press, 1968) at 235. [117] Supra, note 116, at 235–6.

[118] For the transition, and the emergence of the trust, H. P. Glenn, 'The Historical Origins of the Trust' in A. Rabello (ed.), *Aequitas and Equity: Equity in Civil Law and Mixed Jurisdictions* (Jerusalem: Sacher Institute, 1997) 749; and for the inadequacy of the Roman tradition in medieval land law, M. Ryan, 'Ius Commune Feudorum in the Thirteenth Century' in A. Romano (ed.), . . . Collendo iustitian et iura condendo . . . *Federico II Legislatore del Regio de Sicilia nell'Europa del Deucento. Per una storia comparata delle codificazione europee* (Rome: Edizione de Luca, 1997) 51 at 52 ('for obvious reasons silent about vassals and fiefs'); F. Wieacker, *A History of Private Law in Europe*, trans. T. Weir (Oxford: Clarendon Press, 1995) at 185 (feudal character of land-holding 'prevented the Roman law of ownership, despite its superficial presence, from actually being applied').

[119] For incorporation, Stein, supra, note 16, at 61; for survival, H. Lange, *Römisches Recht im Mittelalter*, vol. I, *Die Glossatoren* (Munich: C. H. Beck'sche Verlagsbuchhandlung, 1997) at 89, 90; and for the construction by the glossators of an 'ideal fief', Ryan, supra, note 118 at 62.

[120] For the Lombard feudal law, supra, Ch. 1, *Other common laws of Europe*; Ryan, supra, note 118 at 54–5, citing Accursius, and 63–4 (for expansion northward as ius commune); Coing, supra, note 54, at 36.

became, however, 'just the common law' and while serving as a 'general law for particular territories' was still described as a ius speciale in relation to the Roman-derived texts.[121] It was national legislation which turned attention to the Roman concepts of property. The relations between the two laws were largely harmonious.

Harmony in the relations of common laws would be challenged, however, by their close proximity in a particular territory.

Territories at the confluence of common laws

In the flow of populations, common laws were those which moved or expanded from given territories into others. Territory was not an essential element for common laws, however, since they tended to float, claiming no mandatory application in a particular place. That was the role of the iura propria, which expressed particular, local needs, which had to be met, such that the iura propria did not float but rather bound (or at least claimed imperative application). Common laws did not meet only iura propria in the course of their expansion, however; they also met other common laws. We have already seen the mutual interdependence which this process demonstrated, as different common laws expanded or contracted in influence, and accepted more, or less, of the content of other common laws.[122] This process went on for centuries in Europe with each common law engaged in a double dialectic, with its own iura propria and with other common laws. In each territory there was application of a multitude of laws of different origins. With the nationalization of laws in the nineteenth century, however, the idea came to prominence of a single, national set of laws derived from official, national sources. Each national state, or particular jurisdiction, did what it could to provide an exhaustive set of local norms (the 'local jurisprudence' of Jhering).[123] Within Europe most of the new states appeared to succeed in converting themselves into iura propria within the context of the emerging transnational common

[121] Calasso, supra, note 71, at 53, given what is described as an impossibility of two common laws in a single territory.

[122] See above, this Ch., notably *The common law and the ius commune, The common law and other continental common laws, The ius commune and other continental common laws.*

[123] Supra, Ch. 2, *Territoriality and appropriation.*

laws, of which they themselves were in some measure the origin. They did so by appropriating the common law traditionally most influential within their newly defined state territory, improving on it as best they could. In some cases, however, it proved impossible to crystallize existing common laws into a single, national set of norms. This occurred at points of maximum overlap or confluence of common laws, such that definitive, binding choice between them proved to be impossible. This occurred more often beyond the seas, where loyalties were less fixed, but it also occurred in Europe, at least in Scotland.[124]

Scotland and other similar jurisdictions (South Africa, Quebec, Israel, Louisiana, the Philippines, the list is now lengthening) have been known for the last half century as 'mixed jurisdictions' and there has been much interesting work done recently on their methods and characteristics.[125] The idea of a 'mixed jurisdiction' is itself a product, however, of nationalist legal thought, which ties law to a fixed territory with formal, national sources of law, though admitting that these sources have not (yet) succeeded in overcoming the attractions of different common laws within the territory. From the perspective of common laws, however, it is simply a question of their ongoing interdependence, in this place as in many others. The place is simply one of ongoing confluence, where state laws have not succeeded in the process of exclusive appropriation of one of them. Curiously, the notion of a 'mixed jurisdiction' may therefore decline in the future with the increase in importance in the world of overlapping laws. The condition would become so widespread as not to call for a particular, and exceptional, designation. This would be at some indefinite point in the future. For the moment, jurisdictions at the confluence of common laws provide useful and interesting information on their mutual relations.

Scotland had its own, Celtic, form of European lex non scripta. Like all European unwritten laws, however, it was to go into decline from the eleventh or twelfth centuries. The Scottish kings paid homage to

[124] There are also territories of overlapping common laws on the European continent, as for example in Alsace-Lorraine, as to which see H. P. Glenn, 'The Local Law of Alsace-Lorraince' (1974) 23 I.C.L.Q. 769.

[125] E. Örucü, E. Attwooll, and S. Coyle, *Studies in Legal Systems: Mixed and Mixing* (The Hague: Kluwer, 1996) (chapters on Quebec, Scotland, Basque Country, Australia, Sri Lanka, Turkey, Russian Federation, Tyumen Region of Russia, Hong Kong, Israel, South Africa, Algeria, Mauritius, Malta, Japan, Slovenia, Germany, European Community); V. Palmer, *Mixed Jurisdictions of the World: The Third Legal Family* (Cambridge: Cambridge Univ. Press, 2001) (with national reports); K. Reid, 'The Idea of Mixed Legal Systems' (2003) 78 Tul. L. Rev. 5, with other articles from First Worldwide Congress on Mixed Jurisdictions.

William I and his successors, and English forms of feudalism were introduced into Scotland. Thus began a process of 'Normanization' of Scottish institutions, including adoption of English-style royal writs for use in Scottish courts.[126] Anglo-Norman settlers also arrived, so the process of arrival of a common law replicated in large measure a process taking place across Europe. English law thus made great advances even in the absence of imposition of military or political power, and even Robert the Bruce in 1324 authorized use of 'English law' in Galloway, in south-west Scotland.[127] A 'reception' thus occurred, with both the name 'common law' and much of its content derived from Anglo-Norman practice in England.[128] The expression 'common law' surfaced for the first time in a writ in 1264.[129]

In its important features, the arrival of English law into Scotland demonstrates the major characteristics of a relational common law. Its arrival was due to local measures of adoption which were without prejudice to the survival of local law. While traces of an oral legal tradition are difficult to identify after a millennium, the reception 'did not mark a complete break with the past'[130] and there was 'no outright rejection of the Celtic legal inheritance.'[131] Traces of Celtic law are still found in Scotland today, notably the judge or lawman (breitheamh) of pre-feudal times.[132] The reception was also a dynamic process, subject to local

[126] For 'Normanization', P. Stein, 'Roman Law in Scotland' (1968) Pars V, 13b, Ius romanum medii aevi 3; and for the process of adoption of writs, H. L. MacQueen, *Common Law and Feudal Society in Medieval Scotland* (Edinburgh: Edinburgh Univ. Press, 1993), notably at 246 for English-style writs being 'central in the general development of regularised royal justice in the thirteenth century.'

[127] R. R. Davies, *The First English Empire: Power and Identities in the British Isles 1093–1343* (Oxford: Oxford Univ. Press, 2000) at 157.

[128] W. D. H. Sellar, 'Celtic Law and Scots Law: Survival and Integration' (1989) 29 Scottish Studies 1 at 6.

[129] W. D. H. Sellar, 'The Common Law of Scotland and the Common Law of England' in R. R. Davies (ed.), *The British Isles 1100–1500* (Edinburgh: John Donald Publishers Ltd., 1988) 82 at 86. The term referred to 'law developed by the Anglo-Norman institutions to protect and enforce the new feudal tenures.' J. Cairns, 'Historical Introduction' in K. Reid and R. Zimmermann, *A History of Private Law in Scotland*, vol. 1, *Introduction and Property* (Oxford: Oxford Univ. Press, 2000) 14 at 28. For the expression 'common law' appearing in Italy and England in the late 12th century, supra, Ch. 1, *Mobility of people and mobility of laws.*

[130] Sellar, supra, note 128, at 6.

[131] Sellar, supra, note 129, at 86; and see also W. D. H. Sellar, 'The Resilience of the Scottish Common Law' in D. L. Carey Miller and R. Zimmermann, *The Civilian Tradition and Scots Law* (Berlin: Duncker & Humblot, 1997) 149 at 156 (prior law largely Celtic but also elements of Anglo-Saxon or Anglo-Danish law, demonstrating 'tenacious survival'). Scots thus referred in the 13th century to the 'laws and customs of the realm' as well as to the 'common law.' MacQueen, supra, note 126, at 2.

[132] Sellar, supra, note 128, at 3, 18–20 (also referring to different features of Crown law); and for these judicial officers, G. W. S. Barrow, *The Kingdom of the Scots* (London: Edward Arnold, 1973) at 69–82 (the iudex) and 83–139 (the justiciar).

circumstance, such that the received law itself underwent change. There is thus regular reference in Scotland to 'Scottish common law' and what is meant is that variant of the common law originating in England which came to exist in Scotland.[133] There was nothing inevitable about the adoption of English writs in Scotland. Choice was involved.[134] There were inevitable differences in the manner of implementation.[135]

The common law existing in Scotland being a relational common law, it was open to other common laws, as well as to its own iura propria. What then occurred in Scotland was a relatively rare European occurrence, a shift in allegiance from one European common law to another. Why this occurred will perhaps never be adequately explained, but a number of factors came together. There were differences between the bodies politic, and there were wars, yet these differences at the international level do not necessarily imply radical change in domestic law.[136] More fundamental appears the shift in education of Scottish lawyers from the fourteenth and fifteenth centuries, as more and more Scottish law students travelled to the Netherlands and France for legal education.[137] This was to have a great effect on the future of Scots law. Yet there must have been reasons for the decision of Scottish law students to study abroad, and some disaffection with the common law appears to have already set in by the middle of the fourteenth century[138] and some would have it even a century earlier.[139] So the common law originating in England was not entirely persuasive, in Scotland. This may have had to do with the ongoing influence of Celtic law, and with the strong presence in Scotland of canon law and the wide jurisdiction of ecclesiastical tribunals.[140] These other laws presumed an open court system and the application of rules of substantive law. The common law originating in England was that of a closed court system (requiring the grant of a writ), and a law of procedure and remedies. Scotland already had a decentralized (open) court system, and never saw

[133] Sellar, supra, note 129; Sellar (1997), supra, note 131, notably at 153.

[134] MacQueen, supra, note 126, at 5, 265 (on local determination of rules to be borrowed).

[135] For differences in institutions, use of the writs, Sellar, supra, note 129, at 88; Cairns, supra, note 129, at 31.

[136] Thus it does not appear helpful to conclude that '[i]t was because the common laws of England and Scotland had led different lives that they turned out not to be capable of fusion as James VI and I desired,' as proposed in A. Harding, *Medieval Law and the Foundations of the State* (Oxford: Oxford Univ. Press, 2002) at 337. We still need to know which of the differences were operative, and why.

[137] Stein, supra, note 126, at 40–1 (400 students to continent from 1340–1410, only 11 to England); Sellar, supra, note 129, at 93–4.

[138] Sellar, supra, note 129, at 82.

[139] For the thesis of Lord Cooper to this effect, H. MacQueen, 'Scots Law under Alexander III' in N. H. Reid (ed.), *Scotland in the Reign of Alexander III 1249–1286* (Edinburgh: John Donald Publishers Ltd., 1990) 74 at 76.

[140] MacQueen, supra, note 139, at 76, 77.

the creation of a centrally-controlled system of ambulatory (and closed) royal courts.[141] A move from open to closed, and from substance to procedure, must have appeared problematical. When a central court was eventually established, in the sixteenth century, it adopted an investigative or romano-canonical form of procedure, one which presumes that the judge knows the (substantive) law (jura novit curia) and has an obligation to establish fact, so that the substantive law is correctly applied.[142] The adversarial common law of procedure was rejected, since the preference was for ongoing application of substantive law.[143] Its detailed articulation had to be found in the common laws of the continent. There followed a second 'reception' in Scotland.[144] Yet since reception of common laws is without prejudice to existing laws, the common law originating in England has never lost its influence in Scotland. This influence continued even with the decline of the writs, in the fifteenth century, so that particular elements of the common law could continue to speak to Scottish circumstance.[145] By the second half of the nineteenth century (England having abandoned the writ system), there was even a 'shift in Scotland from continental Europe towards England' and a decline in the practice of continental legal education.[146] There may be still further shifts, in these relations of common laws which have gone on for close to a millennium.

Beyond Europe the territories of confluence of common laws most frequently have resulted from changes in the exercise of colonial authority. We have already seen that European law, however binding it may have appeared at home, acquired inevitably the character of a relational common law abroad. Local unwritten law was thus preserved, and it was also almost always the case that the law of prior European authority was also preserved, Trinidad and Guyana being exceptions.[147] The territories of

[141] MacQueen, supra, note 126, at 66, 253; Stein, supra, note 126, at 5.

[142] Cairns, supra, note 129, at 74; and for the Court of Session being modelled on the Parlement of Paris and possibly the Collegio dei Giudici of Pavia, D. Guth, 'Law' in R. Tittler and N. Jones (eds), *A Companion to Tudor Britain* (Oxford: Blackwell, 2004) 77 at 87.

[143] For an ongoing distinction between the 'procedural justice' of the common law, and the 'substantive justice' of the civil law, A. Jolowicz, 'The Woolf Report and the Adversary System' (1996) 15 C.J.Q. 198, notably at 199, 209. The notion of substantive justice would imply a form of investigative procedure, since substantive rules must be properly applied, to facts objectively ascertained by the judge.

[144] Stein, supra, note 126, at 50; and for the suppletive though highly persuasive character of the civil law, Cairns, supra, note 129, at 73, 101.

[145] For the common law never disappearing in 14th, 15th centuries, MacQueen, supra, note 126, at 3; and for its influence being 'never entirely negligible', Sellar (1997), supra, note 131, at 154.

[146] R. Evans-Jones, 'Receptions of Law, Mixed Legal Systems and the Myth of the Genius of Scots Private Law' (1998) 114 L.Q.R 228 at 232; and for the decline in civil law teaching from 1800, Cairns, supra, note 129, at 167.

[147] Supra, Ch. 2, *The common law as common law, in the world.*

confluence of common laws are thus generally ones in which there is ongoing interaction between indigenous or chthonic law, the common law of an initial European authority, and a European common law of later arrival. In Quebec the common law of France which began to arrive in the sixteenth century was maintained with the arrival of the English in the late eighteenth century.[148] Attempts to graft an English system of writs onto a French system of substantive law and open courts were unsuccessful. South Africa initially received Roman-Dutch law, which was preserved by the English, but there was then a 'general movement' towards English law and institutions.[149] This made itself felt in matters of public law, procedure, and commercial law, which was also the case in Quebec. These are, it should be observed, not the areas of classic private law in which the continental common laws have been most reputed. Israel has known many laws, and many authorities, and the Chief Justice of Israel has recently indicated the openness of courts in Israel to citation of different common laws.[150] Louisana has known native American law, French common law, Spanish common law, and English common law. It makes New Orleans what it is, though there is the music.[151] There is also, however, a phenomenon of voluntary acquisition of multiple common laws, as in Turkey where civil law has been taken from Switzerland, criminal law from Italy, administrative law from France, and criminal procedure from Germany, and there are 'continued relationship[s]' with the jurists of all of these places.[152]

Territories at the confluence of common laws thus demonstrate the ongoing nature of the relations of common laws. Since they are relational

[148] J. E. C. Brierley, 'Quebec's "Common Laws" (*Droits communs*): How Many are There?' in *Mélanges Louis-Philippe Pigeon* (Montreal: Wilson & Lafleur, 1989) 109; H. P. Glenn 'Quebec: Mixité and Monism' in Örucü, supra, note 125, 1.

[149] H. R. Hahlo and E. Kahn, *The South African Legal System and its Background* (CapeTown/Wynberg/Johannesburg: Juta, 1973) at 576.

[150] A. Barak, 'Forward: A Judge on Judging: The Role of a Supreme Court in a Democracy' (2002) 116 Harv. L. Rev. 16, at 113–14; and see generally, R. Levush, 'The Reception of Legal Systems—Implantation and Destiny in Israel' in M. Doucet and J. Vanderlinden, *La réception des systèmes juridiques: implantation et destin* (Bruxelles: Bruylant, 1994) 411, notably at 425 on 'absorption' and preservation of prior laws, and preservation of Ottoman millet system of personal laws.

[151] For debate on the present state of play, S. Herman, '*E Pluribus Unum:* The Paradox that Safeguards Louisiana's Mixed Legal System' (2003) 78 Tul. L. Rev. 457; A. N. Yiannopoulos, 'Requiem for a Civil Code: A Commemorative Essay' (2003) 78 Tul. L. Rev. 379; H. L. MacQueen, 'Looking Forward to a Mixed Future: A Response to Professor Yiannopoulos' (2003) 78 Tul. L. Rev. 410; A. Levasseur, 'La réception du système de la common law par le système législatif francais en Louisiane' in Doucet and Vanderlinden, supra, note 150, at 381.

[152] E. Ürücü, *Critical Comparative Law: Considering Paradoxes for Legal Systems in Transition* (Kluwer: Deventer, 1999), Ch. 6, at 80 ff., notably 95 for 'continued relationship' with source jurisdictions.

common laws, and not binding legal systems incompatible with one another in a single territory, there is no question of one somehow eliminating the other. Common laws cannot be eliminated, since they are beyond the reach of any single, national legislator or judiciary. At most, they can be momentarily eclipsed, as may have happened in the last century or two in some jurisdictions of nationalization of law. Where there is a confluence of common laws, however, the ongoing utility of each of them is demonstrated in the daily processes of adjudication and legislation. Large repositories of information are needed in the process of resolving problems which are ever-new. Common laws concentrate on the merits of problems and make no claims of systemic integrity or necessary application. It is inconsistent with their nature that they be somehow reified, as totalities, and that corresponding efforts be made to ensure their systemic triumph or defeat. There has been no such triumph or defeat as yet, in the long lives of the common laws, and the virtues of equilibrium are becoming more attractive.[153] Language and education, moreover, are important features of the longevity of common laws.

Common laws and language

Common laws have much in common with languages. Both transcend borders, resist appropriation, demonstrate internal discipline (while remaining open to external influence), and achieve sophistication and even beauty in their formulation. Both also exist in multiple form and contribute to the peaceful diversity of the world. The relations between the two are also important and complex.

A common law is a repository of ideas and concepts, a language the means of their expression.[154] To what extent, however, is a common law linked to a particular language, for its formulation and ongoing effectiveness? Very strong necessary relations between particular laws and particular languages have been mooted, as with the relation between Islamic law and Arabic, and there has been a major movement towards

[153] H. P. Glenn, 'Mixing it up' (2003) 78 Tul. L. Rev. 79.

[154] On law prior to language, R. Sacco, 'Mute Law' (1995) 43 Am. J. Comp. L. 455 at 456 ('law existed and operated efficiently in the absence of either lawgivers or lawyers') and 460 (law existing also prior to articulated language); D. Jutras, 'Énoncer l'indicible: le droit entre langues et traditions' Rev. int. dr. comp. 2000.781 (norms only partially rendered by different linguistic efforts to express them).

unification of language and unification of law in the process of construction of western states from the sixteenth century. George Fletcher has also recently spoken of 'the strong connection between English and the common law system,' concluding that 'this system has not lent itself to translation into any other language of the world. English and the common law come together as a cultural package.'[155] Curiously, however, and in spite of an apparently strong association between the common law and the English language in the contemporary world, the history of the common law provides strong evidence against the idea of a necessary and exclusive connection between a common law and a particular language. French was the first language of the judges of the common law for most of its formative period and it has been said that the languages of the common law in the thirteenth and fourteenth centuries were Latin and French, with English 'little in evidence.'[156] John Baker concludes that of the 'three languages of the common law,' French was the foremost, and cites a seventeenth-century King's Counsel, Roger North, to the effect that 'the law is scarcely expressible properly in English.'[157] French as a modern and written language would even have developed first in England and not in France, and multilingualism was so much the order of the day in England that legal proceedings would involve up to five changes between the three languages.[158] Law French continued to be used in pleading in English courts until 1731;[159] an entire contemporary vocabulary of common law in French has been developed by the Canadian federal Government and the University of Moncton's Centre of Common Law in French (for use at the federal level and in Canadian common law provinces); and the common law is now in the process of translation into Chinese, to facilitate legal relations between Hong Kong and the rest of China.[160] Over time the common law has therefore expressed itself in many languages.

[155] G. Fletcher, 'Comparative Law as a Subversive Discipline' (1998) 46 Am. J. Comp. L. 683 at 697.

[156] P. Brand, 'The languages of the law in later medieval England' in D. A. Trotter, *Multilingualism in Later Medieval Britain* (D. S. Brewer: Cambridge, 2000) 63 at 66, 75, and also at 71–2 for early common law legal education in French or, as it was then called, 'roman.'

[157] J. H. Baker, 'The Three Languages of the Common Law' (1998) 43 McGill L. J. 5 at 16, 24; and for the cardinal words of contemporary common law as 'essentially French' (tort, tenement, purchaser), G. Woodbine, 'The Language of English Law' (1943) 18 Speculum 395 at 395.

[158] M. T. Clanchy, *From Memory to Written Record: England 1066–1307*, 2nd ed. (Oxford: Blackwell, 1993) at 18 (for development of French, then only one of many unwritten vernaculars in France) and 207 (for changes of language between jury, justices, clerk, and counsel).

[159] Baker, supra, note 157, at 20.

[160] H. P. Glenn, 'Qu'est-ce que la common law en français?' (2003) 5 Rev. de la common law en fr. 97; J. A. Clarence Smith, 'La Common Law en Français' (1983) 61 Can. Bar Rev. 595; for the work of the University of Moncton, the *Vocabulaire de la common law*, 6 vols. (Moncton: Centre de traduction

Other common laws appear to have been more closely associated with a single language, sometimes to their advantage, sometimes not. Much appears to depend on the nature and (incalculable) fate of the language, though all of the common laws have profited from association with major languages in the world. The ius commune unquestionably profited from the currency of Latin as a language of the elite from the eleventh century.[161] It then declined with the decline of Latin, the rise of vernacular languages, and efforts towards national unilingualism.[162] Language would thus clearly influence the ambit of common laws and their mutual relations, and there have been many statements of common laws expanding or declining in influence in accordance with the fortunes of their principal language.[163] Yet Japanese judges cite Pandectist common law in the original, German language and the influence of German codification in Latin America is clearly beyond the 'language boundary' of Pandectist tradition.[164] There are also translations, of great influence. Pothier in translation

et de terminologie juridique, Université de Moncton, 1980–94) and the collection *La common law en poche* edited by J. Vanderlinden (Cowansville: Yvon Blais, 1996–04); and for an electronic francophone programme of common law commercial law, <www.multidroit.org>; D. Roebuck and King-kui Sin, 'The Ego and I and Ngo: Theoretical Problems in the Translation of the Common Law into Chinese' in R. Wacks (ed.), *Hong Kong, China and 1997: Essays in Legal Theory* (Hong Kong: Hong Kong Univ. Press, 1983) at 185; 'The Common Law: Can it be translated?' City University of Hong Kong Bulletin, Issue 13, June, 1997 (question is not extent to which common law will be changed by translation into Chinese, but extent to which Chinese will be changed).

[161] For the ius commune as a notion entirely dependent on Latin, supra, Ch. 1, *The ius commune, as prototype*, and for Latin as form of cultural unity of various peoples, Ermini, supra, note 72, at 5.

[162] For the decline, F. Waquet, *Latin or the Empire of a Sign: From the Sixteenth to the Twentieth Centuries*, transl. John Howe (London/New York: Verso, 2001), notably at 157 (Paris Law Faculty having to abandon its mediocre use in professorial examinations because of 'jeers of the audience'), 171 (English said by Italians to be 'terrible with their pronunciation'); and for Latin playing a 'fundamental role in the apparatus of power,' its disappearance a 'force for democratization' and liberation, L. Morgan, 'The many deaths of Latin' TLS 17 Aug. 2001, at 24. On the rise of the local languages and laws, R. Jacob, 'Doctrine et culture nationale. La naissance de la littérature juridique en langue populaire en France et en Allemagne' Droits 1994.5 ; H. P. Glenn, 'Droit comparé et langages juridiques' in G. Snow and J. Vanderlinden, *Français juridique et science du droit* (Bruxelles: Bruyland, 1995) at 155.

[163] For the idea of a 'language boundary' (*Sprachgrenze*) of the German legal family or *Rechtskreise*, E. Kramer, 'Der Einfluss des BGB auf das schweizerische und österreichische Privatrecht'(2000) 200 AcP 365, at 371; and for the same idea in the francophone world, J. Bemba, *Devenir avocat dans l'espace francophone* (Paris: Harmattan, 2003) and the *Revue juridique et politique des états francophones* (Paris: Editions Juris Africa). Greek law would not have exercised much influence in Europe for linguistic reasons since the west 'did not read Greek' (*graeca non leguntur*); van Caenegem, supra, note 70, at 86; and for language pressures in Lousiana, South Africa, Israel, and Quebec, A. Levasseur, supra, note 151, at 385; M. Loubser, 'Linguistic Factors into the Mix: The South African Experience of Language and Law' (2003) 78 Tul. L. Rev. 105; C. L. Fassberg, 'Language and Style in a Mixed System' (2003) 78 Tul. L. Rev. 151; W. Tetley, 'Nationalism in a Mixed Jurisdiction and the Importance of Language (South Africa, Israel, and Quebec/Canada)' (2003) 78 Tul. L. Rev. 175.

[164] Supra, Ch. 2, *Pandectist common law, in the world*.

greatly influenced the common law originating in England,[165] while the translation of civilian writers in the United States in the nineteenth century had a great influence on the law of that country.[166] It may even be possible to translate very significant portions of an entire common law, with its attendant vocabulary, such that the law then begins a new (or renewed) life in a new (or rediscovered) language. This has already been seen for the common law in French, and potentially Chinese,[167] but it is also the case for the droit commun originating in France, which exists in codified form in English in Quebec. The new (bilingual) Quebec Civil Code has been influential in Eastern Europe in jurisdictions in the process of codification, in providing English-language versions of long-standing civilian concepts. Moreover, even if common laws have often been expressed only in a single language, they are constantly in the process of meeting, and adjusting to, laws expressed in another language, such that the lawyers involved must work at the interface of languages as well as at the interface of laws. This has recently been splendidly documented for antiquity, and even for the boundaries of Roman law, which was rather unconcerned with such issues.[168] The common law was pleaded in Welsh in Wales,[169] and Scotland's common laws were known in many languages and dialects, including both French and Dutch.[170] New Zealand legislation now includes untranslated Maori expressions.[171]

The open character of relational common laws thus appears to explain much of their facility to traverse and combine languages. Open to different ideas and concepts, they are necessarily open to the languages in which these ideas and concepts are expressed. In this, they recall as well the interdependent nature of languages and the constant process of linguistic

[165] R. J. Pothier, *A Treatise on the Law of Obligations, or, contracts*, transl. W. D. Evans (London: Strahan, 1806).

[166] M. H. Hoeflich, 'Translation and the Reception of Foreign Law in the Antebellum United States' (2002) 50 Am. J. Comp. L. 753.

[167] Supra, text accompanying note 160.

[168] J. N. Adams, *Bilingualism and the Latin Language* (Cambridge: Cambridge Univ. Press, 2003) at 383–90, for 'code-switching' by court officials from Greek to Latin, instructions to beat a Greek witness given in Latin to ensure ignorance until execution. For Roman law and its relations with other laws, supra, Ch. 1, *Roman law and roman universality.*

[169] Smith in Trotter, supra, note 156, at 14–15 (novel disseisin becoming newdd-ddifeddiant).

[170] H. L. MacQueen, *Laws and Languages: Some Historical Notes from Scotland* (Maastricht: Universiteit Maastricht, 2002) (Ius Commune Lectures on European Private Law), also reproduced in vol. 6.2, Electr. J. Comp. L. (July, 2002), <www.ejcl.org/ejcl/62/art62-2.html>, notably at 1 for influence of Dutch language in Scotland (surname Fleming, words such as golf, pinkie, scone, croon).

[171] T. Angelo, 'Culture Protection, Language and Law' in E. Jayme (ed.), *Langue et droit* (Brussels: Bruylant, 1999) 271 at 279; and for a similar phenomenon in Africa, C. de Lespinay, 'Droits de l'oralité africaine et traduction francophone, un compromis difficile' (2002) 44 Droits et Cultures (No. 2 on *Traditions juridiques et culturelles et traductions du droit*), at 61.

transfers from one language to another. In the past, this process was so intense that it was difficult to establish which words belonged to which langage or even clearly to separate languages.[172] Those accustomed to working with common laws in different languages now argue that the use of two languages is a means of facilitating rather than hindering the search for comprehension.[173] The search for comprehension is also conducted, however, through the process of legal education.

Common laws and legal education

Formal legal education in Europe had its beginnings in the eleventh century, at the time of the origination of the common law and ius commune traditions. The first major institution of legal education was that of the University of Bologna. It has been convincingly argued that the model for European university and legal education is to be found in the Islamic madhahib,[174] yet the early Law Faculties of the European continent soon developed a sophisticated curriculum of teaching which was profoundly rooted in Christian and Imperial thought. The Christian Church was seen as a 'universal' church and the Emperor as 'dominus mundi' and these ideas translated themselves into a conception of the emerging ius commune as a unum ius.[175] There was great hostility to recognition of, and certainly teaching of, other laws. On the ground the reconciliation of the ius commune with the various iura propria developed rather rapidly, the ius commune converting itself into a relational common law and thereby ensuring its great longevity.[176] Yet its teaching appears to have been frozen

[172] D. A. Trotter, 'Introduction' in Trotter, supra, note 156, at i, 2 (on frequency of language-mixing within documents), 3; T. Janson, *Speak: a short history of languages* (Oxford: Oxford Univ. Press, 2002) at 113–4 on emergence of French from Latin through abandoning of inflections; P. Petot, 'Le droit commun en France selon les coutumiers' Rev. hist. dr. fr. et étr. 1961.413 at 414, on borrowing from Latin by French.

[173] Jutras, supra, note 154; and for each legal vocabulary reflecting a shadow, second language or 'outre-langue' (as English legal vocabulary is composed of words of French or Germanic origin), N. Kasirer, 'L'outre-langue du droit' forthcoming in *Mélanges Jacques Vanderlinden* (Cowansville/Bruxelles: Yvon Blais/Bruylant, 2005).

[174] G. Makdisi, *The Rise of Colleges: Institutions of Highter Learning in Islam and the West* (Edinburgh: Univ. of Edinburgh Press, 1981); G. Makdisi, 'The Guilds of Law in Medieval Legal History: An Inquiry into the Origins of the Inns of Court' (1985–6) 34 Clevel. St. L. Rev. 3.

[175] Supra, Ch. 1, *The early expansion of the ius unum and the common law.*

[176] Supra, Ch. 1, *The essential tradition of the ius commune.*

in the initial form it assumed in the eleventh and twelfth centuries, as a unum ius. It was to be the Roman texts, and their then contemporary glosses, which were to be taught, eventually complemented by canon law, but the iura propria, the law of the people, had no place in the curriculum of the Universities. It was highly elitist legal education, at its inception more a programme for social control and change than anything useful in everyday life. It spread rapidly throughout Europe, even into the jurisdictions of the other common laws, though there were occasional instances of royal prohibition.[177] Oxford and Cambridge thus taught Roman law, and only Roman law (perhaps not even the ius commune), for centuries. Education in the common law took place in the professionally organized Inns of Court. In Spain Roman law began to be taught with the creation of the University of Salamanca in 1243. It was taught, though 'not directly applied.'[178] All of the schools taught according to the Bologna model,[179] and it has been said that 'no European university offered instruction in the law of the land until the seventeenth century.'[180] When Louis XIV ordered the teaching of French law and created the Royal professorships of French law in 1679 only one course in French law was required to be taken in a three-year programme, and the Royal professors were poorly paid, and poorly treated by their more experienced colleagues.[181] England came later, Blackstone being appointed the first professor of the English common law, at Oxford, in 1753. Viner spoke of the need then to improve 'the study of the common laws of *England*' (emphasis in the original).[182] The visibility and expansion of the ius commune was thus due in large measure to its expression in Latin, but also to its teaching, in Latin, throughout the universities of Europe. The other common laws had no such overarching means of diffusion within Europe, and it was only through expansion on the ground, and overseas, that they acquired their status as relational common laws.

[177] The University of Paris thus provided instruction in canon law but it was only in the 17th century that it could add Roman law to its curriculum. T. Carbonneau, 'The French Legal Studies Curriculum: Its History and Relevance as a Model for Reform' (1980) 25 McGill L. J. 445 at 447; and supra, Ch. 1, *The common law (droit commun) originating from France.*

[178] M. Scheppach, *Las Siete Partidas: Entstehungs- und Wirkungsgeschichte* (Pfaffenweiler: Centaurus, 1991).

[179] Coing, supra, note 79, at 510.

[180] Stein, supra, note 16, at 57.

[181] Carbonneau, supra, note 177, at 448–52; and for the nomination of Huber for the teaching of local law in Holland in 1682, and some prior teaching of local legislation, M. Ahsmann, 'Legal Education of Advocates in the Northern Netherlands (1575–1800)', paper presented to the 1993 Meeting of the Jean Bodin Society for Comparative Institutional History (Copenhagen).

[182] D. Lemmings, 'Blackstone and Law Reform by Education: Preparation for the Bar and Lawyerly Culture in Eighteenth-Century England' (1998) 16 Law & Hist. Rev. 211 at 252.

The reaction to the so-called universalist legal education was, however, severe. It was a highly particularist reaction, and used the same, underlying technique of distinguishing between law which was fit to be taught and law which was not fit to be taught. So with the attempted appropriation of the common laws in the nineteenth century it became only national law which was fit to be taught, and in the local vernaculars. In France a uniform national curriculum was created in 1806, with government inspectors established to ensure its implementation.[183] In Germany the examinations came to be state examinations on state law; in the United States a scientific model of (U.S.) law, through study of the cases, came to be dominant.[184] The new legal teaching was even more discriminating and exclusivist than that of Roman law, however, since it was now not only the law of other people which was excluded, but also largely the law of the past.[185]

The teaching of law in Europe thus demonstrated, and demonstrates, inherent tendencies towards hegemony, since students are taught only one law, in spite of the relational character of the common laws.[186] Their natural inclination is to rely on the only law they know, wherever they may find themselves. To the extent that other laws are contemplated, it is through the prism of conflicts of laws (themselves nationally regulated) or through that of exoticism (in rare, optional, and sparsely attended courses in Comparative Law, which are usually courses in foreign law in which little or no comparison takes place). The fundamental, relational character of the common laws is largely lost in this teaching. It is recovered in large measure, however, in jurisdictions where the relations between common laws and iura propria, and amongst the common laws themselves, are their most intense. Here the law of the land is taught, but not in an exclusivist manner, and the relational common laws originating in Europe are present to a greater or lesser degree, as they are in courtroom practice.

[183] H. Baade, '*Stare decisis* in Civil Law Systems' in J. A. Nafziger and S. Symeonides, *Law and Justice in a Multistate World: Essays in Honor of Arthur T. Von Mehren* (Ardsley, NY: Transnational, 2002) 533 at 541. The traditional faculties of law had been abolished in 1793.

[184] H. Schweber, 'The "Science" of Legal Science: The Model of the Natural Sciences in Nineteenth-Century American Legal Education' (1999) 17 Law & Hist. Rev. 421; B. Kimball, '"Warn Students That I Entertain Heretical Opinions": The Inception of Case Method Teaching in the Classrooms of the Early C. C. Langdell, 1870–1883' (1999) 17 Law & Hist. Rev. 57.

[185] R. Zimmermann, *Roman Law, Contemporary Law, European Law: The Civilian Tradition Today* (Oxford: Oxford Univ. Press, 2001), notably at 44–6 ('The services of the legal historian were no longer required, he could now turn his attention to the lotus flowers'); and for teaching of Roman law 'quasiment disparu' from legal education in France, Rouland, supra, note 3, at 260.

[186] H. P. Glenn, 'Legal Education and Legal Hegemony' in Swiss Institute of Comparative Law, *Imperialism and Chauvinism in the Law* (Lausanne, 2004) at 11.

It is therefore appropriate, in terms of the relational common laws of the world, that various forms of transnational law teaching are now the object of experiments.[187]

Common laws do not, however, only meet iura propria and other European common laws in the world. They also meet non-European legal traditions which are themselves of worldwide significance. Perhaps the most illustrative of these are Talmudic law, Islamic law, and Hindu law.

Common laws and Talmudic law

Jewish people have travelled the world, though the diaspora which began in the sixth century BCE was not at its inception, and often thereafter, a voluntary one. Yet as has been seen in Europe, the mobility of populations brings about a mobility of laws, and various forms of accommodation then become necessary. The Talmud is the principal repository of the law of the Jewish religion, and while it does not pretend to exclusivity it is difficult to escape its influence in Jewish life. It is also represents a brilliant intellectual concept, a book of law which contains endless differences of opinion, from all ages and dealing with all that had gone on before, while seen as never definitively finished and thus leaving room for still more opinions, as each generation engages with it.[188] There is no equivalent to it in any other legal tradition. Jewish law thus has a specific name for its principal source, and while the expression 'common law' is occasionally used it appears to be largely a linguistic transfer from English, indicating some level of generality, without any major functional or descriptive role.[189]

As was the case for mobile European populations, Jewish settlers were assumed to have taken their law with them into new lands. Law and religion being so intertwined in the Jewish faith it would be difficult to

[187] Glenn, supra, note 186, notably programmes of Maastricht University, Hanse Law School, McGill Law Faculty, described on respective websites.

[188] A. Steinsaltz, *The Essential Talmud*, transl. C. Galai (New York: Basic Books, 1976), notably at 47; and for further references, Glenn, supra, note 105, ch. 4.

[189] See, e.g., Z. Falk, *Hebrew Law in Biblical Times* (Jerusalem: Wahrmann Books, 1964) at 40 (among 'important factors of unity was the "common law" of the community,' quotation marks in original); G. Horowitz, *The Spirit of Jewish Law* (New York: Central Book, 1953) at 12, citing G. Moore that Jews during Persian, Greek domination had 'unwritten common law'; J. Neusner, *The Halakhah: An Encyclopedia of the Law of Judaism*, vol. I (Leiden: Brill, 2000) at 5 (exegetical literature investigating 'legal principles embodied in diverse details of a common law').

conceive of any other solution. Forced migration could not be taken as a form of automatic excommunication. The law which Jewish settlers thus took with them was in the form of the classic texts, originally the Torah, accompanied by the oral tradition, then eventually, on its redaction in the fifth and sixth centuries CE, the Talmud. There were also other written texts, making up the totality of Jewish law.[190] Yet it was recognized that all normativity could not be found in halakhah, in presently written sources, and a large place was therefore left for what is referred to in English as custom, or minhag. Minhag was recognized perhaps most frequently in matters of procedure but extended generally to local and folk practices. It need not be rooted in halakhah, though it is said that it was unable to overcome unanimous halakhic opinion, or endorse heresy.[191] Its importance is recognized in long-standing maxims, such as 'The custom of our fathers is Torah,' 'The custom of Israel is Torah' and 'Leave Israel alone' (laws should be allowed to fall into desuetude).[192] Recognition of minhag came inevitably to be used as an argument when the question arose as to the recognition of the law of the new lands of Jewish settlers. Other arguments were also used, such as local sovereignty, implicit contract between king and subject, and ownership of the land of the territory.[193] Since minhag had often assumed 'a national dimension' (minhag ashkenaz),[194] recognition of the law of the new lands did not represent a major deviation from the tradition. A new principle thus emerged by the third century CE, that 'the law of kingdom is law' (dina de-malkhuta dina). Thus, while Jewish normativity continued to be respected, there were 'adjustments to conditions of the non-Jewish environment'[195] and recognition that the situation was 'too complicated to be solved by any neat declaration in terms of 'us' and 'them.'[196]

Over the centuries, there has been ongoing determination of the limits of recognition of the law of the kingdom, or state law as it is now recognized to be. The law of secular communities or kingdoms was

[190] For the Tosefta and the Midrashe Halakhah, Glenn, supra, note 105, at 96, with ref.

[191] L. Jacobs, *A Tree of Life: Diversity, Flexibility and Creativity in Jewish Law* (London/Portland, OR: The Littman Library of Jewish Civilization, 2000) at 206, 210.

[192] Jacobs, supra, note 191, at 206, 215.

[193] G. Graff, *Separation of Church and State:* Dina de-Malkhuta Dina *in Jewish Law, 1750–1848* (Tuscaloosa: University of Alabama Press, 1985) at 11; M. Elon, *Jewish Law: History, Sources, Principles*, vol. I, trans. B. Auerbach and M. J. Sykes (Philadelphia/Jerusalem: The Jewish Publication Society, 5754/1994) at 66–7. L. Landman, *Jewish Law in the Diaspora: Confrontation and Accommodation* (Philadelphia: Dropsie College, 1968) at 35, 44.

[194] B. Jackson, 'Jewish Law or Jewish Laws' (1989) 8 Jewish L. Ann. 15, at 24.

[195] Elon, supra, note 193, at 71.

[196] Jacobs, supra, note 191, at 81.

originally not ambitious, and initial recognition was largely in matters of taxation and expropriation.[197] With the growth of kingdoms and states, and the growth of their law, Jewish recognition has expanded, in recognition of 'the king's interest.'[198] Recognition of state law is now permissible even in private legal relations, providing there is no infringement of religious principle[199] or basic principles of justice and equity, such as non-discrimination.[200] So too is the jurisdiction of secular courts largely recognized, overcoming earlier notions of exclusive jurisdiction of the Bet Din and aversion to high levels of corruption in secular courts.[201] It is even said that state or secular law can be 'incorporated' into Talmudic law, a clear equivalent to the process of 'canonization' of secular law by canonical tribunals.[202] The eventual rabbinic prohibition of polygamy is said to have clearly resulted from such external influence.[203]

In spite of widespread anti-Semitism, secular governmental authorities in Europe often specifically authorized the jurisdiction of Jewish courts and the application of Jewish law. There may well have been financial reasons behind these measures, the Jewish population being a rich source of tax revenues, having turned to commercial activity on being barred from ownership of land. Jewish tribunals existed in England following the arrival of Jews after the Norman Conquest, and there was even a special court, the Exchequer of the Jews, with jurisdiction over disputes between Jews and Gentiles.[204] King John explicitly confirmed that Jewish disputes could be settled by Jewish law.[205] On the continent there were many charters to the same effect.[206] All such measures came to naught, of course, in the face of the mass deportations which occurred from the

[197] Graff, supra, note 193, at 2, 8.

[198] Elon, supra, note 193, at 68; for expansion of recognition at time of Napoleon in France, with codification of French law, Graff, supra, note 193, at 79–80; and for broadening and narrowing of maxim as living conditions demanded, Landman, supra, note 193, at 45.

[199] Landman, supra, note 193, at 148; Elon, supra, note 193, at 70.

[200] Elon, supra, note 193, at 73; Landman, supra, note 193, at 48; S. Shilo, 'Equity as a Bridge between Jewish and Secular Law' (1991) 12 Cardozo L. Rev. 737 at 741.

[201] Landman, supra, note 193, at 86, 103; though see for recognition as expansion of exceptions to exclusive jurisdiction of Bet Din, M. J. Broyde, *The Pursuit of Justice and Jewish Law: Halakhic Perspectives on the Legal Profession* (New York/Hoboken: Yeshiva Univ. Press/KTAV Publishing, 1996) at 41, and 67 for extensive listing of 'public causes of action' determinable in secular courts (securities, environmental protection, taxation, immigration, labour, and administrative law, etc.).

[202] Shilo, supra, note 200, at 738; Elon, supra, note 193, at 73; and for 'canonization,' supra, this Ch., *Common laws and canon law.*

[203] Jacobs, supra, note 191, at 90–1.

[204] J. Rabinowitz, *Jewish Law: Its Influence on the Development of Legal Institutions* (New York: Bloch Publishing Company, 1956) at 250–1.

[205] H. G. Richardson, *The English Jewry under Angevin Kings* (London: Methuen & Co., 1960) at 113.

[206] Graff, supra, note 193, at 9–10, 32–3.

thirteenth to the eighteenth centuries.[207] Yet today a judgment of a Bet Din (to which no notion of stare decisis attaches) may be recognized by a secular, state court in the same manner as recognition is accorded an arbitral award. The relations between secular, western authorities (sources of the iura propria) and Jewish people were therefore irregular. The common laws of Europe, however, would not necessarily have had the same difficulties in relations with Jewish tradition.

In Chapter 2 certain characteristics of a common law were noted in examining the expansion of European common laws beyond the seas.[208] Common laws were found to be relational or non-binding in character, such that they could yield to iura propria and co-exist with them in an ongoing, dialogical manner. This was invariably done through a differentiation amongst peoples, allowing recognizable identities to be maintained while admitting commonalities in the application of law. Common laws also did not purport to abolish or abrogate other laws (being themselves non-positive in character), while the ongoing process of delineation amongst different laws was a large and highly visible process of decision making. It is remarkable how the Talmudic legal tradition also meets these criteria of a relational common law, without making explicit use of the concept or, apparently, having borrowed it from western sources. The underlying relations between western common laws and Talmudic law would thus be those of interdependent common laws, with their techniques of mutual conciliation. The conclusion is drawn, of course, with due respect to the particularity of each of the traditions which have reached this result. Similar questions may thus be asked of the possibilities of reconciliation between western common laws and Islamic and Hindu legal traditions.

Common laws and Islamic law

Like Christianity, but unlike Judaism and Hinduism, the Islamic religion is a proselytizing one. This has contributed greatly to the expansion of Islamic religion and law in the world and to the growth of Islamic peoples, so Islamic law has necessarily developed principles and institutions addressing its relations with other laws. It has done so within the general

[207] Glenn, supra, note 105, at 116.
[208] Supra, Ch. 2, *The nature of the common laws abroad.*

cadre of Islamic law or fiqh, which is essentially doctrinal and non-positive in character, deriving its ultimate authority from the Koran and the teachings of Muhammad.[209] Islamic law, like Talmudic law, does not appear to have developed or relied upon a specific notion of common law, though the expression is sometimes used by western commentators.[210] They do so in part because Islamic law clearly follows Islamic people in the world and therefore fulfils the function, it has recently been said, of a 'major tradition,'[211] with basic, legitimating texts, here of revelatory origin, as well as a massive body of law containing general, overarching principles.[212] Yet because of both the size and diversity of Islamic populations, and the lack of any central authority, there has been acceptance of 'very wide margins of orthodoxy' within the tradition, and this tolerant perspective has necessarily had its effect on relations with other populations.[213]

Like western common laws and Talmudic law, Islamic law has thus developed specific techniques for acknowledging the various iura propria, and common laws with which it has to deal. Urf, or custom, is now said to be 'as if dictated by law' and while originally construed as a narrow exception it has assumed major proportions in the Islamic world since the

[209] For further sources and references, Glenn, supra, note 105, Ch. 7; and for the intensity of earlier English–Islamic relations, with thousands of conversions to Islam bringing about a removal from authority of English law, N. Matar, *Islam in Britain 1558–1685* (Cambridge: Cambridge Univ. Press, 1998), notably at 15, 45.

[210] See, e.g., K. Bälz, 'Europäisches Privatrecht jenseits von Europa? Zum fünfzigjährigen Jubiläum des ägyptischen Zivilgesetzbuches (1948)' ZEuP 2000.51 at 73 (Islamic law as 'ius commune'); L. Rosen, *The Justice of Islam* (Oxford: Oxford Univ. Press, 2000), Ch. 3, on similarities between Islamic law and the common law, notably in emphasizing particular situations, reliance on local experts and witnesses, allowing parties to negotiate, avoiding appellate structures, use of analogy, local custom; L. Milliot and F.-P. Blanc, *Introduction à l'étude du droit musulman*, 2nd ed. (Paris: Sirey, 1987) at 166 ('droit commun des peuples musulmans').

[211] T. S. Dahl, *The Muslim Family: A Study of Women's Rights in Islam*, trans. R. Walford (Oslo: Scandinavian Univ. Press, 1997) at 11 (major tradition deemed applicable to all Muslims, yet numbers of local traditions modifying and differentiating the doctrine).

[212] On such general principles or maxims, J. J. Nasir, *The Islamic Law of Personal Status*, 3rd ed. (The Hague/London/New York: Kluwer Law International, 2002) at 29 ff; S. Jahel, 'Les principes généraux du droit dans les systèmes arabo-musulmans au regard de la technique juridique contemporaine' Rev. int. dr. comp. 2003.105.

[213] H. Gerber, *Islamic Law and Culture 1600–1840* (Leiden/Boston/Koln: Brill, 1999) at 67 (rather the state which has 'had some trouble in tolerating this legal pluralism'); C. Imber, *Ebu's-suùd: The Islamic Legal Tradition* (Edinburgh: Edinburgh Univ. Press, 1997), at 6 (on local autonomy, legal pluralism, Islamic courts as factors of unity); Rosen, supra, note 210, at 183 (on 'equalizing forces of Islamic thought—the emphasis on learning as the only basis for admiration, the assertion that "a difference is not a distinction," the absence of hierarchy'—all contributing to 'ethos of dispersed power').

sixteenth century.[214] Since much conduct is viewed in Islamic law as neither compulsory nor forbidden, there is a wide range of conduct potentially subject to unwritten rules or usages.[215] Much is therefore left to local determination, on condition that nothing would contravene the Koran or the teachings of the Prophet (a process of interpretation).[216] There is also a recognized phenomenon of 'general customs' which become integrated into the body of fiqh, so recognition of custom has been described as a 'long and peaceful process . . . still continuing.'[217]

The wide range of permitted conduct in Islamic law has also been seen as the principal justification for the development of kanun (borrowed from the Greek kanon, or rule), or legislative enactment.[218] So local legislative authority came to be recognized in Islamic law, as did royal and municipal regulation in Europe under the general operation of the common laws. In Islamic jurisdictions the phenomenon would have existed from early times, and has also been known in different parts of the Islamic world as syasa (administrative policy), nizam (ordinance), or marsum (decree).[219] There has, over centuries, been a certain ebb and flow between kanun and Islamic legal authority, usually with a double administration of justice,[220] and during the Ottoman Empire major intellectual efforts were made to effect a synthesis or equilibrium between the two.[221] It is generally understood that analytically the law precedes the state[222] (and it is argued that Islamic states should have no constitution other than the Koran, or constitutions which proclaim its priority), just as

214 Gerber, supra, note 213, at 105; G. Libson, 'On the Development of Custom as a Source of Law in Islamic Law' (1997) 4 Islamic L. & Soc. 131 at 135–7.

215 For classification of conduct into the five basic categories of compulsory, rewarded, permitted or indifferent, disapproved, and forbidden, M Bāqir as-Sadr, *Lessons in Islamic Jurisprudence*, transl. R. P. Mottahedeh (Oxford: Oneworld, 2003) at 56–7; Glenn, supra, note 105, at 201, with refs; and for parties being allowed, explicitly or implicitly, to opt for local law, Libson, supra, note 214, at 152.

216 T. Mahmood, 'Custom as a Source of Law in Islam' (1967) 7 J. Indian L. Institute 102 at 103–5.

217 N. Lubis, 'The State's Legal Policy and the Development of Islamic Law in Indonesia's New Order' in A. Salim and A. Azra (eds), *Shari'a and Politics in Modern Indonesia* (Singapore: Institute of Southeast Asian Studies, 2003) 48 at 64; also on integration, B. Johansen, *Contingency in a Sacred Law* (Leiden/Boston/Köln: Brill, 1999) at 169; and for relations between custom and body of Islamic law as 'positive and enriching,' R. Lukito, *Islamic Law and Adat Encounter: The Experience of Indonesia* (Jakarta: Logos, 2001) at 5.

218 S. Vesey-Fitzgerald, *Muhammadan Law: An Abridgement according to its various schools* (London: Oxford Univ. Press/Humphrey Milford, 1931) at 2.

219 J. Schacht, *An Introduction to Islamic Law* (Oxford: Clarendon Press, 1964) at 54, 87; and for still further designations, Milliot and Blanc, supra, note 210 at 160.

220 Schacht, supra, note 219, at 54 (on double administration of justice), 86 (on religious reform movements aiming to eliminate customary and legislative or administrative law).

221 Gerber, supra, note 213, at 29; Imber, supra, note 213, at 40–1, including feudal law as kanun, in addition to land, tax, and criminal law.

222 Gerber, supra, note 213, at 43.

western states rest on an underlying basis of common public law.[223] Since legislation would thus have to be generally compatible with the Koran there is, in states such as Egypt, constitutional review to ensure that this is the case.[224] Yet there is much kanun in the world today, with a corresponding growth in secular state courts which occupy themselves with state law and even in some measure with western common laws.

The great part of Islamic law is thus relational in character and, like a number of common laws in their relations with the world, would reserve unto itself only a fundamental core of its essential teachings.[225] In both proselytizing yet recognizing local laws, Islamic teaching necessarily differentiates amongst populations, generally between the Islamic population of the world, or umma, and the non-Islamic population, but also more importantly between the umma and those non-Islamic peoples, the dhimmi, living within lands considered to be Islamic. The dhimma is a contract, treaty, or convention by which other 'People of the Book,' in principle Christians and Jews, are accorded residence and status within Islamic lands.[226] It is said historically that minority populations thus fared very well under Islamic regimes and that in the early years of Islamic authority in the Middle East, Islam 'rested as lightly as a mist along the

[223] Supra, Ch. 2, *A common, pan-European process of appropriation.*

[224] K. Bälz, 'Das islamiche recht als Grundlage arabischer Rechtseinheit' in H.-G. Ebert and T. Hanstein (eds.), *Beiträge zum Islamischen Recht* (Frankfurt: Peter Lang, 2000) 35 at 50; though for debate on the type of court which should exercise this function (state or shar'a), M. Q. Zamam, *The Ulama in Contemporary Islam* (Princeton/Oxford: Princeton Univ. Press, 2002) at 88 ff.

[225] For reservations of common laws, variously in favour of public policy, natural law, Christianity, that which is 'tolerable', and against the 'odious,' see supra, Ch. 1, *The essential tradition of the ius commune*, Ch. 2, *The derecho commún originating from Spain, in the world; Roman-Dutch common law, in the world*; and for canon law's resistance to recognition of 'unreasonable' local law or custom, supra, this Ch., Common Laws and Canon Law. Yet for the tentative nature of the decisional reasoning of the islamic mufti, citing al-Shafi ('our opinion is right though it may turn out to be wrong') and echoing the tentative nature of sources of European common laws, T. Ramadan, *Western Muslims and the Future of Islam* (Oxford: Oxford Univ. Press, 2004) at 51; Zaman, supra, note 224, at 97–8 (shari'a best understood not as code but as ongoing 'discursive tradition', not as content but as process).

[226] A. Fattal, *Le statut légal des non-Musulmans en pays d'Islam* (Beyrouth: Imprimerie Catholique, 1958) at 16 ; for history of the concept, A. S. Tritton, *The Caliphs and their Non-Muslim Subjects: A Critical Study of the Covenant of 'Umar'* (London: Frank Cass & Co. Ltd., 1970); and more currently, A. R. Awang, *The Status of the Dhimmi in Islamic Law* (Kuala Lumpur: International Law Book Services, 1994); Royal Academy for Islamic Civilization Research, *Treatment of non-Muslims in Islam* (Amman: Royal Academy for Islamic Civilization Research, 1992). For the Ottoman Empire, R. Ayoun, 'Le statut des juifs dans l'Empire ottoman au XIXe siècle' Rev. hist. dr. fr. et étr. 1992.197, notably at 197 for exercising religion and practising professions in 'total liberty'; E. Örücü, 'The Impact of European Law on the Ottoman Empire and Turkey' in W. J. Mommsen and J. A. de Moor, *European Expansion and Law* (Oxford/ New York: Berg, 1992) 39, notably at 39, 40, for general policy of leaving local laws intact.

contours of what had remained a largely Christian landscape.'[227] A hadith or teaching of the Prophet said that 'whoever harms a dhimmi shall have me for an antagonist.'[228] As custom or urf remained viable elsewhere for people not of the Book, so the dhimmi remained entitled to application of their law and to their own tribunals, though Islamic law remained applicable in Islamic tribunals and generally in criminal matters.[229] The dhimmi paid a particular tax, the gizya, and were generally excluded from public service and political participation, but in private law matters were as fully entitled as Muslim subjects.[230] There is some analogy with the treatment of non-nationals or aliens in contemporary western states. Here there would be a Roman-like division between peoples, courts, and laws, but its effect is greatly reduced by the role of urf and kanun in the contemporary Islamic world.

There are therefore many forms of iura propria encompassed in Islamic teaching, and the importance of their recognition becomes still more significant with respect to Muslims who find themselves in non-Muslim lands. There would initially have been an obligation to return, at least for Muslims in lands falling to foreign conquerors, but the mobility of Muslim populations and the complexity of many historical relationships soon gave rise to many forms of adaptation. Thus by the second/eighth century large numbers of Muslims were living in coastal India and China, and this itself was seen as representing a de facto compromise position.[231] By the early tenth/sixteenth century a fatwah literature had developed on means of adaptation to life abroad,[232] and doctrinal writing fixed on the notion of an implied aman, or agreement of safe conduct, by which the grant of permission to enter foreign territory would imply an obligation to abide by local law.[233] This would be the Islamic equivalent of dina de-malkhuta dina in Talmudic law and the principle of yielding to local iura propria in western common laws. The principle of freedom of religion in western states has facilitated ongoing adherence to Islamic law, particularly in respect to religious obligations, but there is said to be an

[227] P. Brown, *The Rise of Western Christendom: Triumph and Diversity, A.D. 200–1000*, 2nd ed. (Oxford: Blackwell Publishing, 2003) at 306.

[228] Royal Academy, supra, note 226, at 22.

[229] Fattal, supra, note 226, at 72, 79, 127, 347; Awang, supra, note 226, at 88–9, for criminal matters.

[230] Awang, supra, note 226, at 167; Royal Academy, supra, note 226, at 60; Fattal, supra, note 226, at 72, 157.

[231] K. A. El Fadl, 'Islamic Law and Muslim Minorities: The Juristic Discourse on Muslim Minorities from the Second/Eighth to the Eleventh/Seventeenth Centuries' (1994) 1 Islamic L. & Soc. 141 at 145, 175.

[232] S. A. Aldeeb Abu-Sahlieh, *Les musulmans en occident entre droits et devoirs* (Paris: L'Harmattan, 2002) at 31.

[233] Fadl, supra, note 231, at 176, 179; Ramadan, supra, note 225, at 95–6.

ongoing sense of lack of reciprocity, since Muslim populations in western States would not enjoy the same level of entitlement to their law as would the dhimmi populations of Islamic lands.[234]

Hostility to recognition of Islamic law is, however, a mark of the iura propria of the western legal traditions and not of the common laws, inherently open and relational with respect to laws they encounter. In western colonies where common laws were present, Islamic law was invariably recognized, even if relegated to a residual and ignominious category of local custom.[235] As common laws are rediscovered in the western world, moreover, there is increasing recognition within the iura propria of the possibility of collaboration with Islamic law, particularly in the large field of party autonomy or ius dispositum which remains a significant part of state laws. Placing the treatment of Muslim people in Europe within the cadre of private international law or the conflicts of laws is now seriously questioned, since Muslim people have often become integrated into European societies, and for generations.[236] So Islamic tribunals may exist within western states, as they do in Canada and the U.K. and no doubt elsewhere,[237] and there is now a major process under way of reasonably accommodating Islamic law in administrative and labour law.[238] Private law institutions are also being developed which are compatible with Islamic legal principles, such as the prohibition of interest (Islamic mortgages and bonds),[239] while the growth of Islamic

[234] Aldeeb Abu-Sahlieh, supra, note 232, at 46.

[235] A. Christelow, 'Islamic Law' in J. Middleton (ed.), *Encyclopedia of Africa South of the Sahara*, vol. 2 (New York: Charles Scribner's Sons, 1997) 530 at 532; Schacht, supra, note 219, at 87 (Islamic law acquiring higher degree of 'practical application' under colonial administration).

[236] S. Ferrari and A. Bradney, *Islam and European Legal Systems* (Aldershot: Ashgate, 2000) at 7 (suggesting examination of issues raised by Muslim populations in the cadre of constitutional, administrative, and ecclesiastical law).

[237] For the U.K., H. Ansari, *Muslims in Britain* at 23 (London: Minority Rights Group International, 2002); Quebec, *The Gazette*, 20 February 1994 at A-3 (though article 2639 of the Quebec Civil Code excludes arbitration of 'family matters'); and for current debate on islamic arbitration in Ontario, the report of the former Attorney General of Ontario, Marion Boyd, recommending procedural guarantees at <www.attorneygeneral.jus.gov.on.ca/english/about/pubs/boyd/fullreport.pdf>; and for the compatibility of Islamic dispute resolution with German law, M. Rohe, 'Der Islam und Deutsches Zivilrecht' in Ebert and Hanstein, supra, note 224, 35 at 38.

[238] See, for example, M. Rohe, 'Rechtliche Perspektiven eines deutschen und europäischen Islam' RabelsZ 2000.256, at 275–87; L. Panafit, *Quand le droit écrit l'Islam: L'intégration juridique de l'Islam en Belgique* (Bruxelles: Bruylant, 1999).

[239] For the use of an Islamic bond (sukuk) to attract Islamic investment by the German province of Sachsen-Anhalt, Frankfurter Allgemeine Zeitung, 6 November 2003, p. 31. Islamic mortgages have been developed by British banks (essentially a lease of property by bank to borrower, to avoid payment of interest).

investment is entirely compatible with western commercial law.[240] There is even discussion of a so-called 'cultural defence' in western criminal law, which would pay some heed to personal loyalties beyond the state, even if only as a means of assessing mental states.[241] All of these instances of exchange of legal ideas between mutually accommodating laws are compatible with the idea of Islamic law as a common law, comparable to those of the west in spite of the profound particularity of Islamic law.

Common laws and Hindu law

Hindu law has also been described as a 'common law' by at least one western observer, and in this resort to the western concept there is perhaps an effort to describe in western terms essential characteristics of the tradition, in spite of the absence of the concept within the tradition itself.[242] Hindu law, like Talmudic and Islamic law, simply uses the names of its classic sources as a means of identification of its normativity. These appear to have been of sufficient visibility and presence in the minds of adherents that no further designation, such as 'common,' was considered necessary. So Hindu law has its ultimate source in the Vedas, or revealed teaching, and the Vedas were followed by the dharmasutras and then by the great books of law, the dharmasastras, including that of Manu.[243] There were also later Digests and Commentaries, constituting an immense body of law for one of the largest populations of the world, yet the entire mass of law is characterized perhaps most of all by its enormous flexibility and adaptability. The tradition has it that Vedic law arrived with Vedic peoples, some three or four millennia ago, and local people could adhere to it, or not adhere to it, largely as they chose, while the process of choice is ongoing. Where the local people did not adhere to the learned law, their own law continued, in western terms a ius proprium, in unwritten form. In the western language now used in India this is frequently referred to as custom, in the western way stripping it of meaning and content and

240 For the Dow Jones index of Islamic investment, <www.djindexes>.

241 Rosen, supra, note 210, at 204; and generally A. Dundes Renteln, *The Cultural Defense* (Oxford/New York: Oxford Univ. Press, 2004).

242 R. Lingat, *The Classical Law of India*, trans. J. D. M. Derrett (Berkeley/Los Angeles/London: Univ. of California Press, 1973) at 195.

243 See generally, H. P. Glenn, supra, note 105, at 274–7.

leaving it as a surface phenomenon of observable conduct; but in the tradition of south Asia it was sadachara, that which had been done from time immemorial by those who were virtuous. It was that which should be done, for reasons known and understood, and as such could not be simply displaced through some type of formal act. It was sometimes said that practices contrary to revealed teaching were sinful, but the place of sadachara was anchored in the texts themselves and when clearly established could not be overcome.[244] Hindu law thus acted as a suppletive, relational law, defining itself constantly in relation to the laws that it met, and for people differentiated from those who chose to remain themselves.[245] It had no power of abrogation, and determination of the relations between the laws which remained in place was an immense and ongoing process. There is no uniform civil law in India even today, and little likelihood of its creation.[246]

Vedic law had moved into India with the movement of Vedic people, it is usually said, and Hindu law was eventually to move with Hindu people, as they settled in many different parts of the world. A process of recognized reception thus occurred in south-east Asia, notably in Bali, but it is recognized that the process of reception was not a dictated or imposed one, and was rather controlled by the 'donees rather than the Indian donors.'[247] Elsewhere in the world Hindu law does what it did in India, recognizing local law and making no claims of mandatory, territorial application. It is, however, followed by Hindu people, such that in England, for example, it is possible to speak of English Hindu law, the result of the process of adaptation between floating Hindu law and whatever rules of the place may be seen as mandatory.[248] This combination of norms is possible in western states because western states which have themselves become iura propria, within common laws of their own origination, have

[244] Lingat, supra, note 242, at 195–8, 203–4 (comparing Hindu law to Roman law for its suppletive character); J. Derrett, *Introduction to Modern Hindu Law* (Oxford: Oxford Univ. Press, 1963) at 13; W. Menski, 'The Role of Custom in Hindu Law' (1992) 53 Receuils de la Société Jean Bodin (Brussels: De Boeck University, 1992) 311 at 323 (learned law only slowly gaining influence over unwritten law).

[245] W. Menski, *Hindu Law* (New Delhi: Oxford Univ. Press, 2003) at 122 (for custom as the 'major source of law') 127 (ancient texts as 'residual source of law') and 194 (existence of Hindu law in contemporary India not an 'either/or' question but involving 'assessment of the actual extent of more or less invisible Hindu law input in any sphere of life').

[246] Menski, supra, note 245, at 41–2.

[247] A. Huxley, 'The Reception of Buddhist Law in S.E. Asia (200 BCE–1860 CE)' in Doucet and Vanderlinden, supra, note 150, at 142, 144 (local choice of various streams of Indian influence).

[248] W. Menski, 'Legal pluralism in the Hindu marriage' in R. Burghard (ed.), *Hinduism in Great Britain: The perpetuation of religion in an alien cultural milieu* (London: Tavistock, 1987) 180; S. Poulter, *Ethnicity, Law and Human Rights* (Oxford: Oxford Univ. Press, 1999).

appropriated also much of the liberty or freedom inherent in common laws, such that even within the states of appropriation there is much room for optional forms of ordering.

Contemporary relations of common laws

The non-imperative character of relational common laws means that each of them is able to incorporate, or even 'canonize,' elements of the others. Each of them, moreover, has found it necessary to do so over time and this process is continuing today. It is perhaps most evident with respect to large, conceptual questions, as the common law finds increasing room for notions of rights, originally of continental inspiration, and the continental common laws increasingly look to jurisprudence as a source of national and transnational law. The process of mutual support is most visible in the case of countries said to be in transition from former communist regimes, but is equally present in all instances of national law reform. Transnational common laws are invariably looked to, in their various manifestations, and one or another of them will be seen as most useful, depending on the fit between local need and the nature of assistance each common law can provide. The common law is thus often looked to in commercial matters, because of the commercial influence of common law countries, but the amorphous form of the common law, in hundreds of thousands of cases, is often rejected as incompatible with the immediate needs of a transitional or developing country. It is often said today that common laws are in competition with one another, and in the European context even that there is menace to the survival of the common law. These views and remarks are overly dramatic, since there are no winners and losers in the world of common laws, only instances of greater or lesser influence, over time and in relation to particular matters. Survival, moreover, is ensured, since even the major efforts of appropriation and elimination of common laws over the last two centuries have now been shown to be unsuccessful, and all of the common laws of Europe now have firmly established and transnational roots.

SOME CONCLUDING REMARKS

Common laws exist within history. However influential they may be in the world, they are not universal, and do not purport to be. They are bounded by the other common laws of the world, with which they are in constant and inevitably ongoing interaction, and they are bounded by their own iura propria, which constantly remind them of the need to respect local circumstances and local identities. Common laws are thus not imperialistic or aggressive in themselves, towards either the external or the internal world. If territorial expansion of peoples has been an essential condition of their emergence, they themselves are not a cause of such expansion. The common laws have been articulated after such expansion, as a means of reconciliation and equilibrium. They have thus existed as bridges amongst peoples, the existence of which has been taken as a given. Today the notion of territorial expansion or acquisition has become largely obsolescent, yet there are major ongoing problems of reconciliation amongst peoples, who may be sedentary or highly mobile. Common laws are a contemporary means of such reconciliation, as they have been for centuries. This does not prevent imperialism or oppression, even in the name of common laws, but the imposition or appropriation of common laws has always been limited in time and space. Common laws thus eventually re-assert themselves across borders, as various forms of human collaboration and cooperation become necessary and desirable. Technology today accelerates this age-old process. There should be a great future for common laws, as techniques for the conciliation of laws and of peoples.

Index

Argentinian Civil Code 82

Blackstone
legal education and 129
Bartolus
essential tradition of the ius commune 18
Brazilian Civil Code 82

Californian Civil Code 86
Cambridge University
teaching of Roman law 129
canon law
Code of Canon Law 1917 84, 111–112
commentators and 110
common law of England and 112–113
common laws and
generally 108–114
'interdependence yet separateness of the two laws' 110–111
'first modern Western legal system' 109
fusion of, with ius commune of Roman origin
affirmation of the 110
resistance to the notion 110
glossators, and 110
Castilian law
see also **Sieta Partidas**
canon law and 112
chthonic peoples
living legal tradition of chthonic law and 67
recognition of land claims of 105
commentators
canon law and 110
roman law and
influence in Europe 58–59

commercial law
common laws, and
generally 114–116
growth of 115
common laws of Europe
common law originating from England
distinction between the ius commune of the continent and 26
generally 32–35
history of 29
relational common law 32
structurally different from ius commune 31
current debate for a new ius commune 1
derecho commún
fueros 40
generally 75–78
Ordenamiento de Alcala 40
originating from Spain 40–41
Siete Partidas: book of teaching 40, 43; recognition beyond Castile 41; relational common law 41
droit commun
Custom of Paris 36, 42
direct rule of the colonies 70
duality of laws 71
'families' of customs 36
feudal law and the 117
French Civil Code ending 72–75
French colonial territories and the 70
originating from France 35–37
early medieval law and 8–9
expiry of
national codifications and the 44
generally 25–32
gemeine Recht
emergence from substantive commonalities in regional laws 39
Germany and the 37–39
lex non scripta of Saxons 38
Sachsenspiegel 37
similarities to droit commun 39
others
Liber Feudorum 42

Lombards 41–43
Naples 41–43
Piedmont 41–43
Tuscany 41–43
world, *see* **World, common laws of**
commonality of laws
development of 9–10
conflict of laws 43, 130
custom
existence of proven and contrary indigenous law 67
gavelkind 30
Halsbury's Laws, recognition of 31
custom of Paris 36–37, 42, 60, 71

delineation
tribal laws of, by United States Supreme Court 67
derecho commún
ejido 76
fueros 40
generally 75–78
Ordenamiento de Alcala 40
originating from Spain 40–41
Siete Partidas
book of teaching 40, 43
recognition beyond Castile 41
relational common law 41
droit commun
comparison with Justinian 37
Custom of Paris 36, 42
direct rule of the colonies 70
duality of laws 71
'families' of customs 36
feudal law and the 117
French Civil Code ending 72–75
French colonial territories and the 70
Dutch Civil Code 79

European legal history
custom 7

European legal history (*cont.*)
common laws of Europe
derecho commún originating from Spain 40–41, 75–78
droit commun originating from France 35–37
gemeine Recht originating from Germany 37–39
generally 25–32
originating from England 32–35
others 41–43
European common law 8–9, 42–43
introduction 1
ius commune
distinction between common law and 14
essential tradition of the 16–20
prototype 20–25
ius unum
common law and 14–16
lex non scripta 7–9
mobility of law
development of the common law 9–12
mobility of people
development of the common law 9–12
nature of new common laws
in Europe generally 12–14
roman law
'barbarian' peoples 6
common law 3–7
Egyptian law 5
Greek law 5
inadequacies of 17
ius gentium 2–7
ius civile 2–7
Jewish law 5
unwritten law 7–9
European Union
single European ius commune and the 20
territoriality and appropriation of common laws 55–56

feudal law
common laws and 116–118
governed land 24

French Civil Code
absence of national French legal system until 50
ending droit commun in France 72
'general and local customs', contained in 50
influence in Europe 73
influence of world's new codification on 94
pan-European process of appropriation 50
Roman law still pertinent, contained in 50
reduction of common law of France to 37
royal ordonnances 50, 60

gavelkind
local custom of the regions of England 30
gemeine Recht
emergence from substantive commonalities in regional laws 39
Germany and the 37–39
lex non scripta of Saxon law 38
Poland and the Sachsenspigel 38
Sachsenspiegel 37–39
similarities to droit commun 39
German Civil Code or BGB 48, 79–80, 83
glossators
canon law and 110
expansion of the ius unum 15
roman law and
influence in Europe 58–59
Greek Civil Code 82

Halsbury's Laws of England
recognition of local custom 31
Hindu law
common laws and
dharmasatras 140
dharmasutras 140
generally 140–142
sadachara 141
Vedas 140–141
hybridity
common laws and colonization process 66–67

indigenous law
European law not applied where proven and contrary 67
fuero 76
indigenous people
aboriginal people
English law introduced in disregard of 64–65
chthonic law remains as living legal tradition 67
common law judges guarantors of lex non scripta 67
violence towards, in colonization process 67
indirect rule
modus vivendi between common law and particular local law 66
Inns of Court
legal education and the 129
Irish law
Brehon law 33–34
Brehon property law 34
Case of Tanistry 34
Islamic law
common laws and
dhimma 137
fatwah literature 138
fiqh 135–136
generally 134–140
gizya 138
hostility to 139
kanun 136–138
Koran, ultimate authority of 135–137
Muhammad teachings and 135–136
urf 135–138
Islamic madhahib
model for legal education 128
iura propria
application of, on European continent 68
ascendancy of, within operative and functioning common laws 50
commercial law and the 115
essential tradition of the ius commune and the 18
examples of European
Liber Feudorum 42
Lombards 41–43
Naples 41–43

Piedmont 41–43
Tuscany 41–43
Islamic law and 138
legal education and the 129
pan-European process of appropriation 51
territoriality and appropriation of common laws 55
Welsh law 32–33
ius commune
binding law 19
current debate for a new European 1
common law originating in England and the, originating in Italy, relations between 97–103
development of 11
distinction between common law of England and 14–16
essential tradition of the 16–20
European legal history and the 49–50, 68
identification of different forms 24
identity problems relating to common laws originating from Italy 57–58
other continental common laws 105–108
prototype 20–25
relational common law 20
transition from unum ius to 16
vulnerability to local laws 24
ius gentium
Roman law and the 2
ius unum
early expansion of, and the common law 14–16

Japanese, Civil Code 83
Jewish law
code of Maimonides 49
roman law and 5
Talmudic law and common laws
Bet Din 133–134
Exchequer of the Jews 133
generally 131–134
halakhah 132
minhag 132
Torah law 132

judiciary
agent of apparent appropriation 51
federations and the 88–91
Justinian
Custom of Paris, comparison with law of 37
ideas on Roman law 15

Korean Civil Code 83

language
initial common law 14
legal education
Blackstone and 129
common laws and
beginnings in eleventh century 128
Christian and Imperial thought, rooted in 128
hegemony and 130
Inns of Court 129
Islamic madhahib, model for 128
relational character and 130
University of Bologna 128
Inns of Court and 129
Islamic madhahib
model for legal education 128
iura propria and 129
Islamic law and 138
ius commune a conceptual framework 22
lex mercatoria
contemporary common law of international trade 116
lex non scripta
common law judges guarantors of, in colonized world 67
original population of Latin America and 76
Sachsenspiegel and 38
roman law and 7–9

Magna Carta
clause 34, 29
Mexican Civil Code 90
'mixed jurisprudence'
development of common law 13

multiplicity of European common laws
confirmed by transplantation of European law overseas 62
pan-European process of appropriation 50

national codifications
effect of, on expiry of common laws 44
generally 48, 59
Netherlands Civil Code 82

Oxford University
teaching of Roman law and 129

Pandectist common law
expansion of different zones of
Austria 81
Czech Republic 81
Hungary 81
Poland 81
Switzerland 81
influence on codification in the world 79–84
'Rechtskreise' 80
roman law and 24
pan-European common law
character of developments
nationalization of law in nineteenth century 51–53
private law 52–53
public law 52–53
extent of, early history 8–9
implications of new, for world beyond Europe 1
process of appropriation 50

relations of common laws
canon law and common laws 108–114
commercial law and common laws 114–116
common law and other continental common laws
France 103–104
Germany 103–104
Holland 103–104
Spain 103–104
common law originating in England and the ius commune 97–103

relations of common laws (*cont.*)
contemporary relations of common laws 142
feudal law and common laws 116–118
generally 95–96
Hindu law and common laws
dharmasatras 140
dharmasutras 140
generally 140–142
sadachara 141
Vedas 140–141
Islamic law and common laws
dhimma 137
fatwah literature 138
fiqh 135–136
generally 134–140
gizya 138
hostility to 139
kanun 136–138
Koran, ultimate authority of 135–137
Muhammad teachings and 135–136
urf 135–138
ius commune and other continental common laws 105–108
language and common laws
cultural package of english and the common law 125
french common law language 125
generally 124–128
latin common law language 125
process of translation into chinese 125
relation between Islamic law and arabic 124
legal education and common laws
beginnings in eleventh century 128
Christian and Imperial thought, rooted in 128
hegemony and 130
Inns of Court 129
Islamic madhahib, model for 128
relational character and 130
University of Bologna 128
Talmudic law and common laws
Bet Din 133–134
Exchequer of the Jews 133

generally 131–134
halakhah 132
minhag 132
Torah law 132
University of Salamanca 129
territories at the confluence of common laws 118–124
remedies
concentration on, in common law of England 112
roman law
'barbarian' peoples 6
commentators work on
influence in Europe 58–59
common law 3–7
Egyptian law 5
glossators work on
influence in Europe 58–59
Greek law 5
inadequacies of
canon law of the Christian Church 17
feudal law of land owning 17
ius gentium 2–7
ius civile 2–7
Jewish law 5
lex non scripta 7–9
unwritten law 7–9
use of, interpretation of Frankish and Lombard law 13

Sachsenspiegel
common law of continent expanding beyond Europe 57
lex non scripta of Saxons 12, 38
gemeine Recht 37–39
Scotland
ius commune of the European continent 35
Siete Partidas
Castilian texts 40, 43, 77–78
major overarching source of law beyond Europe 61
model behind important instances of English law-making 105
new common laws and 12
recognition beyond Castile 41
relational common law 41

Soviet Civil Code 81
specific performance
influence of Dutch jurists on primary contractual remedy 59
stare decisis
absence of in early history of common law 30–31
binding, enforced through national judicial hierarchy 50, 51
emergence of concept of 44
substantive law
generally 112
new common laws and
historical perspective 12

Talmudic law
common laws and 131–134
Thailand Civil and Commercial Code 83
'tribal' law
survival in United States of America 67

University of Bologna
legal education and the 128–129

Welsh law
existence of, as ius proprium 32–33
World, common laws of
common law as common law in the world
adjusting common law to local particularity 63–64
colony acquired by settlement 64
dislodging of, where colony acquired by conquest 64–65
European continent, application of ius commune and iura propria 68
indigenous people 67
indirect rule 66–67
yielding to local, unwritten law 68
derecho commún originating from Spain, in the world 75–78
droit commun originating from France, in the world
direct rule of the colonies 70
duality of laws 71
French Civil Code ending 72–75
French colonial territories and the 70
essential characteristics

common law in England and the British Isles 69
common laws of the European continent 69
hybridity and fluidity of populations tolerant 69
relational 69
federations
judiciary and 89–91
reason for common law being an important concept 89–91
identity of the common laws abroad
Castile in Spain 57, 61
Continental, expanding beyond Europe 57
English settlers taking common law 56–57
French-derived rules in North America, Africa and Middle-East 59–60
Holland 57
Paris 57
Roman-Dutch law 58–59
influence within common laws of the world 91–94
introduction 44–45
multiplicity of the common laws of Europe
confirmed by transplantation of European law overseas 62
national appropriation of common laws abroad
general model 85
United States of America model 85–88
national appropriation of common laws in Europe
'binding' law 46, 51
Civil Code 46
development of autonomous legal system 47
generally 48–49
invective 47–48
restatement of common law in a national source 47
territoriality of law 47
nature of common laws abroad
affirmations of non-binding character 68
application by imperium rationis and not ratio imperii 68
operation of the common laws in Europe 63
recognition of different groups of people 63
relational character 28, 62–63, 68–69
Pandectist common law, in the world 79–84
pan-European character of developments
nationalization of law in nineteenth century 51–53

World, common laws of (*cont.*)
private law 52–53
public law 52–53
Roman-Dutch common law, in the world 78–79
territoriality and appropriation
emerging pattern of provincial jurisprudence 55
survival of common laws overseas 54
writs
common law 11
concentration on, in common law of England 112
introduction of English writs to Ireland and Wales 15–16